Community Denied

COMMUNITY DENIED:

❖

THE WRONG TURN OF PRAGMATIC LIBERALISM

JAMES HOOPES

CORNELL UNIVERSITY PRESS

ITHACA AND LONDON

First published 1998 by Cornell University Press

Printed in the United States of America

Library of Congress Cataloging-in-Publication Data

Hoopes, James, 1944–
    Community denied : the wrong turn of pragmatic liberalism / James Hoopes.
        p.   cm.
    Includes bibliographical references and index.
    ISBN 0-8014-3500-5 (cloth : alk. paper)
    1. Liberalism—United States—History—20th century.   2. Pragmatism—
History—20th century.   I. Title.
JC574.2.U6H66   1998
320.51—dc21   98-9611

Cornell University Press strives to use environmentally responsible suppliers and materials to the fullest extent possible in the publishing of its books. Such materials include vegetable-based, low-VOC inks and acid-free papers that are also recycled, totally chlorine-free, or partly composed of nonwood fibers.

Cloth printing 10 9 8 7 6 5 4 3 2 1

For John Hoopes, Linda Hoopes, John Barnes,
and in memory of Beverly Barnes

CONTENTS

ACKNOWLEDGMENTS

For comments and suggestions on all or part of this manuscript I am indebted to George Cotkin, John Patrick Diggins, Susan Haack, Carol Hoopes, Kenneth Lynn, and Norbert Wiley. Stephen Collins read parts of the manuscript but made his largest contribution as a close and inspiring colleague whose many hours of discussion and counsel exemplify giving and giftedness. I am grateful to the Babson College Board of Research for a summer stipend which greatly facilitated the writing of this book. For secretarial assistance, my thanks to Peggy Carswell, Jennifer Chan, Mary Driscoll, Lee Payton, Jennifer Tzamos, and Joan Walter.

Somehow the love and understanding of Carol, Johanna, and Ben Hoopes grow more indispensable everyday.

Community Denied

CHAPTER ONE

OUR   DEWEYAN   MOMENT   AND   THE

DANGER   OF   A   SECOND   WRONG   TURN

> Wittgenstein, Heidegger, and Dewey are in agreement that the notion of
> knowledge as accurate representation . . . needs to be abandoned. . . . Yet nei-
> ther Heidegger nor Wittgenstein lets us see the historical phenomenon of
> mirror-imagery, the story of the domination of the mind of the West by ocu-
> lar metaphors, within a social perspective. . . . Dewey, on the other hand, . . .
> wrote his polemics against traditional mirror-imagery out of a vision of a new
> kind of society.
> —Richard Rorty, *Philosophy and the Mirror of Nature,* 6, 12–13.

The last quarter of the twentieth century has been no less difficult intellectually than politically for American liberals. The powerful ideals of
free markets and small, nonintrusive government have brought crashing
down the once resplendent ideals of the mixed economy and the welfare
state, along with the supposed special need for the guiding hands of liberal and expert policy makers to steer the ship of state toward social justice. That liberal vision which dominated the politics of much of the early
and middle parts of this century had its philosophical underpinning in
American pragmatism, whose best known proponent was John Dewey.

Nothing better indicates the paucity of intellectual resources available
to liberals than the fact that the collapse of the Deweyan platform has
led progressives not to reject Dewey but to read him anew under the
assumption that he is the only philosopher available on whom to base
liberal hope. James Kloppenberg says that Dewey's generation created an
"unsteady synthesis [but] . . . it may be time to build bridges back to
their ideas." Robert Westbrook believes that "the history of modern
American liberal-democratic theory is a history of treachery [against]

Dewey's democratic faith." Cornel West argues "that it is with Dewey that American pragmatism achieves intellectual maturity, historical scope, and political engagement." Even a book on Reinhold Niebuhr, Dewey's enemy, tells us that "Niebuhr's analysis actually revealed . . . how close his own prophetic faith was to Dewey."[1]

I sympathize greatly with the hope of these other liberal historians to find a usable past on which to rebuild liberal ideals, but I do not believe that Dewey is the right foundation on which to build. In this book I argue that the reliance on Dewey by twentieth-century political and social theorists amounted to an enormous wrong turn in our intellectual history. It is vital that we avoid a second wrong turn.

Sympathizing with the desire of the above scholars and others not to give up on American pragmatism, I hope to show that there was another pragmatic philosopher—Charles Sanders Peirce—who offered a sounder basis for the liberal dream than Dewey did or does. Peirce is of course almost always acknowledged as the great originative mind of pragmatism, but he is seldom discussed in the context of political and social theory. To open a place for him in liberal political theory, I attempt in this book to expose two myths.

I want first to help scotch the myth that there was *one* school of American pragmatism led by Charles Sanders Peirce, William James, and John Dewey. There were *two* very different American pragmatisms, a Peircean strain and a James-Dewey strain, the latter being what most intellectual historians have in mind when they invoke "American pragmatism." The distinction between the two camps is not a matter of idiosyncratic differences among pragmatists, not a matter of there being "as many pragmatisms as there are pragmatic philosophers."[2] There were real and specific differences in logic and metaphysics between Peirce on the one hand and James and Dewey on the other. Where Peirce's pragmatism was strong and objective, theirs was weak, was at least partly subjective and

1. James Kloppenberg, *Uncertain Victory: Social Democracy and Progressivism in American and European Thought, 1870–1920* (New York: Oxford University Press, 1986), 11; Robert Westbrook, *John Dewey and American Democracy* (Ithaca, N.Y.: Cornell University Press, 1991), xv; Cornel West, *The American Evasion of Philosophy: A Genealogy of Pragmatism* (Madison: University of Wisconsin Press, 1989), 6; Richard Wrightman Fox, *Reinhold Niebuhr: A Biography* (New York: Pantheon, 1985), 165. Cf. James Livingston, *Pragmatism and the Political Economy of Cultural Revolution, 1850–1940* (Chapel Hill: University of North Carolina Press, 1994), 199; Robert N. Bellah, Richard Madsen, William M. Sullivan, Ann Swidler, Steven M. Tipton, *The Good Society* (New York: Knopf, 1991), 8; Casey Nelson Blake, *Beloved Community* (Chapel Hill: University of North Carolina Press, 1990), 5; Alan Ryan, *John Dewey and the High Tide of American Liberalism* (New York: Norton, 1995), 109; Giles Gunn, *Thinking Across the American Grain* (Chicago: University of Chicago Press, 1992), 72.
2. Richard Poirier, *Poetry and Pragmatism* (Cambridge, Mass.: Harvard University Press, 1992), 4.

unpragmatic. I do not claim to be the first to have called attention to the fact that there were two schools of American pragmatism, not one.[3] But the myth of *an* American pragmatism lives on despite the efforts of others, so I want to add my mite toward its eventual demise.

I also hope to help debunk a second myth, the idea that what is commonly called "American pragmatism"—the weak James-Dewey variant—was the best philosophy on which to build progressive social and political theory in the first half of the twentieth century. Influential commentators such as Reinhold Niebuhr and Walter Lippmann, whose writings I analyze in the latter part of this book, accepted at face value the conventional wisdom of their time that William James was the preeminently avant-garde American philosopher at the start of the twentieth century. There were deep problems in their political commentary, an elitist skepticism of democracy in Lippmann's case and an unreasoned suspicion of social groups in Niebuhr's, that are at least partly traceable to the influence of James upon them both in youth. Another less influential, but more profound social commentator, Mary Parker Follett, saw earlier and more clearly the weakness of James's and Dewey's variant of pragmatism. But without knowledge of Pierce, she could find no foundation for the unifying social theory she ardently sought.

James and his heir, Dewey, left to twentieth-century American liberals insufficient intellectual equipment for them to build a communitarian political theory. Because of James's raw empiricism, his individualism, and his vestigial dualism, he bequeathed to mainstream pragmatic liberals a viewpoint that was not nearly as communitarian, not nearly as questioning of the traditional self, not nearly as experimentalist as it was purported to be. These problems in James were attenuated by the social emphasis in Dewey. But Dewey's social emphasis was just that—an emphasis—and rested on vaguely stated metaphysical premises. Although Dewey knew that communication was vital to society, he did not elaborate his metaphysics in sufficient detail to offer a foundation for a well-developed theory of communication. In the absence of a well-developed theory he sometimes slipped, more or less unwittingly, into the individualism against which he meant to protest. He left to twentieth-century American liberals insufficient intellectual equipment for them to build a communitarian political theory.

I am all too aware of the difficulties of thus pairing James and Dewey, aware of the obvious differences between them in regard to their level of

3. A recent excellent study that does this is H. O. Mounce, *The Two Pragmatisms: From Peirce to Rorty* (London: Routledge, 1997).

social concern, aware of the less obvious but vital differences between them in metaphysics. I have no intention of minimizing these differences but only of showing how they shrink somewhat when juxtaposed to Peirce's detailed theory of communication, which surpassed the philosophy of both James and Dewey in its potential usefulness to political theory, a potential almost totally unexploited. I consequently regard twentieth-century liberal political theory as an enormous wrong turn in our intellectual history.

James and Dewey were less communitarian philosophers than Peirce because of their tendency, admittedly less strong in Dewey than in James, toward a metaphysical position that made it difficult to conceive of society as anything more than a mass of atomistic individuals. The difference between Peirce and the other two thinkers is the difference between metaphysical realism and metaphysical nominalism. Nominalism is the view that the only real things in the world are particular, individual things. In this view, a horse is real, but the general class of all four-legged animals we refer to by the name "horse" is only a name, an unreal abstraction. Similarly, an individual human being is real, but "humanity" is, as the nominalists say, only a name, not a reality. It would be too strong to assert that James and Dewey saddled twentieth-century progressives with a nominalist viewpoint, for nominalism was the heritage of most western intellectuals at the start of the twentieth century. James and, especially, Dewey saw from afar the possibility of a new philosophy but did not support it with a theory of communication sufficiently clear and detailed to guide their followers to the promised land. In the absence of the intellectual guidance that would have steered them past nominalism, twentieth-century liberals continued in an important respect the social philosophy of recent centuries. They believed that the individual was real in a way that society was not, a view that made it difficult to recognize the reality of community or shared spirit.

Peirce's realism, on the other hand, allowed for the possible reality of general classes, such as "horse" or "humanity." Metaphysical realists such as Peirce take the opposite view from nominalists such as Dewey and James. Realists hold that not only are individual facts real, but so, in at least some cases, are the general kinds or classes or patterns or laws — universals — by which particular facts are conceived to be related to each other. Realists, of course, admit that general classes such as "horse" are names, but they think that these classes are also sometimes more than names, that they are real in the same sense that the particular facts they denote are real. How Peirce moved from nominalism to realism is one of the subjects of the next chapter. The important point here is that Peirce's philosophy allows for what twentieth-century liberals, laboring under the nominalist incubus, have failed to recognize. Because general classes (a philosopher would say "kinds") may be as real as particular facts, society may be just as real as individual human beings.

Labeling James a nominalist will provoke far less controversy than similarly denominating Dewey, who himself frequently denounced nominalism. I hope that readers who are already certain that Dewey's denunciations of nominalism, combined with the sheer voluminousness of his social commentary, must outweigh any case I can make for his implicit nominalism will nevertheless push on and evaluate the arguments I offer in subsequent chapters. Here I offer the broad qualification that when I speak of Dewey as a nominalist I do not mean to dispute the sincerity of his conviction that the obvious reality of society disproves nominalism. But Dewey did not well examine the implications of his avowed antinominalism for his conception of the individual. Insist as he might on the importance of social experience in the formation of the individual, his conception of the individual remained biological and organic, related to but also distinct from the things of the spirit such as words and thoughts by which human beings are bound together in society. Even granting that Dewey was an avowed antinominalist, whenever his focus was on the human person rather than society, his perspective tended to be biological, organic, and, by implication, individualist and nominalist.

In the conclusion of this book I bring the story down to the present by discussing what the philosopher Susan Haack has aptly called "vulgar pragmatism," which I also characterize as weak pragmatism because of its failure to take as strenuous a path in logic as Peirce. Weak and vulgar pragmatism is the pragmatism of recent antifoundationalists who attempt to claim the mantle of James and Dewey.[4] It is best, according to the antifoundationalists, to abandon the traditional epistemological concerns of modern philosophy as to how knowledge is grounded.[5] The results of such a search, they say, must be trivial and unimportant compared to the present needs of a liberal society concerned with justice. Such a society will "view foundational accounts not as the foundation of political institutions, but as, at worst, philosophical mumbo jumbo, or, at best, relevant to private searches for perfection, but not to social policy."[6] In this view it is a virtue that pragmatic liberals have no vision but only technique, no "Philosophy" as Richard Rorty has put it, but only "philosophy."

4. Susan Haack, *Evidence and Inquiry: Towards Reconstruction in Epistemology* (Cambridge: Blackwell, 1993), 182–202.
5. The major statement of this view is Richard Rorty, *Philosophy and the Mirror of Nature* (Princeton: Princeton University Press, 1979).
6. Richard Rorty, *Philosophical Papers: Objectivity, Relativism, and Truth* (Cambridge: Cambridge University Press, 1991), 184.

I believe that the antifoundationalists confuse metaphysical foundations with ideological dogmatism. The latter is to be avoided. The former are unavoidable. In the final chapter of this book I try to suggest something of Peirce's moderation in metaphysics. His description of the foundational relations, which he believed could be discerned in the world, never slipped into any sort of Cartesian essentialism or preposterous attempt to describe an *ens entium* or unknown substance underlying the qualities we perceive. Peirce never fell into the kind of philosophy against which antifoundationalists understandably protest.

Although I doubt that unconcern for foundational issues will characterize future liberal societies, my concern in this book is with the past. I want to show that in the past, at least one society, our own, was deeply influenced by foundational issues. Philosophical foundations were an important basis of liberalism and pragmatism in the first half of the twentieth century. I do not doubt that, as Rorty claims, "a metaphysical difference can safely be neglected if we cannot tie it in with a difference in practices."[7] But metaphysical differences in American intellectual history cannot be safely neglected, for they have made a difference, an unfortunate difference, in practice.

As I attempt to show below, James and Dewey, contrary to their own occasional disclaimers, were foundationalists, and the result of their philosophy, a variant of traditional nominalism and individualism, was not trivial. It limited or, at minimum, failed to support the social vision of progressive social critics such as Lippmann, Niebuhr, and Follett. The worst effect on these prototypical twentieth-century liberals was that they were never able to conceive of society as real in the same sense that they conceived of individuals as real.

Nearly half a century ago Morton White rebuked Lippmann and Niebuhr for their recurrence to ancient, formalist doctrines, but he did not examine the possibility that their late apostasy might have been at least partly due to inadequacies in the Jamesian philosophy that influenced them both. White's *Social Thought in America,* first published in 1949, was a Deweyan milestone in our intellectual history, beyond which we have even now not much progressed. Revising the book for republication in 1957, White added a new section that dealt largely with the recent writings of Niebuhr and Lippmann. Niebuhr had continued his anti-Deweyan defense of original sin while Lippmann had recently abandoned pragmatism in favor of natural law as a basis for a free polity.

7. Richard Rorty, "Response to Hartshorne" in *Rorty and Pragmatism: The Philosopher Responds to His Critics,* ed. Herman J. Saatkamp, Jr. (Nashville: Vanderbilt University Press, 1995), 34.

White, from his Deweyan perspective, found both the theologian and the publicist full of poor stuff: "it seems to me a sad commentary on the social thought of today that two of the most popular social thinkers on the American scene can produce nothing more original or natural than the doctrines of original sin and natural law as answers to the pressing problems of this age."[8]

One of my objectives in this book is to fill in a gap that White left empty. Although he was critical of the social thought of his day, White did not offer any systematic explanation of the cause of its obvious ennui as represented in the later works of Niebuhr and Lippmann. Never considering the possibility that the reversion to dogma by the publicist no less than the theologian might indicate some weakness in the Jamesian and Deweyan pragmatism to which he himself was committed, White only expressed his dissatisfaction and looked no deeper. Perhaps no more was possible then. With the deeper understanding of pragmatism that is beginning now to be established, it is possible to see that the weak pragmatism of our mainstream liberals limited their social vision. Desperately searching for community standards, Niebuhr and Lippmann were eventually driven back from pragmatic nominalism toward older, more absolutist systems of thought that pretended to greater universality. Follett, whom White did not discuss, had never been so deeply snared by pragmatism, so her reaction against it was not absolutist. But she remained a practicing nominalist, unable to articulate a theoretical basis for the communitarian social theory she sought.

What might have strengthened liberal foundations was Peirce's pragmatism as opposed to James's and Dewey's. As Lippmann in his last years finally evolved away from James's nominalism, he could have profited from Peirce's realism, but he did not know of it. Instead, he adopted his natural law position without much metaphysical explanation or defense. Neither was Niebuhr's commitment to individual transcendence examined from any philosophical point of view, though in his early years he unquestioningly supposed it was supported by James's pragmatism. In later life Niebuhr realized the narrowness of James, the incompatibility of James's metaphysics with any notion of the transcendent, despite the sympathy James manifested in *Varieties of Religious Experience*. Niebuhr turned to no other philosopher. His skepticism about human potential began in Christian faith and, to him, was confirmed less by philosophy than by events. Follett, a more avid and thorough student of philosophy

---

8. Morton White, *Social Thought in America: The Revolt against Formalism* (Boston: Beacon, 1957), xii.

than either Lippmann or Niebuhr, nevertheless found nothing better than physiological psychology, limited perforce to the individual organism, as a basis for political theory.

The weakness of the philosophic foundations they inherited from James vitiated the communitarianism in Lippmann's and Niebuhr's political thought. Although both thinkers suffered briefly from socialist fevers in their youth, neither was ever in any danger of succumbing, not only because of temperament but because of the influence of Jamesian pragmatism upon them both. But while James may have helped save them from socialism, he also denied them access to communitarianism. Lacking much knowledge of Peirce, neither Lippmann nor Niebuhr had a way to conceive of any human group or society as anything other than a group of atomistic individuals. While Lippmann unsuccessfully wrestled for his entire career with what James, following Plato, called the problem of "the One and the Many," the young Niebuhr more or less unquestioningly accepted the side of James's disjointed metaphysics that supported individualism. While Lippmann accepted the theory that groups required elite leadership before they could act effectively, Niebuhr held groups incapable of spirituality or even morality and therefore believed groups could resolve their differences only by power and force. Between them Lippmann and Niebuhr represent and helped create the two aspects of liberalism that have made it seem anticommunity to many people—the one aspect, undemocratic decision making by elitists eager to manage the lives of others and, the other aspect, resolution of conflict by countervailing power among amoral, self-interested groups.

Follett better kept the liberal faith. She searched for a democratic relation between experts and citizenry. She also rejected the power politics of self-interested groups. But she was unable to explain how her proposed method of "integration" or resolution of social conflict by communication and inclusion would work at any level beyond the local.

Since they knew little or nothing of Peirce, neither Lippmann nor Niebuhr nor Follett was capable of achieving a model of democratic decision making that acknowledged the inescapability of elite managers and special interests but nevertheless also recognized an element of spirituality and mentality within groups. Such recognition might have led Lippmann to embrace elite managerialism a bit less enthusiastically, might have led him to show a bit more respect for democracy and public opinion. Niebuhr might have been a little less contemptuous of those who hoped democracy could rise above realpolitik, might have allowed for a liberalism less cynical and more respectful of the ability of a community to act together sometimes in behalf of its better ideals. Follett might have been able to rise above her penchant for the local and conceive of a national community with a public culture subsuming the particular individual differences she sought to integrate.

In telling this story of missed opportunities, my target is James as well as Dewey. From the time of Randolph Bourne (1886–1918), politically radical critics of American pragmatism have launched numerous assaults on Dewey while largely ignoring James, an error whose essence lies less in criticism of Dewey than in leniency toward James. As I show below, both Niebuhr and Lippmann, even though they were both famously critical of Dewey, were deeply influenced by James, and not for the better. Part of the reason James got off posterity's hook was his death at the outset of the cultural and political wars of the 1910s, in which Dewey had to stake out positions. Moreover, Bourne and many other cultural radicals have been drawn to the warmth of James's personality and put off by Dewey's staidness. I confess to partiality for the dull Dewey over the sainted James. Dewey came closer than James to the spirit of Peirce's rebuilding of modern philosophy, though with nothing like Peirce's attempt to provide a new metaphysics. But if Dewey came closer than James to the spirit of Peirce, he never entirely escaped James's atomistic individualism.

Even though I have James in my sights as well as Dewey, I characterize our contemporary time in the history of American political and social theory as the "Deweyan moment," not the "Deweyan Jamesian moment," because Dewey's reputation has recently undergone an astonishing rebirth. Of course in some liberal circles his reputation never waned. But in recent years, many liberal intellectual historians have abandoned the legacy of Bourne and attempted to remake Dewey into a model American communitarian and participatory democrat. Much of our Deweyan moment falls within the frame of a recognizable American tradition, the search for a usable past. The search is worthy, but I fear that the Deweyan terrain, so assiduously prospected at present, is poorer than it appears and will not yield the hoped-for riches. Nevertheless, I share with our latter-day Deweyans a conviction that our pragmatic heritage has been too soon abandoned and urge only that we consider the possibility that Dewey and James may have helped start us on the wrong path, the path of weak pragmatism rather than the strong pragmatism of Peirce. If, as I think, liberals' original faith in Dewey and James was a false step, our present revival of interest in Dewey runs the risk of becoming a second wrong turn.

Not all of the recent scholarship on the history of American social theory is Deweyan, but that which is not escapes the influence of Dewey less by a reexamination of pragmatism than a Niebuhrian rejection of it. In *The Origins of American Social Science* (1991) Dorothy Ross's viewpoint, whether intentionally so or not, is essentially Niebuhrian. She is skeptical of the Deweyan project of modeling social science on natural science because social and historical patterns, unlike natural law, are continuously interrupted and reshaped by human action.[9] The late Christopher Lasch, in *The True and Only Heaven: Progress and Its Critics* (1991), wrote out of what might be called "neofundamentalist" convictions, according to which anyone who ever displayed concern about the arrogance of liberal optimism—from sophisticated thinkers like Niebuhr to visceral defenders of traditional values—has more to offer to political thought and communitarian values than liberal intellectuals. Lasch's book is an emphatic reminder of how bereft of resources the conventional Deweyan account of American intellectual history leaves those who are in search of some real communitarianism in our liberal tradition. Similarly, John Patrick Diggins's *The Promise of Pragmatism* (1994) criticizes pragmatism not from within but from the tragic perspectives of Niebuhr and Henry Adams. Although Diggins distinguishes himself among intellectual historians by devoting as much attention to Peirce as to Dewey and James, he adopts the customary notion that Dewey's philosophy was the best that pragmatism had to offer to political thought.

Even though I sympathize less with Niebuhr than with pragmatic liberalism and the attempt to provide it with a usable past, I agree with Diggins that not much usable is provided by our contemporary cry of "Back to Dewey!" By lamenting the failure of Dewey's vision and then reinvoking his vision without reexamining its philosophical basis, we act as if social theory is nothing but a matter of keeping our spirits up. We must not only celebrate Dewey's admirable goals but examine the content of his philosophy to ascertain whether it was genuinely supportive of his goals and therefore still usable. We need at least to consider the possibility that Dewey's pragmatism might have contained within itself some of the origins of the problems it has encountered as the more or less official philosophy of American liberalism.

I think a usable past is more likely to be found in Charles Sanders Peirce's pragmatism than in Dewey's. It is customary in histories of American philosophy to lament Peirce's isolation, but there is often something

9. Still, Ross sees Dewey and his pragmatic interest in change as superior to social science in general: "The distance that will remain between Dewey and the main body of American social science is a significant measure of how reluctant the social science disciplines were to come fully to grips with historicism" (Ross, *The Origins of American Social Science* [Cambridge: Cambridge University Press, 1991], 162).

smug about those lamentations, as if Peirce, poor untenured devil, was the only sufferer from his tortured personal life and self-inflicted professional woes. This study aims to suggest that something was lost to us all when Dewey rather than Peirce became the avatar of American pragmatism and that it is possible to recover and use some of what has been lost.

I do not advocate Peirce simply because his philosophy, more than James's or Dewey's, has political implications that I admire. That would be expediency of a kind too characteristic of much contemporary political discussion. I see Peirce's thought as more true than James's or Dewey's for reasons that are first of all philosophical, not political. Readers of my *Consciousness in New England: From Puritanism and Ideas to Psychoanalysis and Semiotic* and of *Peirce on Signs,* my edition of his writings on semiotic, will understand that I came to my admiration of Peirce first of all through his philosophy. Only in recent years have I begun to see that his philosophy, especially his realism, supports a mild communitarianism which I find appealing and from which I believe contemporary liberalism could benefit.

By the words "community" and "communitarian" I refer both to a traditional notion of social responsibility on the part of individuals and to a somewhat more radical idea that the community has claims on us because we belong to it in a more integral way than most of modern Western philosophy has seen. Much of twentieth-century liberalism has emphasized political rights and social benefits more than duties and responsibilities. The rights are admirable and, if some benefits have been overdone, there are nevertheless others much needed such as universal health insurance and care for young children of working mothers. I claim no special insight in noticing that such benefits are possible only in societies that equally emphasize social responsibility, which until recently has not been considered a prominent feature of liberalism. But I think there is, within the tradition of American pragmatism, a neglected and original approach to the difficult problem of justifying the sacrifices entailed by responsibility to the national and even international community against such powerful but lesser claimants as myself, my ethnic group, my interest group, and other local loyalties.

Peirce's philosophy, far more than James's and Dewey's, makes it possible to see that our relation to society has some of the same kind of integration, some of the same kind of reality, as do the relations within us that constitute our individual minds and selves. Society, according to Peirce, has some of the same reality as does the individual. If he is right, then it follows that society has some of the same claims on our resources as do our individual selves. Peirce's philosophy, esoteric as it may seem, is therefore a social resource that we, unlike progressives a century ago, can no longer afford to ignore in favor of James and Dewey.

Nowhere is the weakness of Dewey's and James's pragmatism more clear, and their potential contributions to liberal politics more deeply undermined, than in their conservative logic, their failure to follow Peirce in making logic formal and objective. Their philosophy contained elements of an old-fashioned, subjective logic that prevented James and even Dewey from entirely escaping an illogical individualism. Dewey and James were not nearly as tough minded and empirical as both they and many of their historians have believed. They preferred a logic that was at least partly intuitive—a matter of what seemed reasonable to them—over Peirce's formal, symbolic logic which he eventually identified with his semiotic or general theory of signs. Peirce's logic was far more tough minded and empirical, based as it was on objective relations among external signs rather than intuitive, subjective feelings of reasonableness. By steadily focusing on interpretive relations among objective signs, Peirce's logic, far more than Dewey's and James's, opens up new possibilities for understanding social relations. Indeed, Peirce's communitarianism, as I attempt to show in the next chapter, was based far more in his logic than, as is generally believed, in his science.

Contemporary misunderstanding of Peirce is often based in the same failure as James's and Dewey's, the failure to understand the centrality of Peirce's logic to his pragmatism. Richard Rorty, the leading antifoundationalist, tells us that the present rebirth of pragmatism rejects radical empiricism in favor of an emphasis on language and interpretation somewhat akin to Peirce's famous claims that a person is a sign and that the self is an interpretation rather than a substantial entity. But antifoundationalists "regret that these are passages to which neither James nor Dewey, nor even Peirce himself paid much attention." [10] Most readers familiar with Peirce must surely be astonished to hear that he paid little attention to his own emphasis on interpretation and semiotic. How could Rorty commit so large a misreading? There is a clue in Rorty's later acknowledgment that his first philosophical publication had to do with Peirce, but "It was, of course, the Peirce of Evolutionary Love, rather than the Peirce of the Logic of Relatives, whom I admired most." [11] Rorty evidently supposes that the holism of "Evolutionary Love" was at odds

---

10. Rorty, "Dewey between Hegel and Darwin" in *Rorty and Pragmatism*, 2. The philosopher who has best answered Rorty's antifoundationalism by suggesting that Rorty's opposition to a "God's-Eye View" is itself a "God's-Eye View" is Hilary Putnam, *Realism with a Human Face* (Cambridge, Mass.: Harvard University Press, 1990), 25.
11. Rorty, "Response to Hartshorne," 30.

with or at least distinct from Peirce's logic. My view is just the opposite; Peirce's holism and communitarianism were based in his symbolic logic.

At our moment in time it rings false to find seeds of communitarianism in symbolic logic, but this is only because the chronology of twentieth-century philosophy suggests an opposition between social awareness and technically sophisticated philosophy. Dewey's sort of concern with social issues dominated early twentieth-century American philosophy, only to be succeeded at mid-century by analytic philosophy which, in turn, has given way in recent decades to a rebirth of socially concerned pragmatism. This seeming opposition between philosophical rigor and social concern is not the result of irresolvable differences between them. In the next chapter I argue that Peirce's communitarianism stemmed from his logic. Peirce was a moderate in logic and never subscribed to belief in the possibility of an utterly abstract, purely formal logic, or what later became known as "logic without ontology" of the Russell-Schroeder-Frege variety. Peirce points to a sort of middle road in philosophy that has been utterly missed in our twentieth-century veerings between abstract logic and social concern.

This book is not a defense of symbolic logic, but it is an attempt to get straight the origins of pragmatism in Peirce and the reason for its relative political weakness in the hands of James and Dewey. Perhaps the turn of contemporary philosophy away from symbolic logic is justified, but it is important not to forget that the original appeal of formal logic lay in its promise of escape from Descartes' clear and distinct ideas, supposedly intuited subjectively within the individual mind. Peirce turned instead to external and objective symbols, which offered the prospect that logic could be recognized as a basis rather than a result of social experience. It was scarcely coincidence that Peirce, one of the creators of symbolic logic, was also the author of the pragmatic maxim emphasizing that the meaning of a thought was nothing other than its imaginable external effects: "Consider what effects, that might conceivably have practical bearings, we conceive the object of our conception to have. Then, our conception of these effects is the whole of our conception of the object." [12]

It cannot be too strongly stressed that pragmatism had its origins in Peirce's commitment to symbolic logic. Peirce's logic was premised on the notion that all thought has an objective element. Therefore, he believed that logic could be studied just as well, and probably better, by focusing not on our subjective experience of thinking but on objective symbols

---

12. *Peirce on Signs: Writings on Semiotic by Charles Sanders Peirce*, ed. James Hoopes (Chapel Hill: University of North Carolina Press, 1991), 169.

and the form of their relations to their objects. In its beginnings pragmatism was a matter of treating thought itself as practical action, as objective activity, not simply a matter of considering the practical consequences of acting on our thoughts.

In other words, pragmatism had its origins in a new conception of what thinking is—an objective process of representation and interpretation in time and space rather than, as Descartes had thought, unmediated apprehension of the contents of the unextended substance of mind. Peirce's logic did not require the notion of immediate, unrepresented, uninterpreted apprehension by which Descartes had believed that mind grasped the meaning of its thoughts. In Peirce's formulation even human thought is external in the sense that it is objective brain activity rather than the immaterial substance of mind described by Descartes. And the meaning of a thought is not grasped immediately or intuitively in the way that Descartes described but is an interpretation of a brain state as a sign or representation of yet some other object or some prior brain state. Therefore, according to Peirce, a person's knowledge of even his or her own thoughts is representational and interpretational, not unrepresented or immediate.

Neither James nor even Dewey completely escaped the notion that thought, albeit a natural process, is also a privileged experience, somehow different from the rest of nature. This was a largely unnoticed lapse in their much remarked break with the tradition of English empiricism according to which we are trapped in a veil of subjective representation and cannot know the world as well as we know our minds. James and Dewey questioned the Lockean denial of knowledge of the external world but shared the Lockean and Cartesian confidence in our knowledge of the meaning of our thoughts. James remained committed to an old-fashioned faith in the immediacy of self-knowledge. He believed that introspection or consciousness was undeniably empirical knowledge of our minds' workings, as for instance in his faith that consciousness must be a continuous stream for no other reason than that it feels continuous. Dewey did not go down that path but neither did he go down any other on the question of the metaphysical constitution of thought. Confident that all of human experience attests to the vital importance of thought, he stayed close to home, so to speak, and consequently never formulated arguments as clear and detailed as Peirce's for the reality of thirdness—thought or semiosis—as a category of the universe at large, not just of human experience.

James and Dewey thus led pragmatism away from Peirce's conception of thought as objectively real as the rest of the universe. As a result, there was an element of dualism and false subjectivity in James and even Dewey that made them somewhat antipragmatic pragmatists. If they were not "vulgar pragmatists" like many of their self-proclaimed heirs, they were "weak" pragmatists—at least weaker than Peirce—because of their distrust of formal logic and their corresponding skepticism of the objectivity of thought. For all their vaunted empiricism, their logic was not entirely empirical. They were sometimes left with no better test of truth than what seemed reasonable to them, a test of truth contradictory to Peirce's view that truth is a sign's objectively accurate representation of its object.

James's and Dewey's vitiation of the logical spirit of Peirce's pragmatism had immense implications for the political theory of mainstream American liberalism. For Peirce's logic was at the heart of his communitarianism and his realism. When Dewey and James failed to follow Peirce's logic they made it impossible for *their* followers, such as Lippmann, Niebuhr, and Follett, to arrive at any communitarianism like Peirce's. In turn, this antilogical viewpoint has come to influence some historians' view of Peirce. James and Dewey are so historically influential that they have succeeded, so to speak, in "Deweyizing" Peirce. It is therefore understandable that some intellectual historians believe Peirce's logic to have been based on social processes rather than vice versa. The highest test of reality, according to this interpretation of Peirce, is the opinion of the community, especially a community of experts.[13] I believe that those who interpret Peirce in this way overemphasize his confidence in experts. Much as he valued learned opinion he never considered it a test of reality, never considered the thinking of experts a logical standard. Rather, I think the texts show the opposite, show him to have believed that social processes and all communication are a form of logic, believed thought to be constrained by reality, and believed logical relations to be objectively real.[14] Based in symbolic logic, Peirce's communitarianism had a much firmer foundation than Dewey's, which was mainly a hopeful insistence on the obvious correctness of the proposition that no man is an island.

The supposed radicalism of Dewey's emphasis on the social has therefore been enormously overestimated. Dewey can always be counted on to

13. Thomas L. Haskell, *The Emergence of Professional Social Science: The American Social Science Association and the Nineteenth-Century Crisis of Authority* (Urbana: University of Illinois Press, 1977), 238–39. Haskell usefully modifies this opinion and defends Peirce's fallibilism against Rorty by dealing with Peirce's realism in his essay, "Justifying the Rights of Academic Freedom in the Era of 'Power/Knowledge,'" in *Legal Rights: Historical and Philosophical Perspectives,* ed. Austin Sarat and Thomas R. Kearns (Ann Arbor: University of Michigan Press, 1996), 147–50.
14. Carl R. Hausman, *Charles S. Peirce's Evolutionary Philosophy* (Cambridge: Cambridge University Press, 1993) is an excellent survey of Peirce's thought from this point of view.

insist that community is a real and obvious fact. But when he gets down to specifics he is unable to explain how boundaries between persons are crossed. His naturalist emphasis on biology and his metaphysical vagueness as to the nature of the relations constituting the self led him to conceive of the self as stopping at the body's limits. For Dewey there was a sharp boundary between self and society. Society influenced but also kept its distance, so to speak, from the self. The self was as individual and real as the organism, but Dewey never showed how "society" might be anything other than a mere collection of atomistic selves, with no more spiritual unity among them than physical unity among distinct organisms. The Progressive Era social theory Dewey helped foster was not as complete a rupture with traditional, atomistic individualism as it is often thought to have been.

We late twentieth-century heirs of progressive theory have been overconfident of its recognition of social forces. Having known no other political theory, we have difficulty seeing how there could have been a more radical transition from individual to group analysis in social theory than was undertaken by Dewey, George Herbert Mead, and Charles H. Cooley. Earlier liberal sociologists such as Lester Frank Ward had begun with the assumption that the individual organism and its responses to stimuli were the source of all behavior. Dewey and his followers asserted instead that human association was the key factor in human behavior, an assertion which enabled them to recognize the importance of communication and "symbolic interaction," as Mead later put it. Yet out of concern for adequate acknowledgment of biological factors, the school of Dewey and Mead never looked for any larger social being than the individual organism. They saw human association or society as a decisive factor in behavior, but it was still the individual that behaved. "Society" was not a *community* but only the sum of associated individuals. In this sense, the Deweyans were every bit as committed to atomistic individualism as their predecessors.

It is scarcely any wonder, then, that many of Dewey's followers, lacking any knowledge of Peirce's strong pragmatic notion that society might possess some of the same kind of spiritual unity as an individual human being, developed elitist conceptions of leadership. It follows from Dewey's biologism that only individuals, not societies, are sufficiently unified to be capable of spirituality or mentality. Dewey was notoriously vague on the details of how and by what means society should employ his method of intelligence. But on the basis of his implicit nominalism it is a reasonable inference that society's decisions must finally be made by individual minds who ought, of course, to be the best among us. Recently Dewey has been defended against such charges by the assertion that liberal elitism is a matter of "treachery" against Dewey's ideal of participatory de-mocracy.[15] I believe the story is more complicated. Dewey often invoked participatory ideals, but as a philosopher he must be judged not only by his political invocations but also by his philosophy, which in its implicit nominalism and vestigial individualism, left no philosophical basis for a communitarian understanding of social reality and of how leadership might be accomplished in a participatory democracy.

The possibility of Dewey's philosophical inadequacy was raised, briefly, in one of the most dramatic episodes in American intellectual his-tory when Randolph Bourne, protesting Dewey's support of American entry into the First World War, asked of pragmatism, "What is the mat-ter with the philosophy? . . . Is there something in these realistic attitudes that works actually against poetic vision, against concern for the quality of life as above machinery of life?" Dewey's claim that frenzied abuses of civil liberties were merely misdirected social energy suggested to Bourne that "the attitudes which war calls out are fiercer and more incalculable than Professor Dewey is accustomed to take into his hopeful imagina-tion, and the pragmatist mind, in trying to adjust itself to them, gives the air of grappling . . . with a power too big for it."[16]

Eighty years later the doubts Bourne expressed in regard to Dewey's support of war might be asked in regard to the relation of Deweyan phi-losophy to the welfare state and the social fabric in general. Dewey's phi-losophy of control by intelligence, his confidence that society could be at least partly managed by scientific technique, seems everywhere to be in tatters. In the face of all this, the latter-day disciples who have created the Deweyan moment seem only to replicate the inadequacy of earlier Deweyans' response to the First World War. By its harshness and the dire situation that justified its harshness, Bourne's condemnation of his gen-eration of intellectuals does not apply to our contemporary Deweyans. But if we remove the word "pitifully" from the following quotation, there is still an analogy to our time: Bourne wrote of the "intelligentsia, trained up in the pragmatic dispensation, immensely ready for the executive or-dering of events, pitifully unprepared for the intellectual interpretation or the idealistic focusing of ends."[17]

Intellectual historians interested in political theory have not elabo-rated the complexity of pragmatism with much precision, partly because they assume that Peirce's intense focus on logic, which distinguished him

---

15. Robert B. Westbrook, *John Dewey and American Democracy* (Ithaca, N.Y.: Cornell University Press, 1991), xv.

16. *War and the Intellectuals: Essays by Randolph Bourne, 1915–1919,* ed. Carl Resek (New York: Harper and Row, 1964), 54, 59.

17. Ibid., 59.

from Dewey and James, also made his philosophy less relevant to political theory. Usually, they acknowledge the founding role of Peirce and then devote most attention to the other two thirds of the pragmatist triumvirate.[18] A reader acquainted with only this historical literature might think the nature of pragmatism to have been well agreed on among its great originators and would perhaps be surprised to find a contemporary philosopher, a supposed disciple of Dewey, criticizing the "tendency to overpraise Peirce" whose "contribution to pragmatism was merely to have given it a name, and to have stimulated James."[19] As that insecure and mistaken assertion might lead one to suspect, in some philosophical circles, Peirce's star is today ascending faster and higher than James's or Dewey's.

Those intellectual historians who have written extensively about Peirce have done little to draw out the political implications of his philosophy, an omission that needs correction but is nonetheless understandable. For as opposed to Dewey and even James, Peirce was politically inactive. In later life, he seems to have objected to American imperialism in the Philippines, and he spoke sentimentally of Civil War monuments as a sign of the moral force that preserved the Union. But on slavery, the largest social issue of his lifetime, the young Peirce was a distinct reactionary, mystified as to why the issue was worth the upset. In this he followed his family and diverged from the family's social circle, the Cambridge intelligentsia that included the James, Holmes, and Longfellow families, with strong social ties to the Concord transcendentalists. The Peirces' reactionary Civil War politics brought the family some measure of social isolation, perhaps not a great measure, since the young philosopher mixed well enough in Cambridge society in the late 1860s and early 1870s. Nevertheless, his reactionary Civil War politics may have helped Peirce along toward the disastrous debacles of his worldly career. Or rather, since he seems to have needed little help in ruining his life, whatever estrangement there was between his family and the liberal Cambridge intelligentsia may have helped deny him the safety net he so desperately needed.

A year after the Civil War, as the nation wrestled with the issue of how thoroughly southern society should be reconstructed, Peirce, the brilliant

18. For a recent example of this tendency to justify leaving Peirce out of consideration when discussing pragmatism and social theory because logic is supposedly irrelevant to social theory see James T. Kloppenberg, "Pragmatism: An Old Name for Some New Ways of Thinking?" *The Journal of American History* 83 (June 1996), 102 n. 3.

19. Richard Rorty, *Consequences of Pragmatism: Essays 1972–80* (Minneapolis: University of Minnesota Press, 1982), 160–61.

young logician, lectured a Cambridge audience on the limited value of any single syllogism:

> If therefore we find a single syllogism which seems to be of great avail we should scrutinize it carefully to see whether it is not false. We often hear it said
>
> All men are equal in their political rights
>
> Negroes are men;
>
> ∴ Negroes are equal in political rights to whites.
>
> Far be it from me to say anything which could hinder justice from being done to that people whose guardianship the people of the North have assumed. . . . But this argument which seems to carry us so far, becomes suspicious from the very fact that it does carry us so far while it is only a syllogism. The Declaration of Independence declares that it is "self-evident that all men are created equal." Now men are created babies and therefore, in this case, *men* is used in a sense that includes babies and therefore nothing can follow from the argument relatively to the rights of Negroes which does not apply to babies, as well. The argument, therefore, can amount to very little.[20]

Peirce's logic may be close, but his mastery of political context, whether of the Civil War or Revolutionary eras, leaves much to be desired.

Peirce's illiberalism did not end with slavery and race. Norbert Wiley has pointed to Peirce's bitter statement in old age, in which he says that he is "ultra-conservative. I am, for example, an old-fashioned christian, a believer in the efficacy of prayer, an opponent of female suffrage and of universal male suffrage, in favor of letting business-methods develop without the interference of law, a disbeliever in democracy, etc. etc."[21] Yet Wiley finds that Peirce's philosophy is a powerful tool for modern social theory in fields such as anthropology and sociology which are not notoriously conservative.

Similarly, even though Peirce's specifically political commentary was sparse and often reactionary, he had many radical insights to offer to political theory. His commitment to community went far deeper than

20. "Lowell Lecture VI," in *Writings of Charles S. Peirce: A Chronological Edition,* ed. Edward C. Moore, et al. (Bloomington: Indiana University Press, 1982), 1:444.

21. Quoted in Christian J. W. Kloesel, "Charles Peirce and Honoré de Clairefont," *Versus* (January–April 1988), 15–16, and in Norbert Wiley, "Peirce and Social Theory: The Discovery of Culture," American Sociological Association Convention, August 1995, Washington, D.C. I am grateful to Professor Wiley for calling Peirce's quote to my attention and supplying me with a copy of his ASA paper. The original source of the quote is MS 645, Peirce Papers, Houghton Library, Harvard University.

his much remarked devotion to the scientific community. His metaphysics was communitarian, for it argued that logical relations were real constituents of the universe and thus ensured not only the possibility of human understanding of nature but also the possibility of communication among human beings. Human thought could fathom the natural world because thought is natural, is a part of nature and even "develops there" (230).[22] He cited the shape of crystals (such as the silicon chips used now in computers) as an example of the presence of thought in nature. Scientific study was actually a form of human communication with the thought of the universe.

Since human beings are not separate from nature but share its logic, they can use nature as a means to communicate with each other, which means that human beings are not of necessity atoms, not necessarily isolated from one another. Communication between people is so real, according to Peirce, that a group of people becomes one person to the degree that they communicate and share thoughts. Yet Peirce's metaphysics was supremely tough minded and allowed for plenty of recognition of what separates people as well as joins them. There is, in short, a basis in Peirce's philosophy for an extremely sophisticated social and political theory (187–88).

Peirce never followed up his metaphysical conception of community with a full blown sociological theory, though he at least once suggested that he intended to do so. He had equally little to say about the sociological theories of others except for an occasional expression of disgust with Herbert Spencer, social Darwinism, and celebrations of selfishness in laissez-faire economic theories. Yet with our growing understanding of pragmatism in general and Peirce in particular, the greatest American philosopher may yet have some influence in social and political theory. What Peirce offers to political theory is the most profoundly realist metaphysics of the modern era, a metaphysics that makes it possible to conceive of society as more than an abstract name for a collection of atomistic individuals.

In what, for Peirce, does the reality of a human being consist? Like James and Dewey—and twenty years before them—Peirce came to see the human self as a series of relations. But he laid far more emphasis than they on the interpretive, representative aspect of these relations—as in his famous statement that "man is a sign" (255). Since life is a train of thought and since thought, according to Peirce, is a semiotic process, a human being is a sign. A human being, in other words, consists of his or

22. The page numbers in parentheses through the end of this chapter refer to *Peirce on Signs*.

her thoughts, the meaning of which are not unmediated, as Descartes had believed, but are only known through an act of interpretation. There were implications of metaphysical idealism in Peirce's declaration that persons are constituted by thought, but his idealism was moderate and did not exclude the material. For Peirce always insisted also on a material quality in thought, insisted that the semiotic relations that constitute the person are in turn constituted in the body and, especially, the brain.

Peirce's notion that human identity rests on relations of thought within the person—or, as he sometimes said, on the person's existing within thought—makes his conception of the person social in a more profound sense than in Dewey's philosophy. When Dewey said a person was essentially social he meant that the person was formed in relation with other people, but he never laid out a metaphysics showing that the relations that enable people to communicate with each other are the same kind of relations out of which their individual identities are constituted. In Peirce, on the other hand, the same kind of relations—semiotic relations—that create society also create the self so that there is no impassable barrier between self and society. Indeed, in a strict sense, for Peirce, there is no such thing as an individual but only relations. Even if there were only one person on earth, that "individual" would actually be, not an individual, but so to speak, a society of thoughts and feelings within that person's body.

Just as a person is a society, so may society be a person. To say that society is real in the same way that a person is real is to say that rather than being a mere collection of atomistic individuals, society may have enough spiritual or mental unity to be not merely many persons but also one "greater person":

> All that is necessary, upon this theory, to the existence of a person is that the feelings out of which he is constructed should be in close enough connection to influence one another. . . . if this be the case, there should be something like personal consciousness in bodies of men who are in intimate and intensely sympathetic communion. It is true that when the generalization of feeling has been carried so far as to include all within a person [i.e., an individual human being] a stopping-place, in a certain sense, has been attained; and further generalization will have a less lively character. But we must not think it will cease. Esprit de corps, national sentiment, sympathy, are no mere metaphors. None of us can fully realize what the minds of corporations are, any more than one of my brain-cells

can know what the whole brain is thinking. But the law of mind clearly
points to the existence of such personalities (229–30).

Clearly, Peirce is using the word "person" in a very broad sense. His
point is not that society has the *same* coherence as a human being but that
it has some of the same *kind* of coherence. Semiotic relations within an
organic brain constitute a human person, while relations among human
beings give society its personhood. Peirce is not proposing an exact analogy between a human person and society. Society is bound to be more
complex, less coherent, and less vital than a human person. Beyond the
human self, the generalization of feeling that also makes society a self or
person will be "less lively." Society, considered as a person, is less alive
than a human being, who will therefore not be able to see himself or
herself simply writ large in society. Yet the relations among the human
beings who comprise society are intense enough to give society some of
the same coherence of feeling, some of the same life, that makes a human
being a self.

This notion of vitality and coherence in the societal person, in comparison to the human person, saves Peirce's idea of society from slipping
into totalitarianism. In order to guard against some extremist misunderstanding that society as a self has all-encompassing claims on our personal selves, I occasionally speak of society as merely an "emergent mind"
or else say that it has coherence and identity that begins to "approach"
that of a human being. To claim that society and human beings have the
same degree of coherence or personhood would miss Peirce's firm attention to the different material relations or, in Peirce's words, "secondness"
on which are based the "thirdness" or semiotic relations that constitute
persons. Because of the difference in the secondness out of which citizens
and society are composed (human bodies, in the one case, plus instruments of communication, in the other), there is less danger of losing
sight of the difference between individuals and groups than in vague, organic notions of society as a larger self to which we owe unswerving loyalty. In Peirce's view of society as a "person," the claims that society may
rightfully make on us can scarcely be total. Yet we are not only part of
that "greater person" but to some degree owe ourselves and our minds to
it, just as it owes its personhood to us and our relations with other people.

If Peirce allows for such large differences between society and human
beings, it might be asked, why use the word "person" to describe society?
But here I think Peirce's literary instinct is sound. We need to be re-
minded of commonalities more than differences. "Person," applied both
to a human being and to society, captures Peirce's point that the same

kind of communicative, semiotic relations that give a human being personal identity are involved, albeit in a less "lively" way, in creating a holisitic society. "Person" keeps our attention focused on the difficult task of relating human beings to society rather than the easy job of separating them from it.

As a "greater person," society is formed by communication among ordinary persons: "two minds in communication are, in so far [as they communicate], 'at one,' that is, are properly one mind in that part of them" (255). Just as interpretive relations within the brain create the self, the extension of those relations via words and other communicative media may bring human "individuals" into close enough spiritual communication to form a still larger self. If as Peirce believed, the individual human self is constructed of interpretive, semiotic relations, there is nothing to prevent those relations being extended by words and other signs to include other human beings. The same sort of mental or semiotic relations that constitute a person are capable of constituting society and giving it some of the same sort of reality or spiritual unity as individual human beings. Although others had preceded Peirce in arguing for a conception of the state as a personality, they did so in idealistic, Hegelian terms, which left the idea sounding vaguely hopeful.[23] Peirce actually explained how community feeling could make society a person.

Peirce's discovery that society can be a person is a potentially important contribution to political theory because it shows the boundary between self and society to be permeable on the basis of a sophisticated theory of communication. For Peirce there is no separation of kind or essence between self and society. Each is constituted of interpretive relations that may flow into the other. Peirce of course acknowledged the element of organicism that also weighed so heavily in Dewey's conception of individual human beings. But Peirce showed how the boundaries between organic bodies are crossed. The relations constituting the individual self are organic and neurological while the relations constituting society take the form of speech, newspapers, television, and other media. But however the relations are constituted, the signs they carry may be interpreted as having the same meaning, so that both individuals and social groups (or "greater persons") may think the same thoughts. Interpretive relations among individuals therefore enable them to join and become, to some extent, one. Self and society merge, not indistinguishably, but fluidly in Peirce's metaphysics.

23. Wilfred M. McClay, *The Masterless: Self and Society in Modern America* (Chapel Hill: University of North Carolina Press, 1994), 135.

Dewey, on the other hand, never allowed for the possibility of greater persons, never allowed for the possibility that human beings might share some spiritual quality, might possess some degree of unity amounting to an identity resembling in some respects the personal identity of an individual human being. When Dewey spoke of the self as social he meant only that the human self was a product of society, not that society may be a self. At least he never spelled out a theory of communication comparable to Peirce's clearly showing how a human being and society may each share some of the same kind of selfhood. Legions of commentators have lamented Dewey's failure to spell out the details of his vision of participatory democracy. But even if Dewey had offered specifics, they would have been unlikely to have much improved the mechanics of democracy. The real problem is that nowhere does Dewey ask, let alone answer, the question, can the inevitably imperfect mechanisms of democracy be aided by a deeper spiritual unity than is allowed for in the prognostications of liberal technocrats, be they managerial elitists, pessimistic practitioners of realpolitik, or skillful integrators of opposed positions?

Perhaps some reader more steeped in Dewey than I will point out a passage where Dewey did describe society as possessing some holism, even amounting to a kind of emergent mind or personhood. I have looked for such a description of society in Dewey's works but have not found it. Certainly, he often spoke of the wrongheadedness of atomistic individualism and announced his confidence that society cannot be described in nominalist terms. Sometimes he spoke of mind as "emergent" or arising out of social interaction. But this always seems to come back to the mind of the individual organism emerging out of social interaction. In Dewey I have found no description of society as an emergent mind, after the fashion of Peirce's description of society as a "greater person." If I have missed such a passage in Dewey, I will be grateful to be corrected but will still be convinced of the soundness of my argument for Peirce's greater usefulness in social and political theory.

For unlike Peirce, and of this there can be no doubt, Dewey had no well-developed theory of communication to explain how such social holism might emerge. Dewey was probably the most widely read American philosopher in the first half of the twentieth century. The absence in his writings of any attempt to explain how, not just assert that, society was more than a nominalist aggregate of separate individuals left twentieth-century political theory with nowhere to turn for such an explanation. Peirce's theory of communication by semiotic relations could have provided such an explanation, but Peirce fell into oblivion at least partly because James and Dewey misrepresented him to subsequent generations as the originator of *their* kind of pragmatism. Liberal political theory was therefore built on James's and Dewey's weak pragmatism with its implicit support of nominalism because of its lack of a vital theory of communication. Liberal theory became skilled at spotting nominalist particulars that separate us from each other but less able to identify the universals or generals that unite us as a society.

Our Deweyan twentieth-century liberal tradition has proven deft in recognizing the divisive forces in our society, but a Peircean approach might enable us also to recognize what supposedly tough minded liberals have missed and, in missing, have perhaps also helped rend: the reality of shared spirit, or in Peirce's words, "greater persons." It is not that special interests, racial prejudice, ethnic antagonisms, and the countervailing powers to which liberal social theorists have devoted so much attention are unreal. They are as real as the divisive forces within any individual self. Clashing desires, unresolved inner conflicts, and impractical ideas make individual selfhood incomplete and unsatisfying for many people but nonetheless real. So may be the case with the reality of society at large.

Neither James nor Dewey offered a detailed theory of communication similar to Peirce's demonstration that, just as a person is social, society may have some of the same kind of spiritual integration as a person. Weak pragmatists, confident of their originality in conceiving of the human self as a social creation, never considered the possibility that their implicit nominalism focused their attention on the individual and led them to dismiss the society as unreal. They laid the basis for the individualism of twentieth-century liberal democrats such as Lippmann and Niebuhr who could not conceive of the political process in ways other than as the machinations of the inside expert or the power plays of groups practicing realpolitik. Their pragmatic nominalism prevented these two social critics from conceiving of a spiritual or mental role for the people. The masses' reciprocal contempt for liberal democrats suggests that liberals could have used some of the humility that might have accompanied acceptance of Peirce's notion of groups as "greater persons."

Our contemporary Deweyans are too certain of their uncertainty. The problem with the revival of supposed pragmatic social thought—and its daring acceptance of knowledge without foundations, of signs and language without objective representation, and of the need to act without certainty—is the extraordinary confidence of the latter-day Deweyans that this point of view is not only au courant, but positively the last word.

The restoration of a bit of humility to liberalism might make a lot of people more accepting of liberals, and also make liberals more accepting of intellectual innovation.

Unlike contemporary Deweyans, who can only offer an old world view to confirm, Peirce offers a new one to explore. He helps us understand our contemporary social and political theory as what it most likely is, not postmodern but primitive. Peirce can help restore a healthy sense that the world, including its social and political aspects, is a place we are only beginning to understand. Celebrating the Deweyan past more or less on its own terms has led to the unsurprising conclusion that it is a usable past. A Peircean approach allows us to critically reexamine that past.

Heirs of Dewey and James that we intellectual historians mostly are, we do not easily criticize our forebears. It is not simply that like all people we are created by our heritage but that ours is a heritage of weak pragmatism containing a nominalist and even antiintellectual bias. Rightly committed to a reconstructionist rather than a deconstructionist approach to history, we have nevertheless not sufficiently allowed that recovering the past as it was is consistent with also interpreting and criticizing it in order to make a better future. This may be one reason why, despite a fairly secure institutional base in universities and colleges, intellectual history is an isolated scholarly field that exerts little influence on other historians and other academic disciplines, and virtually none on any broader public. More engagement, more questioning of the past, is not only consistent with accurately reconstructing the past but can also help make intellectual history a more vital part of the intellectual life of our own time.

Intellectual historians need not merely to engage the past but to engage it intellectually. Antifoundationalists have suggested that philosophers ought to write more like historians. But I believe intellectual historians should write a bit more like philosophers. Oftentimes our attention is more on contexts than on texts. More attention to texts would let us ask questions about the influence of texts on their readers and on the texts those readers themselves create. In the absence of closer readings of texts, there is a danger of relying too heavily on thinkers' self-descriptions as to what they are or were about. James said he was realistic and Dewey proclaimed himself an antinominalist in social theory, but their pleas in behalf of their own philosophy should not be accepted at face value. Rather, we must ask if they actually created texts useful in steering twentieth-century liberals, including themselves, past self-justifying elitism, excessively cynical realpolitik, or locally constrained good intentions. In this book I argue that they did not, and I base my argument on their philosophical writings and their influence on, or lack of assistance to, three prototypical liberal political thinkers, Lippmann, Niebuhr, and Follett. I hope that those who disagree with my argument will not do so by citing James's and Dewey's statements about their philosophy or Lippmann's, Niebuhr's, and Follett's self-proclaimed descriptions of their social and political theories. Rather, I hope that they will examine and argue from the philosophical and historical texts themselves.

"Intellectual history" ought to allow for the influence of thought in life, but the influence of thought will be missed if we look for it only in responses to dramatic political events. For example, one of this manuscript's anonymous readers has offered an evaluation indicative of the difficulty intellectual historians have in understanding the potential political usefulness of a thinker who wrote little about politics and social theory: "my major reservation is that Hoopes needs to show us Peirce thinking, not as a logician or a semiotician, but as a social thinker, thinking about power, justice, liberty, and so forth. . . . When one thinks of Lippmann and Niebuhr addressing so many political issues, and facing reality as it broke out in the daily news, it is hard to believe they would have thought differently about politics, war, revolution, social disruption, etc. had they thought as Peirceans."

The point of this book is not to suggest that if Lippmann and Niebuhr had better understood Peirce they would have thought differently about, say, the depression or fascism as these events "broke out in the daily news." Rather, I want to show that their conception of the democratic process was unduly constrained by the tradition of weak pragmatism in which they were educated. I also want to show that Peirce's strong pragmatism could have improved their understanding of democracy and therefore might prove similarly useful to us. Knowledge of a philosophy like Peirce's that allows for the reality of "general persons" might have made their view of democracy less discouraged than it was, might have allowed in Lippmann a little more confidence in public opinion and in Niebuhr a little more hope that groups might sometimes have morals. Less harmful, perhaps, in their day than in ours, Lippmann's elitism and Niebuhr's realpolitik foreshadowed and helped create our contemporary liberalism that, despite its rhetorical flair, is intellectually timid, and, despite its pious avowals, sometimes antisocial.

More generally, my goal is to show that the political culture of twentieth-century American liberalism was weakened by being built on philosophical premises mistakenly thought by many, at the end of this century as well as at its beginning, to have been the best available in our pragmatic tradition. This subject does not require showing Peirce as a

"social thinker." I am the first to admit he was no such thing. To be asked
to show him in this light is a bit like being asked to comment on
Napoleon as a theologian. But if Peirce was not a social thinker he created a philosophy potentially more fruitful for social and political theory
than the pragmatism of James and Dewey. I will be content if I convince
some readers that there were problems in the philosophy of James and
Dewey and problems in the political thought of Lippmann, Niebuhr,
and Follett that a more accurate understanding of Peirce might have
helped resolve. Accomplishing even that much might encourage others
to elaborate in the present and future, as Peirce in the past admittedly did
not, the potentially fruitful implications of Peircean philosophy for a realistic political theory.

Although elaborating a Peircean political theory is beyond the scope
of the present study, not to mention my present means and energy, I will
offer a small summary of the qualities that I believe such a theory might
have contributed to twentieth-century liberalism, qualities that we still
very much need. Peirce's realist understanding of human groups as
"greater persons" might have informed liberalism with a conception of
leadership that was more truly democratic, a conception in which leaders thought of themselves as a part of society instead of its top-down
managers and policy makers. An understanding of society as real and of
ourselves as part of something larger might have meant that the left as
well as the right, with its organic metaphors and Burkean sentimental-
ism, would have had a vocabulary of social responsibility. A metaphysical alternative to Cartesian essentialism and confidence in unmediated
self-knowledge—which Peirce's semiotic provided in detail but Dewey's
philosophy suggested only vaguely—might have somewhat mitigated
intolerance and the shrill, unreasoned certainties bandied about the
political arena. Had such things been possible they would have been
important contributions to a democratic polity. Perhaps they are still
possible.

PEIRCE'S LOGICAL

COMMUNITARIANISM

Dust as we are, the immortal spirit grows
Like dark harmony in music; there is a dark
Inscrutable workmanship that reconciles
Discordant elements, makes them cling together
In one society.

  —William Wordsworth, *Lines Composed a Few Miles above Tintern Abbey*

Any argument for the usefulness to social theory of the philosophy of
Charles Sanders Peirce must frankly acknowledge that many of his contemporaries and some scholars since have thought him, with some justice, to have been an antisocial fool. Greater gifts and opportunities have
seldom been bestowed and even less seldom spent so recklessly. Son of
one of the country's leading mathematicians, Peirce got a running start
in intellectual life. His father, Benjamin, was a Harvard professor and
head of the U.S. Coast Survey, which provided Charles with employment as a working scientist for much of his life and made him one of the
foremost geodesists of his time. Peirce's irresponsible behavior eventually
led to feuds with all of his employers—the Harvard Observatory, the
Coast Survey, and Johns Hopkins University, where for five years he held
his only philosophic appointment. Equally disastrous were his marriages.
The first, to an active feminist, ended in a divorce disturbing to middle-
class sensibilities of the time. The second marriage, to a mysterious
French woman who went by the name of Juliette Pourtalai and whose
true name remains unknown, grew out of a love affair conducted with far
less discretion than prevailing proprieties required. When the president
of Johns Hopkins, Daniel Coit Gilman, learned that the "marriage made

no difference in the [sexual] relations of the parties," Peirce's academic career was brought to an end.[1] Peirce was evidently also an adulterer and wife beater, and there are indications that a painful facial neuralgia led to drug addiction. Combined with all these troubles, Peirce's delusions of powerful enemies, his grandiose dreams of a fortune around the next corner, and his insistence on a lavish lifestyle plunged him into poverty and isolation in his later years.

In those later years, Peirce was dependent on William James, who came to Peirce's aid by arranging monetary support, by crediting Peirce with the creation of the pragmatic philosophy that helped to make James famous, and by arranging lectures in Cambridge. The depth to which Peirce's reputation had sunk may be measured by the fact that he lectured in Cambridge but not on the Harvard campus; President Charles William Eliot refused to sanction his visit. Peirce responded gratefully to James's aid and even adopted in old age the middle name "Santiago" (Saint James) as a tribute to his benefactor. Yet he also often expressed dismay with what James and other popularizers had done to his ideas. In preparation for some 1898 lectures in Cambridge, Peirce was urged by James to abandon the mathematical elements of his philosophy in favor of "topics of a vitally important character."[2] During the lectures, Peirce replied to James's comment, asserting that "*vital importance* seems to be a very low kind of importance" as compared to the mathematician's pursuit of the "real potential world."[3] Furthermore, "A Neglected Argument for the Reality of God," Peirce's 1909 essay and almost his last philosophical breath, ended with an implied rebuke of James for "such confusions of thought as that of active willing (willing to control thought, to doubt, and to weigh reasons) with willing not to exert the will (willing to believe)."[4]

A century later, the sad story of Peirce's life less and less obscures his philosophical achievements, but his ever increasing recognition as the greatest American philosopher has far outstripped intellectual historians' general understanding of his philosophy and especially its political

1. The quotation is from Gilman's informant and Peirce's Hopkins colleague, the distinguished scientist Simon Newcomb. Interestingly, Newcomb was Arthur Conan Doyle's model for Professor Moriarty, the dastardly enemy of one of fiction's great semioticians (*Boston Globe*, 5 January 1993, 3). For Newcomb's real-life treachery, see Joseph Lancaster Brent, *Charles Sanders Peirce: A Life* (Bloomington: Indiana University Press, 1993), 151–52.
2. James's letter to Peirce, 22 December 1897, quoted in Kenneth Laine Ketner and Hilary Putman, "Introduction" to Peirce, *Reasoning and the Logic of Things: The Cambridge Conference Lectures of 1898*, ed. Ketner (Cambridge, Mass.: Harvard University Press, 1992), 25.
3. Peirce, *Reasoning and the Logic of Things*, 121.
4. *Peirce on Signs: Writings on Semiotic by Charles Sanders Peirce*, ed. James Hoopes (Chapel Hill: University of North Carolina Press, 1991), 278.

implications. The general tendency is to assume that because his best known writings involving the conception of community were on science, his social experience as part of the rising community of professional scientists must have been responsible for the communitarian emphasis of his philosophy.[5] This assumption is just an assumption and rests on little textual or biographical evidence other than the fact that Peirce was a scientist as well as a philosopher and that his father was a major figure in the professionalization of science in the nineteenth century. There is no doubt something to the assumption that Peirce's experience as a working scientist affected his notion of community, but the assumption has obscured the fact that Peirce's vocational preference was not science but logic, even if he was only able to earn a living as a logician for a few years. Even those who see Peirce's communitarianism as an "elegant epistemological rationale" for the authority of experts admit that there is no evidence to suggest the relationship was anything other than "indirect and unintentional."[6] Close attention to his writings, however, reveals a direct and intentional relation between his logic and his communitarianism.

At least part of the reason for the neglect of Peirce's logic by historians of pragmatism and political theory is that broad synthetic studies can draw on intellectual historians' vast spadework on James and Dewey, but historians have done much less work on Peirce's life and thought. This is true despite Joseph Brent's well written and widely praised biography of Peirce. Although this book is a valuable mine of information about Peirce's personal life and social situation it offers only a superficial look at his thought, and in the end it merely reinforces the conventional and by no means inaccurate notion of Peirce's personal life as impassioned but troubled and somewhat antisocial:

I imagine him as a confidence man and prestidigitator—a frenzied juggler elegantly dressed in harlequin costume, on a flimsy but deceptively substantial stage of his own devising, gambling everything on keeping too many improbably seductive objects in flight, while trying to decide which one to snare. At the end, he stands there in tatters, surrounded by the melancholy debris of his life. . . . But all the while, this poor fool, behind the scenes and between the acts, has been building piece by piece the

5. Thomas L. Haskell, *The Emergence of Professional Social Science: The American Social Science Association and the Nineteenth-Century Crisis of Authority* (Urbana: University of Illinois Press, 1977), 239. See also Raymond Jackson Wilson, *In Quest of Community: Social Philosophy in the United States, 1860–1920* (New York: Oxford University Press, 1970).
6. Thomas L. Haskell, *The Authority of Experts: Studies in History and Theory* (Bloomington: Indiana University Press, 1984), 209.

armature of a most marvelously intricate universe, so beautiful it trans-figures him amidst the wreck of his afflictions, and we gratefully see the signs around us with new eyes.[7]

While there is much truth to this picture of Peirce at the end of his life, it offers no help in understanding the relationship between his preco-cious intellectual development and his early commitment to a commu-nitarian philosophy. Here, too, Brent's biography, rather than breaking new ground, merely fills in the conventional outline. Brent describes Peirce's contemptuous dismissal of most of his secondary school and Harvard College teachers, thus pointing toward the adult character flaws that caused the philosopher so many difficulties: "I imagine Charles in 1857, at age eighteen, brilliantly discoursing in class 'that the PERFECT is the Great Subject of Metaphysics,' elegantly dressed, in negligent pos-ture, completely self-assured and cool, the picture of the arrogant Dandy." As for Peirce's youthful commitment to logic, Brent gives us only well known stock scenes of Peirce's family history: his adored father, Ben-jamin, a Harvard professor of mathematics, showing the teenage Charles flaws in the arguments of Kant, Spinoza, and Hegel; or again, Peirce re-calling himself at twelve, "picking up Whately's [Elements of] Logic, in my elder brother's room, and asking him what logic was. I next see myself stretched on his carpet, devouring the book. . . . From that day to this, logic has been my passion."[8]

Those intellectual historians such as Murray Murphey and Bruce Kuklick who have paid the most attention to Peirce's actual writings rather than merely the social circumstances of his life have recognized the centrality of logic to his thought but have not related it to his em-phasis on community.[9] As opposed to those who emphasize Peirce's par-ticipation in the professional scientific community to explain his communitarianism, these writers emphasize his isolation from the pro-fessional academic community to explain what they see as shortcomings in his philosophy. Between the two camps of intellectual historians—those focused on Peirce as a logician and philosopher and those focused on his science and communitarianism—there is a void that has pre-vented recognition of the importance of his logic in committing him to communitarianism.

7. Brent, *Charles Sanders Peirce*, 203.
8. Quotations in ibid, 57 and 48.
9. Murray Murphey, *The Development of Peirce's Philosophy* (Cambridge, Mass.: Harvard Univer-sity Press, 1961); Bruce Kuklick, *The Rise of American Philosophy, Cambridge, Massachusetts, 1860 – 1930* (New Haven: Yale University Press, 1977).

If Peirce's social experience is taken, as it surely ought to be taken, to include his impassioned participation in the nineteenth-century community of logicians as well as scientists, it is possible to see that his communitarianism was based far more deeply in his social experience as a logician than as a scientist. Unlike scientists, however, nineteenth-century logicians were relatively few in number and not yet beginning to organize in professional associations. Still, Peirce's work as a scientist may well have been more void of congenial human society than his work as a logician, since his primary scientific field—geodesy—involved fieldwork in distant, often dreary places, with little expert assistance or scientific companionship.[10] Peirce's participation in the community of logicians also often took place at a distance and mainly involved communication through reading, writing, and lecturing—social activities in which he engaged far more prolifically as a logician than as a scientist.

In the common view Peirce and Dewey were both spokesmen for the method of science, but the common view misses the point that Peirce, as a formal logician, was far more critical of the ordinary assumption that science was concerned only with particular facts and that it denied the reality of general ideas. Peirce took general ideas to be the basis of mind, religion, communication, and most relevant to this book—community. Science, Peirce said, is not necessarily connected to nominalism, the notion that the only realities are singular facts or individuals. Science is therefore not "necessarily connected with doctrines of a debasing moral tendency" (2:486).[11] The eclipse of Peirce's pragmatism by Dewey's was a tragedy for liberal political theory because there was not in Peirce, as there was in Dewey, a profound breach between an implicitly nominalist metaphysics focused on particulars and a social philosophy attempting communitarian perspectives. If it is possible to show here that the origin of Peirce's views on community lay at least as much in logic as in science, a window may be opened through which intellectual historians can begin to see the complexity of pragmatism, see that it offered not only the Deweyan tradition of empirical respect for particular facts and individuals, but also a path not taken, the Peircean tradition of logical respect for general ideas and communities.

The common error that this study aims to avoid is the lifting out of the context of his realist metaphysics Peirce's frequent statements to the effect that logic is rooted in social life. Peirce's most fundamental view

10. Brent, *Charles Sanders Peirce.*
11. Throughout this chapter all in-text citations refer to volume and page numbers of *Writings of Charles S. Peirce: A Chronological Edition*, ed. Edward C. Moore et al. (Bloomington: Indiana University Press, 1982–present).

was that it is the other way around, that "the social principle is rooted intrinsically in logic." [12] Although he was undoubtedly speaking with conviction when he said that logic is social, such statements reflected his deeper commitment to the idea that society is founded in logic, that logic has a metaphysical basis infinitely broader than the human relations constituting society. As a metaphysical realist who believed in the reality represented by general ideas, Peirce believed that community was an expression of those ideas, not vice versa.

This common but mistaken notion that Peirce believed in a socially determined logic has been used to sanction subjectivist views about knowledge and expertise that Peirce would have found abhorrent. In science Peirce was a fallibilist. That is, he believed that it is impossible to know with certainty that any particular theory is true. But he also believed that countless numbers of our ideas are true, even if we do not know for certain the truth of any particular one. We have reached the truth about many things because our thoughts are constrained by the logic of those things, by the logic of objective reality. But since we cannot know for certain that any one thought is true and since our errors also are innumerable, inquiry may go on to infinity. But it does not follow from these views, as one prominent interpretation has it, that "sound opinion becomes that opinion which wins the broadest and deepest support in the existing community of inquiry; there is, according to Peirce, no higher test of reality." [13] For Peirce the final test of the soundness of opinion is not agreement among the community of inquiry but consistency with the logic of reality itself.

This mistaken view that Peirce makes the community the final arbiter of sound opinion ironically reflects and is occasionally used to support subjectivist academic practice in our own time, when scholars sometimes seem to know more about each other's views than the disciplines they ostensibly study. The more or less self-conscious creations of small communities of scholars who answer to no higher standard of reality than their own mutually agreed upon and supposedly expert opinions is one of the diseases of modern humanistic scholarship. On a smaller scale but in a perhaps more insidious guise, such self-appointed elites embody in contemporary scholarship the nominalist philosophical errors in political theory against which this book argues. What Peirce would have thought

12. *Peirce on Signs,* 113.
13. Thomas L. Haskell, *The Emergence of Professional Social Science,* 238–39. Haskell modifies this view by taking note of Peirce's realism in his essay, "Justifying the Rights of Academic Freedom in the Era of 'Power/Knowledge,'" in *Legal Rights: Historical and Philosophical Perspectives,* ed. Austin Sarat and Thomas R. Kearns (Ann Arbor: University of Michigan Press, 1996), 147–50.

of such self-justifying cliques is suggested by his comment on the danger of gentility in science: "Wherever there is a large class of academic professors who are provided with good incomes and looked up to as gentlemen, scientific inquiry must languish."[14]

What begins to make it possible to escape our past misunderstandings of Peirce is the ongoing publication of the *Writings of Charles S. Peirce: A Chronological Edition.* Although the series will not be completed in this century (nor in the next if new funding is not found), five of the projected twenty volumes have appeared, and these carry the story well past Peirce's formative years as a philosopher. They reveal that the young Peirce was anything but isolated and that there was a significant audience for his logic, an audience for whom he worked hard at clear expression and who probably influenced the communitarian tendency of his thought. Although the later Peirce was certainly no "public philosopher" who spoke to general audiences about issues of broad public concern in the manner of his voluble fellow pragmatists James and Dewey, the early essentials of his philosophy were expressed in public discourse.[15]

As a young man Peirce even seems to have attempted something like a career as a public philosopher. Between the ages of twenty-four and thirty, he spoke approximately three dozen times on philosophic subjects to non-specialists—in an address at his high school reunion, in two lecture series on logic for Harvard alumni, and in a third series of lectures on logic at the Lowell Institute. Also, he presented a series of difficult but important papers on logic to the American Academy of Arts and Sciences. For a young man with no academic appointment and relatively few publications, it was a considerable achievement to be called on to speak so many times, often to audiences of a hundred or more, about such a difficult topic as logic (especially as challenging a logic as his). Although Peirce conceded little to his audience's lack of expertise, his lectures were euphonious and contained a good bit of moralism that could be appreciated without comprehending the logic. Moreover, he was reputed to have oratorical talent.[16] With his dark good looks, piercing eyes, and air of omniscience, Peirce probably had no trouble making the lectures an enjoyable experience, even for those who did not understand them.

The young Peirce was, then, something of a public philosopher and was certainly much more so than the young James or the young Dewey,

14. "The Scientific Attitude and Fallibilism," in *Philosophical Writings of Peirce,* ed. Justus Buchler (New York: Dover, 1955), 45.
15. For the useful concept of "public philosopher," I am indebted to George Cotkin, *William James: Public Philosopher* (Baltimore: Johns Hopkins University Press, 1990).
16. Brent, *Charles Sanders Peirce,* 57.

both of whom were far more cloistered in their early careers. Only later did they grow into the role of public philosophers, just at the time the older Peirce was sinking into miserable seclusion. Indeed, Peirce's early opportunities to address the public may well have been crucial in bringing him to philosophic maturity. Unable to earn a living as a philosopher, he was embarking on a demanding scientific career in the U.S. Coast Survey. Even though his overriding passion continued to be philosophy rather than science, he may have needed the stimulus provided by lecture requests to continue to develop his logic. The lectures outlined nearly all the important ideas he subsequently expressed in his well-known early publications—the 1867 "New List of Categories," the "cognition series" of 1868–69, the 1871 review of Fraser's edition of Berkeley, and the 1877–78 series, "Illustrations of the Logic of Science." That he thus eventually made his ideas ready for print may have had much to do with the earlier demand for their oral expression. In any case, rather than being the result of hermetic isolation, Peirce's logic was early articulated and refined in public.

Peirce's lectures show that whatever the connection to his scientific work his interest in community was also strongly stimulated by his being a logician interested in the question of how human minds should think, communicate with each other, and relate to nature. Unable to support himself as a logician, he probably reconciled himself to a career in science as the best way, both practically and intellectually, to further his overriding interest in logic.[17] His philosophical lectures were the crucial experience in formulating his ideas on community as well as logic. And lecturing on his logic to a nonspecialist public may have led him to further highlight his logic's communitarian implications as a way of making his lectures more appealing and relevant to that public.

It is even conceivable that Peirce, as an alternative to science, toyed with the idea of an Emersonian career as a sort of delphic prophet addressing the broad public in popular lectures. Consider his remarkable address on "The Place of Our Age in the History of Civilization," which he delivered at his high school reunion in 1863. The recently married twenty-four-year-old philosopher could not afford a roof of his own and had brought his bride to live with his parents. In search of a vocation he tried on the mantle of Emerson, whom he knew personally and whom he approvingly quoted to his classmates: "Things are in the saddle, and ride mankind." The young philosopher's style and tone were unmistakably Emersonian: "Our age is brilliant. . . . But is it never to end . . . ? Are

17. Max H. Fisch, "Introduction," in *Writings of Charles S. Peirce*, 1:xxiii.

we then to go on forever toying with electricity and steam, whether in the laboratory or in business, and never *use* these means in the broad field of humanity and social destiny? . . . So then our age shall end; and, indeed, the question is not so much why should it not, as why should it continue" (1:112–13).

Peirce's poor qualifications for the role of Emersonian prophet were confirmed by his high school reunion address, which has a loftiness that even the ethereal sage of Concord would have had trouble matching. Can one imagine Emerson taking up the topic of the historic moment in 1863 and never even mentioning, as Peirce did not that night, that his country was embroiled in Civil War?

Yet there is also a mundaneness in Peirce utterly missing in Emerson. One can almost hear Emerson saying that "the time is coming when there shall be no more poetry," as Peirce did, but Emerson would have bypassed poetic expression in favor of direct, spiritual communication with the Oversoul. Peirce, however, counted on science to make "us familiar with the body of all things, and the unity of the body of all" (1:114). When Peirce said that he wanted to *use* electricity and steam "in the broad field of humanity and social destiny," he had something much more practical in mind than the sort of symbolic or metaphorical uses by which Emerson would have tried to improve the human spirit.

The new wife whom Peirce was attempting to support was Melusina Fay, a zealous social reformer and feminist for whom he had written several of his earliest philosophical manuscripts (1:xxxi). Some of the germinal ideas in those manuscripts would sprout in his public addresses between 1863 and 1869 and then blossom in his best-known philosophic publications in the next decade. "Zina," as Peirce's wife was called, believed human improvement required much more than spiritual insight. So did her husband, who told his high school classmates that since Descartes, humanity had been living in an age of "reason" and must push on to ages of "imagination," "desire," and "action," which is reason's "purpose; and to say that it is not, is the essence of selfishness and atheism" (1:114).

Where Emerson celebrated the internal gaze as the path to the highest truth, Peirce urged humanity to look outward. In 1865, two years after the high school reunion address, he delivered a series of lectures on the logic of science to Harvard alumni. Beginning with a discussion of logic in general, he contradicted the tradition according to which logic's subject was introspective examination of the mind's right workings and its object to learn to think by rules derived from introspection: "we ought to adopt a thoroughly unpsychological view of logic." People wish to think logically "because we wish our thoughts to be representations or symbols of fact" (1:164, 166). Therefore logic pertained to the symbolic element of thought. Peirce informed his audience of what he would announce to the world two years later in his "New List of Categories": logic properly took as its subject, not simply normative rules for the operation of the human mind, but the relations of all symbols to their objects. Symbols might "just as well be studied in the sensible representation as the mental" (1:167; cf. 2:157). In fact, Peirce believed that study of sensible or physical representations, such as marks on paper rather than ideas in the mind, put logic on a far sounder footing by avoiding the mistaken notion that the workings of the mind are immediately observable.

The great question of community is the relation between the general and the particular, the group and the individual, and already in Peirce's public lectures on logic he tended toward rejection of the nominalist notion that general kinds of things—say "horse" as opposed to a particular horse—cannot be real. In the middle of the 1860s Peirce was clearly moving toward realism even though, as Max Fisch said, Peirce was a "professing nominalist" until the time of his 1868–69 cognition series (2:xxvi). But Peirce's nominalism grew increasingly qualified in the 1860s. A nominalist denies the reality of universals. Peirce accepted the name of nominalist because he based his belief in universals upon signs, that is, upon representations which are embodied in particulars. But he did not deny the reality of universals, for he was "quite opposed to that individualism which is often supposed to be coextensive with nominalism" (2:175). And as early as 1865 he was lecturing his Cambridge audience to the effect that, at least in cognition, generals precede particulars, which is a realist rather than nominalist view. The elements of every logical judgment must be brought to unity, but "the world of self, the world of the feelings does not contain such a unity. Much rather does this unity contain the feelings. The world of feelings then is not a world of self but of instances of self." True, "we know our feelings immediately," but they achieve meaning or logic only by being unified mediately in an interpretive judgment: "This consistent unity since it belongs to all our judgments may be said to belong to us. Or rather since it belongs to the judgments of all mankind, we may be said to belong to it" (1:167).

Peirce's notion that the unifying relations of thought create selves rather than selves creating the unity of thought is what makes him a more communitarian philosopher than the Transcendentalists and also separates him, to a significant degree, from his fellow pragmatists James and Dewey. Where the Transcendentalists looked within their individual selves in order to raise their thoughts to the level of divine unity, Peirce

looked outward in order to insure that the logic by which his self was created was the logic of the universe. James and Dewey were eventually
ready to call the self an interpretation of a series of relations, but they
never quite escaped nominalism. Consequently, their philosophy was less
consistent with communitarianism than was Peirce's realism. For Dewey,
the individual biological organism, striving for a successful relation to its
environment, was the source of all thought. James eventually settled on
dyadic relations among "bits" of experience to create the self but never
explained how those discontinuous relations could establish the continuity of thought in which he also believed. Both Dewey and James were left
with nominalist or individualist elements in their philosophy difficult to
reconcile with any notion of community. But Peirce, with his complex,
relational view of reality, was left with no vestiges of atomism or particu-
larism. For him community could never be constituted of individuals,
but, individuals always, of a community of relations.

> You never can narrow down to an individual [Peirce told his Lowell In-
> stitute audience in 1866]. Do you say Daniel Webster is an individual? He
> is so in common parlance, but in logical strictness he is not. We think of
> certain images in our memory—a platform and a noble form uttering
> convincing and patriotic words—a statue—certain printed matter—
> and we say that which that speaker and the man whom that statue was
> taken for and the writer of this speech—that which these are in common
> is Daniel Webster. Thus, even the proper name of a man is a general term
> or the name of a class, for it names a class of sensations and thoughts. The
> true individual term[,] the absolutely singular *this* and *that*[,] cannot be
> reached. Whatever has comprehension must be general (1:461).

Peirce demonstrated to his Lowell Institute audience the usefulness of
logic by "adopting our logic as our metaphysics" and announcing to his
auditors the idea, which he would not publish for two more years, that a
person is a symbol (1:490). By the time the idea reached print, Peirce
would say that a human being is a "sign," rather than a "symbol," for he
was moving toward the terminology of his mature semiotic (2:241).
Descartes had bequeathed to the modern world the notion of the human
being, in Peirce's summary, as "essentially a soul, that is, a thing occupying a mathematical point of space, not thought itself but the subject of
inhesion of thought, without parts, and exerting a certain material force
called volition" (1:491). But Peirce, had already told the Lowell audience
what he would later write in his revolutionary "cognition series"—that
there is no such thing as "intuition" or an immediately known thought.

Rather, all thought is inferential interpretation of symbols ("signs" in the "cognition series"). Since life is a train of thought, "at any instant then man is a thought, and as thought is a species of symbol, the general answer to the question, What is man? is that he is a symbol" (1:494).

In order to help the audience of his Lowell lectures master so strange a notion, Peirce compared the symbolic nature of human beings to the symbolic nature of words. Mere waves of sound or lines on paper, words obviously differ from "the body of a man [which] is a wonderful mechanism" (1:494). But that is the only essential difference. A human being has self-consciousness, "the *I think,* the unity of thought; but the unity of thought is nothing but the unity of symbolization . . . and belongs to every word whatever." Consciousness also involves feeling or sensation, which a word cannot have: "But has it not something corresponding to feeling? Every feeling is . . . a mental sign or word. Now the word has a word; it has itself; and so if man is an animal feeling, the word is just as much a written feeling" (1:495). And so on, with perception, learning, denotation, connotation, interpretation, and even procreation! Acknowledging to his audience that this notion of "a true analogy between a man and a word" must seem "very paradoxical to you," Peirce admitted that "it did to me, at first. But having thought it over repeatedly, it has come to seem the merest truism" (1:498).

The fact that a human being is a sign makes it possible for an individual human being to belong to a genuine community. Speaking to an audience, Peirce dealt with an issue that, as far as I have found, he never touched in print, the issue of whether it diminishes human beings to find that the only essential difference between them and words is that people have organic bodies while words are embodied merely in puffs of air or marks on paper. His answer was that putting human beings on the same level as words did not reduce the human soul but, rather, enlarged it. Descartes had lodged the soul in the pineal gland, but by the middle of the nineteenth century conventional opinion held "that the soul is either spread over the whole body or is all in all, and all in every part" (1:498). Why stop there? Having expanded from the pineal gland to the entire body, was there any reason, Peirce asked, why the soul should not go beyond the body?

Are we shut up in a box of flesh and blood? When I communicate my thoughts and my sentiments to a friend with whom I am in full sympathy, so that my feelings pass into him and I am conscious of what he feels, do I not live in his brain as well as in my own—most literally? True, my animal life is not there; but my soul, my feeling, thought, attention are.

If this be not so, a man is not a word, it is true, but is something much poorer. There is a miserable material and barbarian notion according to which a man cannot be in two places at once; as though he were a *thing!* A word may be in several places at once . . . because its essence is spiritual; and I believe that a man is no whit inferior to the word in this respect (1:498; cf. 2:124).

This symbolic view of both people and words as things of spirit was an essential part of Peirce's communitarianism. Words enabled people not merely to communicate but to unite, to become literally one. The satisfaction people take in communication, in understanding and being understood, confirmed, according to Peirce, this unity of people via words and symbols: "man is conscious of his interpretant, his own thought in another mind . . . is happy in it, feels himself in some degree to be there" (1:499). This view clearly distinguishes Peirce from postmodernist literary theorists who believe that nothing can be repeated and explains why Peirce rather than, say, Saussure, is the source of modern communication theory. Peirce qualified his faith in communication by saying that he did not claim people were "immediately conscious" of their communicational unity (1:499). But this was no concession at all since Peirce believed that all cognition involves symbolic mediation rather than unmediated awareness of thought's meaning.

Symbols not only make it possible for there to be a community in space but also a community in time, which was why Peirce announced a doctrine of immortality to the audience of his Lowell lectures. Since symbols make it possible to live outside the body they make it possible to live forever, provided only that a person is a true rather than false symbol. That six represents twice three "is eternal truth; a truth which always is and must be; which would be though there were not six things in the universe to number. . . . Thus the necessary and true symbol is immortal." A human being is a symbol and can therefore be immortal, "provided he is vivified by the truth." When one person carries another "along with him in his opinions and sentiments," he has achieved in that second person a strictly spiritual existence based on "sympathy [and] love—this is what serves as evidence of man's absolute worth, and this is the existence which logic finds to be immortal." Such immortality via symbolic participation in the lives of others both now and later is of course different from the immortality most of us long for, since it lacks the animal feeling of our individual bodies. But Peirce insisted that symbolic immortality was "not an impersonal existence," for personality lies in cognitive unity "which belongs to every symbol" (1:500). The "foundation" of this theory, the young Peirce assured his audience, "is the rock of truth," and the theory "will serve to illustrate what use might be made by mightier hands of this reviled science, logic" (1:502). In time as well as in space, according to Peirce, the general, symbolic relations constituting the community also give life to the individual rather than the individual giving life to the community.

When Peirce described this theory of immortality via participation in the lives of others by true symbols, he was already planning such a future for himself. On March 23, 1867, he wrote in his private logic notebook, "I cannot explain the deep emotion with which I open this book again. . . . I cannot forget that here are the germs of the theory of the categories which is (if anything is) the gift I make to the world. That is my child. In it I shall live when oblivion has me—my body." On May 14, 1867, he delivered to the American Academy of Arts and Sciences his paper "On a New List of Categories," the paper which in later life he called "my one contribution to philosophy" (1:xxvi).

In the "New List," Peirce offered five fundamental conceptions necessary to bring first impressions of sense to the unity of a thought:

BEING
   Quality
   Relation
   Representation
SUBSTANCE

In the language of Peirce's essay, BEING is the manifold of impressions that must, by an interpretive act, be brought to the unitary idea of the SUBSTANCE before us. Any *quality*—say, the color red—in our impressions can be known only through comparison or contrast to another quality— say, blue—which makes a conception of *relation* indispensable in thinking of quality. This second conception—relation—requires a third, a mediating *representation* to join the things related by representing one of them to be itself a representation of the other.

What was new in Peirce's list, apart from its brevity, was *representation* since Aristotle and Kant both included *quality* and *relation* in their longer lists of categories. But placing representation next to substance was a revolutionary step in metaphysics. It opened the way for Peirce's general theory of signs which he would soon begin to articulate in a famous group of essays called the "cognition series." Moreover, he would shorten his list of categories still further. Since it is impossible to imagine anything incognizable, there is no reason to posit such unknown categories as being and substance. Peirce thus whittled his list of categories down to three, which he would eventually rename *firstness, secondness,* and *thirdness.*

Thirdness, Peirce's distinctive category, is intimately related to his semiotic and to his contribution to communication theory. Thirdness accounts for the phenomena we call mental. Secondness is the merely material relation which occurs when a first object is related immediately to another, a second. In thirdness, however, a first object is represented to a second by a third, a sign. Thirdness constitutes reality because it is a representation, because reality is a representational process.

Peirce soon had a chance to pursue in print the question of how representation could constitute reality. He had gotten involved in a published correspondence with William Torrey Harris, leader of the St. Louis Hegelians and editor of the *Journal of Speculative Philosophy.* Harris challenged him to show how, on the basis of his symbolic logic, the laws of logic could be demonstrated to be objectively valid. Hence the name "cognition series" for the three articles Peirce published in Harris's journal in 1868 and 1869. But the overriding thrust of the series was metaphysical rather than cognitive and depended on proving that reality could be representational since, if that could be established, the laws of symbolic logic could be objectively valid.

Evidently still hoping to play the part of public philosopher, Peirce thanked Harris for publishing the cognition series: "I prefer the Journal to other periodicals or to the American Academy's proceedings for my purposes" (2:159). The appeal of Harris's journal to Peirce almost certainly lay in its being the first specifically philosophical journal in the world, thus offering a special chance to reach other philosophers. But Peirce still saw philosophy as a matter of general importance to the community, not just to other philosophers. In the letter to Harris that opened their correspondence Peirce had spoken of "the national importance of your undertaking" (2:143). He probably saw his articles in *The Journal of Speculative Philosophy* as having, if not specific political content, at least political implications. Peirce wrote the series, he later said, "to prove and to trace the consequences of certain propositions in epistemology tending toward the recognition of the reality of continuity and of generality and going to show the absurdity of individualism and of egoism" (2:524–25).

His argument for the reality of generals, which are of necessity representational, boiled down to radical phenomenology. Since we cannot know the *noumena* or things in themselves apart from the way in which they are represented to us, we should not concern ourselves with the manner of their existence independent of representation: "a realist is simply one who knows no more recondite reality than that which is represented in a true representation" (2:239). Nominalists (and now, postmodernists) suppose themselves tough minded in their assertion that, because particulars are essentially unrepeatable, general ideas must inevitably be inaccurate representations of them, mere figments of our imagination. But nominalists admittedly have no knowledge of those particulars that they nevertheless claim to know to be unrepresentable. This self-contradictory claim to *know* that particulars are *unknowable* means that it is actually the nominalists who believe in a "metaphysical figment." "Modern nominalists are mostly superficial men, who do not know, as the more thorough Roscellinus and Occam did, that a reality which has no representation is one which has no relation and no quality" (2:239–40).

Peirce's pragmatism derives directly from his position that reality is representational, though this has often been missed. His emphasis on the method of science as the highest stage in logic has misled many commentators, and for that matter some pragmatists themselves, to cast Peirce in the role of traditional empiricist. Nothing could be more mistaken. As Max Fisch observed, "pragmatism was the natural and logical next step" from the semiotic realism in the cognition series (2:xxxvi). Peirce pushed his representationalism in the early 1870s at meetings of the Metaphysical Club in Cambridge and then summed it up in the famous pragmatic maxim that he first published in the 1877–78 series on the logic of science: "Consider what effects, which might conceivably have practical bearings, we conceive the object of our conception to have. Then, our conception of these effects is the whole of our conception of the object" (3:266).

The presence of the word "object," plus the fact that Peirce left the series unfinished and did not relate his semiotic to his science as he seems to have intended to do, has obscured for some readers that as a method in logic, the pragmatic maxim is representational and interpretational rather than blindly empirical. Years later, after James and others had begun to twist pragmatism away from its origins in the general logic of signs toward an emphasis on particular experiences, Peirce attempted to call attention to his "sedulous exclusion" from the pragmatic maxim "of all reference to sensation. . . . This maxim is put forth . . . as a far-reaching theorem solidly grounded upon an elaborate study of the nature of signs." [18] It is not the object that Peirce wishes to make clear but our conception of it, since his goal is to teach us to think logically and clearly. We achieve clear, logical thought not by worrying about the object in itself but by asking ourselves how we think about the object, how we represent it,

18. *Pierce on Signs*, 247.

what effects we "conceive" it to have and then recognizing that this representation is the sum total of our knowledge, "the whole of our conception of the object."

Our conceptions are of course not necessarily correct, and indeed, in the "cognition series" Peirce used representational error to prove the existence of both the individual and the community. The conceptions of reality and unreality result from the experience of correcting ourselves, which suggests that there are such things as truth and illusion. The conception of illusion or unreality proves the existence of our individual selves, for the conception of unreality implies "an *ens* relative to *private* [italics added] inward determinations" (2:239). The concept of reality, on the other hand, implies "an *ens* such as would stand in the long run," an *ens* independent of the private self (2:239). Since this *ens* involves representation it is intellectual as well as physical and therefore involves thought. But since this real *ens,* as opposed to the unreal *ens,* is not private, it must be public: "Thus, the very origin of the conception of reality shows that this conception essentially involves the notion of a COM-MUNITY, without definite limits, and capable of an indefinite increase of knowledge" (2:239).

The concept of reality implies community, not vice versa. There are many passages in Peirce which, read out of context, suggest that a representational reality must also be subjective or arbitrary, and the cognition series is no exception: "reality depends on the ultimate decision of the community" (2:241). One prominent interpretation treats such passages as an attempt to escape from epistemological skepticism. The idea is that Peirce was justifying expert authority as the final arbiter of opinion in a world impossible to know with certainty. The undemocratic (and of course unintentional) implication of such a reading of Peirce is clear, for dependence on the authority of experts would leave the individual at the mercy of the community, at least intellectually, with no basis for disagreement with the community's experts.

Such implicitly undemocratic interpretations reverse Peirce's actual views, according to which reality is knowable and according to which reality, not an expert, is the final arbiter of community opinion, as Peirce would eventually make clear in his review of Berkeley: "The arbitrary will or other individual peculiarities of a sufficiently large number of minds may postpone the general agreement in that opinion indefinitely; but it cannot affect what the character of that opinion shall be when it is reached. This final opinion, then, is independent, not indeed of thought in general, but of all that is arbitrary and individual in thought; is quite independent of how you, or I, or any number of men think" (2:469).

The Berkeley review also contains Peirce's statement, which has shocked some readers, that the realist wants "to see questions put to rest. And if a general belief, which is perfectly stable and immovable, can in any way be produced, though it be by the fagot and the rack, to talk of any error in such belief is utterly absurd" (2:471). The crucial qualification is the words "perfectly stable and immovable." In Peirce's view, an "immovable" belief is immovable because it is true, not because it is produced by oppression. In the 1877–78 series on the logic of science, Peirce would make clear his view that the method of authority is a faulty logic and must fail to fix belief, for "even in the most priestridden states some individuals will be found who . . . possess a wider sort of social feeling; . . . they cannot help seeing that it is the mere accident of their having been taught as they have, that has caused them to believe as they do and not far differently. And their candor cannot resist the reflection that there is no reason to rate their own views at a higher value than those of other nations and other centuries; and this gives rise to doubts in their minds" (3:251–52).

Even in the cognition series, Peirce is somewhat less forthright on this question of the arbitrary will of the community in determining knowledge. Representation is an essential aspect of reality as it is represented to us. Therefore, what cannot be represented is unreal. Thus, any proposition in which the infinite community of inquirers, working to infinity, can find no representational error, must contain no error and must accurately represent reality as it is: "There is nothing, then, to prevent our knowing outward things as they really are, and it is most likely that we do thus know them in numberless cases, although we can never be absolutely certain of doing so in any special case" (2:239). The individual who disagrees with the community has recourse to a superior court, reality itself, which indeed may persuade the community to change its mind. Although Peirce's concerns here are philosophical rather than political, it is clear that he leaves no room for those who would invoke him as a supporter of the implicitly undemocratic idea that the opinion of a community of experts is the ultimate test of reality.

Yet as we have already established, Peirce's philosophy is no celebration of the individual, who only knows himself to exist through the fact of error. The only reason that the individual in all his imperfection can contribute to the community is because it too is imperfect. The community in the here and now is only partial and will not be complete until "the ideal state of complete information" is achieved (2:241). Even then there would be individual differences, as Peirce observed in private notes in 1872. Even if everyone knew everything we would still have different minds to some degree "because while one of us was attending particularly to one thing another might be attending to another, and our desires might to a certain extent centre about ourselves and our surroundings as they do now." Still, Peirce clearly approved of the fact that in the ideal state of complete information, where everyone was omniscient, "the barriers of individuality would be partly broken down" (3:57). In the cognition series he reaffirmed this early conviction that individuality in and of itself is nothing to be proud of and invoked Shakespeare in defense of his idea that, looking inward in the manner of Descartes, the individual mind can achieve nothing: "The individual man, since his separate existence is manifested only by ignorance and error, so far as he is anything apart from his fellows, and from what he and they are to be, is only a negation. This is man,

> proud man,
> Most ignorant of what he's most assured,
> His glassy essence" (2:241–42).

The theory of immortality that Peirce had elaborated to the audience of his Lowell lectures became central to the communitarian emphasis of the cognition series: "What shall it profit a man if he shall gain the whole world and lose his own soul." If a person is a sign, to live forever he or she must be a sign in the process of becoming true. The individual self is far less effective at finding truth than is the community, for truth is the opinion on which all are fated to agree after an infinity of inquiry. Therefore the fate of the self depends on the success of that community: "nothing which can happen to a man's self, should be of more consequence to him than everything else   He who would not sacrifice his own soul to save the whole world, is illogical in all his inferences, collectively. So the social principle is rooted intrinsically in logic" (2:271).

As with traditional pietism, which such passages in Peirce eerily resemble, redemption depends not on achieving moral heroism but only in recognizing that logic demands heroism. For if a man only "recognizes the logical necessity of complete self-identification of one's own interests with those of the community," even if he is incapable of actually doing it, he will nevertheless believe that only a man who is capable of doing it is logical. The selfishly illogical man may thus share a belief with the justly logical man, and "so far as he has this belief, he becomes identified with that man" and with his communitarianism (2:271).

Soon after publication of the cognition series, Peirce pursued the question of the relation of the individual to the community in a series of fifteen lectures on British logicians that he delivered to graduate students at Harvard in 1869–70. These Harvard lectures did not constitute a teaching appointment; Peirce was one of a number of local philosophers, including Emerson, Francis Bowen, John Fiske, and Frederic Henry Hedge, who were invited to lecture that year. Little written material from Peirce's lectures survives since he had discovered that he got better attention from his audience when he did not read aloud to them, and "Besides I wish them [the lectures] to be Conversational. So that questions may be asked & doubts raised by you" (2:534).

Yet enough written notes survive to show that these Harvard lectures on the history of logic were instrumental in formulating the communitarian sentiments in Peirce's famous 1871 review, "Fraser's *Berkeley*." In the lectures Peirce anticipates his famous account in the Berkeley review of the dispute between medieval realists and nominalists. Also, in the lectures, just as in the Berkeley review, he defended the schoolmen's contempt for individuality of opinion, a contempt he thought characteristic of modern science but not, unfortunately, of modern literature. And finally, the moving peroration of the Berkeley review, in which he defended the practical importance of the realist-nominalist controversy by citing its relevance to the community, is anticipated in the lectures on British logicians:

"British Logicians"	**"Fraser's *Berkeley*"**
But it is not true that it is of no practical moment whether we believe in Nominalism or Realism, whether we believe that eternal verities are confined entirely to the other world (for a Nominalist may certainly be a Spiritualist or even a Platonist) or that they are matters of everyday consequence, whether we believe that the Genus homo has no existence except as a collection of individuals and that therefore individual happiness, individual aspirations, and individual life is alone of account or that men really have something in common—and that their very essence—so that the Community is to be regarded as something of more consequence and of more dignity than any single men (2:336).	But though the question of realism and nominalism has its roots in the technicalities of logic, its branches reach about our life. The question whether the *genus Homo* has any existence except as individuals, is the question whether there is anything of any more dignity, worth, and importance than individual happiness, individual aspirations, and individual life. Whether men really have anything in common, so that the *community* is to be considered as an end in itself, and if so, what the relative value of the two factors is, is the most fundamental practical question in regard to every public institution the constitution of which we have it in our power to influence (2:487).

Thus by 1869–70, when he was only thirty years old, Peirce had expressed in public lectures on logic, not science, most of the ideas of relevance to the communitarian aspect of his philosophy. It would be eight more years before he published the 1877–78 essays illustrating the logic of science from which intellectual historians draw their conventional conclusion that Peirce's communitarianism was modeled after his participation in the scientific community of his day.

The 1869–70 lectures on logic were not to have been the end of Peirce's career as a public philosopher, for he was engaged again by Harvard for another series of lectures on logic in 1870–71, an engagement he could not keep owing to his departure for Europe to spearhead American participation in international observation of the solar eclipse of 1870. Had his scientific work not interfered, perhaps he could have parlayed these Harvard lecture series into a teaching appointment. His invitations to lecture indicate that he was not yet persona non grata at Harvard as he would be by 1898 when James invited him to lecture in Cambridge but not on the Harvard campus.[19] An early teaching appointment at Harvard would have been of inestimable value to him and to philosophy. Peirce might have helped academic philosophy maintain the balance between technical issues in logic and larger issues in philosophy, as he had done so superbly in his early career. For at the same time that he had been working on the metaphysical and communitarian speculations of the cognition series he was also writing his 1870 American Academy paper on the logic of relatives, one of the most important papers in the history of modern logic, which would help set the direction of formal logic for the next century.[20] Absent Peirce and his metaphysical concerns about community, logic as it was taught in the universities became formal indeed.

When Johns Hopkins did finally offer an appointment in philosophy in 1879, the appointment, and with it any hopes for an academic career, were ignominiously ended after only five years by marital troubles, quarrels with other faculty, Peirce's genuinely difficult personality, and the strain of teaching logic while simultaneously carrying on his geodetic experiments for the U.S. Coast Survey in far-flung railroad tunnels and mineshafts. Similar problems at the Coast Survey would soon also end his career as a working scientist. The aged Peirce was free to return to logic and metaphysics, but in isolation and misery that would help to prevent his contributions to philosophy having any substantial effect on twentieth-century social and political theory.

In his isolated post-Hopkins years, Peirce developed the concept of social groups as "greater persons," as already discussed in chapter one.

19. Ketner and Putnam, "Introduction" to Peirce, *Reasoning and the Logic of Things*, 18.
20. *Writings of Charles S. Peirce*, 2:359–429. For a thoughtful estimate of Peirce's place in the history of logic see Hilary Putnam, "Peirce the Logician" in Putnam, *Realism with a Human Face* (Cambridge, Mass.: Harvard, 1990), 252–260.

But by then, James was well along toward philosophical preeminence in America. When James popularized pragmatism, he stamped it with the nominalism from which even Dewey failed fully to escape, the nominalism that therefore came to dominate twentieth-century pragmatic liberalism.

As for Dewey, not philosophy alone, but also political considerations tilted him toward nominalism, for he mistakenly assumed that metaphysical realism—a commitment to the reality of general classes and principles—was inevitably conservative. His assumption was that general principles can only be fixed principles, such as, say, laissez-faire economic theories, which will usually reflect prevailing social mores and will therefore usually support the status quo. Only late in his life, as I show in chapter four, did he understand Peirce well enough to understand how mistaken was his assumption that metaphysical realism is inevitably conservative. For in Peirce's realism, general ideas are not fixed and static but developmental and evolutionary.

The kind of developmental growth implied by Peirce's realism can best be illustrated by returning to his conception of a person or self as a sign and therefore constituted in thought. A personality, Peirce says, is not a particular or individual thought, but is general, is "some kind of coordination or connection of ideas." Coordination is a temporal process. A personality may develop or evolve because it "has to be lived in time." Moreover, the coordination of thought involved in a personality is not mechanical or determinative. A personality is indeterminate, "is more than a mere purposive pursuit of a predeterminate end; it is a developmental teleology. . . . Were the ends of a person already explicit, there would be no room for development or growth for life."[21]

Therefore, the main idea of the first chapter, the idea that society is a "greater person," is not necessarily socially conservative. Neither, of course, is a "greater person" necessarily radical or severed from the past. The coordination of ideas involved in the general idea constituting a personality, be it an individual or a "greater person" may imply elements of both conservatism and evolutionary development.

Early twentieth-century liberals committed to a progressive, evolutionary society, as were Walter Lippmann, Reinhold Niebuhr, and Mary Parker Follett, could have profited from Peirce's philosophy had they known of it. Instead, they ended up with large unresolved problems in their work in political theory. Lippmann viewed thought as a strictly individual process and concluded that experts must intervene between

21. Carl R. Hausman, *Charles S. Pierce's Evolutionary Philosophy* (New York: Cambridge University Press, 1993); Charles Hartshorne and Paul Weiss, eds., *Collected Papers of Charles Sanders Pierce.* (Cambridge, Mass.: Harvard University Press, 1931–58), 6:156.

government and public opinion. Niebuhr also viewed thinking as an individual process which led him to deny the spiritual reality of groups, led him to deny groups' capacity for moral judgment. Follett came closest to the spirit of Peirce since she believed that thinking was a process so integral to group relations that groups might take on some of the characteristics of persons. But without knowledge of Peirce, she did not understand how communication could create such personhood in groups that were more than local and therefore not in close, immediate contact.

All three of these political thinkers—Lippmann, Niebuhr, and Follett—could have profited from Peirce's recognition that to give society its due recognition as a general idea or a "greater person" with some of the same kind of spiritual unity as individuals is not to surrender to the status quo, but to recognize the shared vitality, the life, that can evolve toward the future. Peirce never developed these ideas in any detail. Living in the neglect and isolation that some would say, perhaps rightly, were his just reward for all his flaws of character, Peirce had little opportunity or encouragement to expand on the social and political implications of his philosophy. But all of us were the poorer for it when American philosophy and its potential contribution to the idea of community were left in lesser hands.

JAMES'S ILLOGICAL INDIVIDUALISM

And new philosophy calls all in doubt,
The element of fire is quite put out;
The sun is lost, and the earth, and no man's wit
Can well direct him where to look for it.
And freely men confess that this world's spent,
When in the planets, and the firmament
They seek so many new; then see that this
Is crumbled out again to his atomies,
'Tis all in pieces, all coherence gone;
All just supply, and all relation:
Prince, subject, Father, Son, are things forgot.
   —John Donne, *An Anatomy of the World*

Elite students of the late nineteenth and early twentieth centuries encountered William James at Harvard before going on, as Walter Lippmann did, to help modernize their country and, indeed, the world. Some who started farther down the social scale but eventually also became part of the cream of their generation—for example, Reinhold Niebuhr—made the acquaintance of James not in person, but through his philosophical and popular writings. Either way, these youths went forth armed, they mistakenly believed, with a radical new philosophy perfectly adapted to deal with an uncertain and changing society, a pragmatic philosophy that celebrated change, made uncertainty a virtue, and accepted raw experience at face value. Such was the legacy of William James to American political and social theory.

Son of Henry James the theologian and brother of Henry James the novelist, William considered careers in art and medicine before finally settling on psychology and then philosophy. He attached himself to Harvard at an opportune time, which helped settle the difficult question of a career, and he seems thereafter to have experienced little wanderlust. Although he once famously expressed contempt for the "gray plaster temperament" of Ph.D.'s, James directed the first American doctoral dissertation in psychology and was a preeminent figure in the modernization of university life. He made his early career on the Harvard faculty with a fair amount of smooth maneuvering, but it would be inaccurate and unfair to see him as a prototype of the careerists now so common on college and university faculties.[1]

We take a truer measure of his character if we emphasize his earnestness and note that his good cheer obscured for both his generation and posterity a certain hauteur in his philosophy. James was a wonderfully warm, open minded teacher and a somewhat perverse puncturer of conventional views. His correspondence remains a delight to read, and his easy, vivid, personal style of expression carried over into his lectures and books, somewhat shielding them from searching criticism. Liberal biographers and historians have been happy to perpetuate the Jamesian myth with a hagiography that celebrates the intellectual origins of their own world view. We can begin to cut through the hyperbole that shores up James's reputation by asking if despite his literary charm he does not come across as taking himself a bit too seriously. Compared against the wisely foolish ebullience of his father's theology and the sly, ironic humor of his younger brother's fiction, the cosmic avuncularity of James's philosophy suggests that the older son may well have been a bit stiff intellectually.

So often has it been remarked that James was the most sociable of men, that little attention has been paid to the fact that he is difficult to know. Despite the work of a legion of biographers and intellectual historians, James remains a distant presence. Yes, we know about his extraordinary family, his youthful battle with neurasthenia, and his long search for a vocation. We know him to have been a loyal friend, a warm-hearted companion, and a sensitive observer of human nature. And he is not known ever to have committed a moral offense. Where rumors of immorality dogged Peirce, James wore a halo during his life and ever after. That is just the trouble. He is the George Washington of American intellectual history, possessed of something—self control? inhibition?— that separates him from other mortals and even makes him seem a little cold and distant beneath the surface warmth.

James's philosophy is as difficult to know as James the man, mainly because his philosophy changed a great deal over time and because it is

1. Howard M. Feinstein, *Becoming William James* (Ithaca: Cornell University Press, 1984), 330–40.

inconsistent and illogical at heart. Where, by the age of twenty-eight, Peirce had made what he called his "one contribution" to philosophy— his list of categories—James struggled for most of his life to reach a basic point of view in philosophy. His first book, *The Principles of Psychology*—twelve years in the making and published when he was forty-eight—was written from the stance of metaphysical dualism, which had the advantage of saving the traditional idea of the soul from the grubby hands of science. By the time of the book's publication, James had abandoned dualism and was moving in the direction that would culminate in his radical empiricist phase. There he sacrificed the soul by urging that the universe was composed of bits of "pure experience."

Because of his insistence on empiricism, James would admit no concept of intangible thirdness or mediation to relate his bits of pure experience to each other. He thus made it difficult to account for coherence, including even that of the human person, not to mention society at large. James was fond of saying that the central issue in philosophy was not the mind-body problem but the question of the relation of "the one and the many." He never found a consistent answer to that question and his legacy to American liberalism was an anticommunitarian nominalism.

By emphasizing the anticommunitarian aspects of James's philosophy I do not mean to contradict recent scholarship showing James to have been alert to social issues and appalled by the social injustice around him.[2] I question neither James's citizenship nor his human decency but only the usefulness of his philosophy to progressive social theory. Such interrogation of his thought, as I suggested in chapter one, is the meat and potatoes of intellectual history, which has too often provided thin gruel for thought. I propose to test James's social vision not according to his heartfelt desire for a better society but against his actual philosophic writings to ascertain whether they offered a way out of the Cartesian individualism that so dominated the ideology of his age and stood in the way of a progressive social vision. For all his inspiriting good cheer, James, unlike Peirce, did not offer the metaphysical basis on which to build a more communitarian philosophy.

It is ironic to find James and Peirce linked so closely together in textbook accounts of pragmatism. Beyond the fact that both called themselves pragmatists, they have little in common. Peirce argued that all cognition is in signs and that therefore the idea that introspection offers immediate self-knowledge was an error. James thought that for psychol-

2. George Cotkin, *William James, Public Philosopher* (Baltimore: Johns Hopkins University Press, 1990) and Deborah J. Coon, "'One Moment in the World's Salvation': Anarchism and the Radicalization of William James," *Journal of American History* (June 1996), 70–99.

ogy to become an empirical science, it must accept introspection at face value, even though he did not always do so in practice. Peirce believed that knowledge was the basic condition of freedom while James opted for effort and what might be called muscular morality. Peirce thought that the path to reality lay through the mediation of signs, which required logical interpretation. James believed that reality presented itself immediately to the senses which therefore had priority over logic.[3] Peirce held that the "spirit" of a word or thought could be shared by two people, but James believed that every thought is singular and unrepeatable. Where Peirce's realism and semiotic logic led to communitarianism, James's nominalism and empiricism pointed toward individualism.

One is torn between gratitude to James for rescuing Peirce's pragmatism from the embers of oblivion and disappointment that he so mangled it in the process. In 1898 when James was invited to lecture at the University of California at Berkeley, Peirce's pragmatic maxim had lain unremarked for twenty years in *Popular Science Monthly*. Peirce had intended the pragmatic maxim as a means of clarifying thought by focusing on its relation to its object: "Our idea of anything *is* our idea of its sensible effects."[4] James, author of a famous essay on "The Will to Believe" and engaged in the investigations that would result in *The Varieties of Religious Experience*, called attention to Peirce's pragmatic maxim not to clarify thought but to justify religious belief: "God's famous inventory of perfections . . . implies certain things that we can feel and do . . . which we could not feel and should not do were no God present. . . . So far as our conceptions of the Deity . . . involve such definite experiences, God means something for us, and may be real."[5]

Although James's opponents may have overshot the mark when they accused him of denying an independent reality, his use of the pragmatic maxim muddied thought rather than clarified it. Peirce's metaphysics left space for the reality of the subjective and spiritual experiences James held so dear. But Peirce would have used the pragmatic maxim to clarify our idea of God by not mistaking any "mere sensation accompanying the thought for a part of the thought itself."[6] Peirce was interested in distinguishing "mere sensation" from an object's "sensible effects," the latter of which is our true idea of the object. James, however, used pragmatism to

3. See William James, *Pragmatism: A New Name for Some Old Ways of Thinking* (New York: Longmans, Green, 1907) 67, 78, 229, 288, 296.
4. *Peirce on Signs: Writings on Semiotic by Charles Sanders Peirce*, ed. James Hoopes (Chapel Hill: University of North Carolina Press, 1991), 266.
5. "Philosophical Conceptions and Practical Results," appendix to *Pragmatism*, ed. Frederick H. Burkhardt et al. (Cambridge, Mass.: Harvard University Press, 1975), 264.
6. *Peirce on Signs*, 266.

justify including subjective sensations in our notions of external objects. James did not deny that reality might differ from subjective experience, but he made it difficult to distinguish the one from the other, the very opposite of Peirce's intention in creating the pragmatic maxim.[7]

James's pragmatism also differed from Peirce's by avoiding generals. Even in the act of calling attention to Peirce's pragmatism, James objected to its generality and insisted on limiting it to singulars. Peirce had emphasized that clarifying our ideas is important in order to develop correct general ideas of how to act. James thought Peirce's focus on general principles of action excluded too much inner, passive experience, and James preferred to focus on particulars, as he made clear in the 1898 Berkeley speech where he resuscitated but crippled Peirce's brainchild: "I should prefer for our purposes this evening to express Peirce's principle by saying that the effective meaning of any philosophic proposition can always be brought down to some particular consequence . . . ; the point lying rather in the fact that the experience must be particular than in the fact that it must be active."[8] No doubt unwittingly, James, in the act of reviving Peirce's pragmatism, read out of it the logical communitarianism that was its most promising contribution to social theory.

"Every thought tends to be part of a personal consciousness," James had said in *The Principles of Psychology* and then gone on to define "personal consciousness" in a way that perfectly expressed his nominalist bias: "My thought belongs with my other thoughts, and your thought with your other thoughts. . . . Each of these minds keeps its own thoughts to itself" (1:220−21).[9] Introspection convinced James that any thought was restricted to the person who thought it. Where Peirce believed that objectivity in logic required abandoning the method of introspection, James believed that introspection was psychology's only empirical safeguard against misleading abstractions. Yet he never considered the possibility that his concept of personal unity was itself an abstraction, a representation. Reflecting on the then recent discovery of subconscious thought, he held that these "buried feelings and thoughts," if not part of the conscious self, must be parts of "*secondary personal selves.*" The notion that the self might sometimes think consciously and other times subconsciously appalled his empirical spirit, his bias toward the view that all

7. Vincent Colapietro, *Peirce's Approach to the Self: A Semiotic Perspective on Human Subjectivity* (Albany: State University of New York Press, 1989).
8. James, "Philosophical Conceptions and Practical Results," 259.
9. William James, *The Principles of Psychology*, ed. Frederick H. Burkhardt et al. (Cambridge, Mass.: Harvard University Press, 1981). Page numbers to most subsequent citations of this work will appear parenthetically in the text.

selves have immediate awareness of their thoughts. If there were two different kinds of thought, they must be the work of two selves — conscious thought the work of a conscious self and subconscious thought the work of a subconscious self. James cited the French psychologist Pierre Janet as authority for the abnormality of "these secondary personalities . . . [which] result from the splitting of what ought to be a single complete self into two parts" (1:222). The whole thrust of James's psychology was always toward singulars.

This nominalist bias made it as difficult for James to explain how different thoughts were joined in one mind as it was difficult for him to explain how different people are joined in a community. Accepting the supposedly empirical evidence of introspection, James held that thought was not an association of ideas as Descartes and Locke had held, but rather a unity: "Consciousness, then, does not appear to itself chopped up in bits" (1:233). Moreover, according to James every thought was unique and therefore not sharable or repeatable. This was in part a result of the dualism he imposed on *The Principles of Psychology*. He accepted the conventional notion that thought was one thing and brain activity another. Since brain activity always accompanied thought, James slipped illogically and probably unconsciously from the premise that no brain state can ever be repeated to the conclusion that no thought can be repeated (1.228-29). It never occurred to him, as it did to Peirce, that if two people think, say, the number six, it means the same thing to each of them and thus that they share the same thought even though it is physically based in different brains. James's nominalist skepticism of the proposition that thought can be repeated or communicated with exactness is suggestive of the weakness of his philosophy for any theory of community.

There was no chance that James would ever reach anything like Peirce's view that just as a person is a community of thought, a community can be a person. Late in life, in *A Pluralistic Universe*, James did abandon his opposition to the idea of subconscious thought and accepted the possibility of "co-consciousness." Yet he used this insight mainly to establish the possibility that pantheistic or "superhuman unities of consciousness exist." [10] The possibility of "co-consciousness" did not suggest to James that human beings might be capable of better social communication in the here and now. He never explicitly abandoned his early denial of the idea which was the basis of Peirce's communitarianism, the idea that one thought may be shared by two people. "Each of these minds," James had

10. William James, *A Pluralistic Universe* (Cambridge, Mass.: Harvard University Press, 1977), 134.

said in *Principles of Psychology,* "keeps its own thoughts to itself. There is no giving or bartering between them. No thought even comes into direct *sight* of a thought in another personal consciousness than its own. Absolute insulation, irreducible pluralism, is the law. It seems as if the elementary psychic fact were not *thought* or *this thought* or *that thought,* but *my thought,* every thought being *owned.* . . . The universal conscious fact is not 'feelings and thoughts exist,' but 'I think' and 'I feel'" (1:221).

When James used the phrase "Social Self" (1:281), he meant nothing so profound as Peirce's view that the self is a community of thoughts and feelings. Rather, he meant only what became the commonplace of twentieth-century social psychology—that one's self is formed partly in relation to the image that others have of that self and the image that one wishes others to have. This basic concept of twentieth-century American progressivism was fundamentally atomistic. It allowed for an effect of society on the self but nevertheless viewed society as a mere collection of atomistic individuals. Peirce's view was that "the very highest and most metaphysical conceptions"—say God or, better for our purposes, self and society—are complex relations.[11] But James leaned toward simplicity and unity. If Peirce saw the self as itself a complex community, James saw the self as an individual atom. James tried but never succeeded in explaining how this atomistic individual might relate to others.

The seeds of James's atomistic understanding of the individual lay in his famous notion of the "stream of consciousness," which he set out in *The Principles of Psychology,* and his attempt to explain personal identity on the basis of it. On the one hand, introspection empirically demonstrated the simple unity of thought: "Our Thought is not composed of parts." James consequently ridiculed Kant's categories as "mythological" (1:344). Since thought is unified to begin with, no categorical conceptions are needed to unify it. Yet despite James's desire to "leave the mind simple," he was forced to complicate it as soon as he approached the question of personal identity (1:343). If consciousness is a continuous stream which leaves some old facts behind as new ones float in, how does it achieve personal identity? The only possible answer for so strong a nominalist as James was an atom within the atom. Personal identity depends on an "identifying 'section' of the stream [that] 'owns' some of the past facts which it surveys, and disowns the rest,—and so makes a unity" (1:321). James's hypothetical "identifying 'section' of the stream" which "makes a unity" obviously has exactly the same function as those hypothetical categories of Kant's which James ridiculed as "mythological"! Yet

11. *Peirce on Signs,* 74.

James believed he had succeeded in keeping the mind simple by resorting to an atom within the atom, a *section* of the stream of consciousness.

James's confusion in *The Principles of Psychology* was due to his inability to choose between his empiricist, nominalist bias and his realistic recognition that knowledge always involves multiple elements which must somehow be brought together in thought. A thinker so helpless in the face of the problem of the one and the many was scarcely likely to offer much useful guidance to social theorists and political commentators, yet in the first half of the twentieth century James was to exert great influence on such figures as Walter Lippmann, Reinhold Niebuhr, and Mary Parker Follett.

There is a fascinating passage in *The Principles of Psychology*, a missed opportunity where James was clearly attracted to, but finally rejected, the possibility "that *all* that is experienced is, strictly considered, *objective*" and therefore "not immediately *known*. . . . It is only known in subsequent reflection" (1:290). This was the conclusion Peirce had reached a quarter of a century earlier and that had led to his semiotic in order to explain mediated knowledge. James, in his later radical empiricist phase would, of course, embrace the idea that all knowledge is objective, but his commitment to empiricism prevented him from ever even exploring the possibility that all knowledge, including self-knowledge, is mediated. Despite his close personal acquaintance with Peirce in the 1860s and 1870s, James seems not to have understood that Peirce viewed all knowledge as mediated and that he had resolved the logical difficulties of this position by positing the real existence of triadic relations where one object is represented to a second by a third, a sign. James's ignorance of the semiotic basis of Peirce's philosophy is indicated by his statement in *The Principles of Psychology* that the idea that we do not have "a direct awareness of the process of our thinking" contradicted "the fundamental assumption of *every* philosophic school" (1:291).

Always committed to introspection as providing immediate, empirical knowledge of thought, James never accepted the basic thrust of Peirce's semiotic—that there is no such thing as intuition or immediate perception of the meaning of a thought, but rather that thinking is inferential interpretation of signs. James was committed to making psychology a science and to seeing science as based on raw empiricism that involved no interpretation: "Every natural science assumes certain data uncritically," he wrote in the preface to *The Principles of Psychology* (1:6), a notion to which Peirce took exception in his review of James's book: "The notion that the natural sciences accept their data *uncritically* we hold to be a serious mistake." The data James accepted uncritically was thought as it appeared to the introspective observer. His best known contribution to psychology—the stream of consciousness—was based on the crudely empirical assumption that thought must be whatever it seemed to be.

James eventually had to retreat from this raw empiricism in regard to the issue of whether or not the content of thought is complex, and he had to admit that thought has parts even though thought appears to itself to be simple and unitary. His *Principles of Psychology* was vigorously assaulted on this point at the 1893 meeting of the American Psychological Association. James gave in at the next year's meeting and agreed "henceforward that mental contents should be called complex." [12] He was ready by the middle of the 1890s to admit what our contemporary antifoundationalists deny even while claiming James's pragmatic mantle, ready to admit "that no conventional restrictions *can* keep metaphysical and so-called epistemological inquiries out of the psychology books." [13]

One of the attractions of James to broad minded students of psychology today is the range of issues he was willing to admit into his discipline, yet in another sense, a still broader sense, James's openness as a psychologist was a reflection of his philosophical narrowness. For he did not so much let philosophy into psychology as enlarge his psychology till it contained his philosophy and, unfortunately, confined that philosophy within a very narrow, empirical range. That is, James enlarged his psychological empiricism into a metaphysics—radical empiricism—in which being was identified with experience. Thus, despite his supposed broad-mindedness, James never abandoned the psychological viewpoint and the empiricism he associated with science. The fact that his vaunted empiricism had failed him in *The Principles of Psychology* and that the failure had forced him to admit that metaphysics was necessary in psychology did not lead him to question empiricism. Rather, he made empiricism into a principle of metaphysics and posited that there was nothing but experience in the universe, that the knowledge relation was simply a relation between two "bits" of pure experience.

In metaphysical terms, James's radical empiricism was a mixture of nominalism and naive realism. Not only were the "bits" of pure experience real and immediately known, but so were the relations by which they were brought into contact with each other. James took the position that because two immediately known elements or bits of experience were brought together in a thought, the relation between them must also be

12. William James, "Knowing of Things Together," in *Essays in Philosophy* (Cambridge, Mass.: Harvard University Press, 1978), 88.
13. Ibid.

immediately known. James would have nothing to do with anything like Peirce's semiotic where the two elements are related by a third element, a sign, which is interpreted as representing the first to the second, because such a notion involved interpretation. Scientific meaning, for James, could be had not through interpretation but only through empiricism which to him meant immediate experience. In any case, he saw no need to bring in a third element to relate the other two: "*the change itself is one of the things immediately experienced.* 'Change' in this case means continuous as opposed to discontinuous transition. But continuous transition is one sort of a conjunctive relation; and to be a radical empiricist means to hold fast to this conjunctive relation of all others. . . . The holding fast to this relation means taking it at its face-value, neither less nor more; and to take it at its face-value means first of all to take it just as we feel it and not to confuse ourselves with abstract talk *about* it." [14]

Yet James seemed to have two different positions on the nature of the relations between his "bits" of pure experience, and his approach to these relations was more interpretational and less empirical than he admitted. Whenever he focused on the fact that two bits of pure experience were thought together, he would confidently affirm that the relation between them was experienced immediately and therefore amounted to a kind of internal relation rather than a "third external thing." [15] But this assertion of internality was based on inferential interpretation rather than immediate experience, as became clear elsewhere when James abandoned the idea that relations between experiences are "internal" because that seemed to suggest a need for a containing third element that cannot be experienced. [16] One of James's contemporary opponents, F. H. Bradley, pointed out the contradiction between, on the one hand, James's frequent assertion that relations are immediately experienced realities and, on the other hand, his assertion that experience is composed of discrete bits with no third term to relate any other two: "Are terms and relations . . . abstractions and mere ideal constructions, or are they given realities? The above two views to myself are irreconcilable, and to myself Prof. James seems committed to *both* of them." [17]

There was a deep fear of logic in James, a fear that logic would lead him away from reality. Despite James's famous commitment to openness and pluralism, there was also a side of him that craved certainty and tilted

14. William James, *Essays in Radical Empiricism* (Cambridge, Mass.: Harvard University Press, 1976), 25.

15. Ibid., 40.

16. James, *Pluralistic Universe*, 41.

17. F. H. Bradley, *Essays on Truth and Reality* (Oxford: Clarendon Press, 1914), 151.

him toward naive confidence in appearances whenever appearances were contradicted by logic. One of the appeals of radical empiricism was that it seemed to support the notion of total perceptual accuracy, with no need for any correcting logic. Whenever he had to choose between logic and experience as the basis of a philosophical position, he chose experience in the hope that it would bring him closer to things as they are. He dreaded, for instance, the infinite regress implied by triadic relations and opted for dyads, which in the absence of thirds, he could only explain as immediate relations. This left him with an illogical commitment to two diametrically opposed positions. First, he subscribed to the notion that consciousness was constituted of *discontinuous,* dyadic relations. But he also held that consciousness was *continuous* because that was the way it appeared to him. Unwilling to abandon either of these positions, James decided to *"give up the logic"* that made them seem contradictory.[18]

James's antirepresentationalism was based in his desire that appearance and reality be the same thing, with no need for any intervening logic or interpretation to pass from the former to the latter. When he said that experience was pure he meant that it was identical with appearances. A pure experience, he said, "is made of *that,* of just what appears, of space, of intensity, of flatness, brownness, heaviness, or what not."[19] For thousands of years the central problem of epistemology had been "the paradox that what is evidently one reality should be in two places at once, both in outer space and in a person's mind." Representational theories resolved the paradox by positing a third element, a mediating representation between the knowing subject and its object. But James believed that such notions, however logical, "violate the . . . sense of life, which knows no intervening mental image" but seems to see the object just as it exists.[20] Always fearful of being cut off from reality, James had no trouble deciding to throw out both logic and the representationalism logic seemed to require. That way he could accept experience at face value: *"To know immediately, then, or intuitively, is for mental content and object to be identical."*[21]

James was now ready, as he had not been in *The Principles of Psychology,* to frankly abandon traditional conceptions of the soul or self as a transcendental container of experience in favor of the notion that experience precedes and creates the self: "a 'mind' or 'personal consciousness' is the name for a series of experiences run together by certain definite

18. James, *Pluralistic Universe,* 96. Emphasis in original.
19. James, *Radical Empiricism,* 14–15.
20. Ibid. 8.
21. William James, *Collected Essays and Reviews* (London: Longmans, 1920), 379. Emphasis in original.

transitions."[22] Here at last James had begun to approach what had been Peirce's view for nearly half a century.

Yet because James believed that the relations that constituted the self were unmediated, he found it difficult to explain how such relations permitted human social life, permitted communication among human beings. On this question he held to an illogical, self-contradictory mix of interpretation and experience. James broached the question of communication in his discussion of how, if mental content and the object known are identical, two people can know the same thing. He argued that two minds could meet in the same object just as two lines could cross in one point. Yet this scarcely proved that two minds did so meet or even that there were other minds besides one's own. No one has immediate experience of anyone else's mind, and it was a basic postulate of radical empiricism that "things of an unexperienceable nature . . . form no part of the material for philosophic debate."[23] James understood that his radical empiricism posed a problem for the existence of minds other than his own. So as often happened with James, he abandoned experience and resorted to inferential interpretation without acknowledging or perhaps even realizing that he was temporarily abandoning the principles of his radical empiricism: "To me the decisive reason in favor of our minds meeting in *some* common objects at least is that, unless I make that supposition, I have no motive for assuming that your mind exists at all. Why do I postulate your mind? Because I see your body acting in a certain way. Its gestures, facial movements, words and conduct generally, are 'expressive,' so I deem it actuated as my own is, by an inner life like mine."[24]

Having thus established the existence of another person's mind on the basis of *interpretation* of that person's bodily movements, James slipped back in the very next paragraph to the position that knowledge of those bodily movements amounted to *immediate knowledge* of that person's mind! "In that perceptual part of *my* universe which I call *your* body, your mind and my mind meet and may be called coterminous." Or again: "Your mind and mine *may* terminate in the same percept, not merely against it, as if it were a third external thing, but by inserting themselves into it and coalescing with it."[25] No space was left for a representational or interpretive relation even though it was originally on the basis of an interpretive relation that James had posited the existence of the second

---

22. James, *Radical Empiricism*, 39.
23. William James, *The Meaning of Truth* (Cambridge, Mass.: Harvard University Press, 1975), 6-7.
24. James, *Radical Empiricism*, 38.
25. Ibid., 38, 40.

person's mind. Rather, James held that knowledge of other minds was given in the same immediate experience on which he based any and all knowledge whenever he was in an explicitly epistemological mode.

In addition to the contradictory and inconsistent reasoning by which James reached his view that other minds are known immediately, the idea is unconvincing because it implies a level of communication and sociability far surpassing the actual experience of human beings. If two minds can communicate in the absence of any interpretive representation or triadic relation, they ought to achieve perfect understanding. In such a world human beings ought to be able to communicate perfectly. The very concept of "society," with its obverse concept of "individual," ought to be superfluous. Since human beings obviously do not communicate perfectly, James's position is difficult to accept precisely because it so obviously contradicts the actual experience to which he believed himself loyal. James's conscious commitment to empiricism and unwitting use of inference whenever it was convenient thus led him away from reality rather than toward it.

The entire tangled knot of James's thinking on human communication would be a dreary, unimportant footnote in the history of philosophy if he had not succeeded in bequeathing his radical empiricism to progressive social theorists of the early twentieth century. Some of them would embrace his belief in immediate experience as the supposedly most radical and avant-garde philosophy available to them. They would not understand that James had never escaped the seventeenth-century Cartesian model of knowledge as unmediated perception of the meaning of ideas. Even after he abandoned the Cartesian model of the human self or soul as a preexistent container of experience, he continued to cling to that model's notion that the meaning of experience is immediately known. Despite his giving up the transcendental self, his epistemology was insufficiently radical to create a world of signs like Peirce's, where nothing, not even the self, was known immediately but only through an act of semiotic interpretation. Surely one of the reasons for James's immense popularity in his lifetime was precisely his straddling the question of subjectivity versus objectivity. Of all the late Victorian and Edwardian thinkers who doubted that the self or soul came ready made into the world as a container or relater of subjective experiences and instead viewed objective relations as constituting the self, James posed the least challenge to the traditional notion of the atomistic individual as living a privileged internal life of immediately known ideas.

James's enormous appeal as a turn-of-the-century moralist was due to a significant degree to the fact that he worked within, not against, the dominant strain of individualism in the culture. Recognizing, indeed having experienced personally, the insecurity and even terror that predominant cultural values might provoke in the individual, he nevertheless did not challenge the culture. Rather, he attempted to offer his audiences the bracing courage they needed to deal with such a culture through the example of his inspiring belief in free will and the accompanying possibility of self-control. By contrasting James's views on free will with Peirce's it is possible to show not only how individualist and traditional James was but how much weaker his pragmatism was than Peirce's, which addressed the free will question as a matter of logic rather than moralistic longing.

Through the ages, the arguments for and against free will have boiled down to two apparently contradictory experiences. Against freedom, there is the common experience of overwhelming temptation, the experience of succumbing in moments of inner conflict to gluttony, greed, or lust despite one's contrary effort or at least misgivings of conscience. On the side of freedom there is the equally common human feeling that in many of our actions we choose freely, the feeling that we could choose to do differently than we do.

James came down on the side of the latter argument, the idea that human beings must have free will because they feel free, a feeling which he interpreted as empirical evidence in behalf of free will. This was not a radical approach, as James believed, but the standard pap of Victorian moralists who often cited the evidence of consciousness, the subjective feeling that we could have done differently than we did, as empirical evidence for free will.[26] Basing free will on the seeming empirical experience of choice was one of the era's common intellectual chestnuts. This supposedly empirical evidence leant a certain aura of science or at least tough mindedness to Victorian moralists' sentimental defense of free will.

James, as I have emphasized, shared the conventional psychological wisdom of the nineteenth century, according to which human consciousness was the mind's direct and unmediated knowledge of its thoughts and operations. The mind's feeling of free choice, a feeling of direct and unmediated knowledge of its own workings, was therefore also empirical evidence of free will. Always interested in the evidence of introspection, James asserted in *Principles of Psychology* that "if we admit, therefore that our thoughts *exist,* we ought to admit that they exist after the fashion in which they appear," and in the next paragraph he added that thought "certainly appears to us indeterminate" (2:1175).

---

26. Frank Hugh Foster, *A Genetic History of the New England Theology* (Chicago: University of Chicago Press, 1907), *passim.*

Having described the scientific evidence as inconclusive but tilting toward free will, James then "permitted" himself a "few words" (several thousand, in fact) of frankly unscientific speculation where he asserted that if the will is free, "freedom's first deed should be to affirm itself" (2:1176, 1177). There is no more rhetorically rousing appeal to muscular spirituality and self-control in all of nineteenth-century literature than the lengthy passage where James identifies "the amount of effort which we can put forth" with human selfhood, "the substantive thing which we *are*": "He who can make none is but a shadow; he who can make much is a hero. . . . The world thus finds in the heroic man its worthy match and mate; and the effort which he is able to put forth to hold himself erect and keep his heart unshaken is the direct measure of his worth and function in the game of human life. He can *stand* this Universe. . . . And hereby he becomes one of the masters and the lords of life" (2:1181). The individual, depending only on his own effort, should live strenuously and heroically alone against the universe.

The danger of moral defeat could then be met by reminders to exert the free will to which consciousness testified. In his well-known description of how faith in free will lifted him out of his youthful spiritual crisis, James cited the influence of the French philosopher Charles Renouvier: "I . . . see no reason why his definition of Free Will—'the sustaining of a thought *because I choose* to . . .' need be the definition of an illusion." [27]

James's supposedly empirical treatment of the question of free will was simplistic compared to Peirce's approach to the issue as a problem in pragmatic logic. Traditional moralists such as James emphasized that it was always possible for a person to have done differently. Peirce agreed with this but emphasized that this did not prove free will: "the question of what would occur under circumstances which do not actually arise is not a question of fact, but only of the most perspicuous arrangement of them." Advocates of free will arrange the facts in order to show the truth of the statement that "if I had willed to do otherwise than I did, I should have done otherwise." [28] But since I did not will otherwise, no actual fact in the case supports free will. On the other hand, when a person tries and succeeds in choosing a moral course, advocates of determinism say that "even if you had not tried, you would have done it." But the fact is that I did try, and therefore no actual fact of the matter supports the determinist position. Contrary to the beliefs of the partisans themselves, the propositions of free will and determinism "are perfectly consistent." [29]

27. *The Letters of William James*, ed. Henry James (Boston: Atlantic Monthly Press, 1920), 1:147.
28. *Writings of Charles S. Peirce: A Chronological Edition*, ed. Edward C. Moore et al. (Bloomington: Indiana University Press, 1982–present), 3:267.
29. *Writings of Charles S. Peirce*, 2:260, 261.

Judged by the pragmatic maxim that an object's conceivable effects are the whole of our knowledge of the object, the entire free-will debate turned out to be organized around two arguments with no actual difference in my action: *I could have willed differently but did not* and *If I had tried to will differently, I would have failed.* Either way, I did what I did. The free-will debate was meaningless except as an example of the waste of time and energy to which human beings have been driven by bad, unpragmatic logic with nonfactual premises.

The logical difference between James's pragmatism and Peirce's may be illustrated by noting that James used exactly the same argument as to the non-factual premises of both sides in the free-will debate, not to move past the pointless debate but to continue it. Six years after "How to Make Our Ideas Clear," in which Peirce had used the free-will debate as an example of the futility of pursuing nonpragmatic logic, James spoke on "The Dilemma of Determinism" at the Harvard Divinity School and pointed out that neither side could cite facts. Determinists held to the counterfactual hypothesis that no other volition could have occurred while voluntarists sustained the equally counterfactual proposition that some other volition was possible. But James did not go on like Peirce to conclude that the debate was an example of bad logic. Rather, James used the lack of a logical difference between the two sides to continue the argument. Since free will was only a question of language rather than facts, James chose the language of free will, not because it was more accurate but because it made him feel better. Even if the determinists were right, "may you and I then have been foredoomed to the error of continuing to believe in liberty." [30]

Peirce's own view was that human beings are free but that the will is not free, at least, insofar as "the will" is understood to mean the internal entity or power of generating effort and restraining impulses that had been posited by traditional moralists. "I cannot admit that the will is free," Peirce wrote to James in 1897. [31] According to traditional moralists such as James, willing is an internal mental decision that takes place before physical action. Thus, in every moral decision there is a potentially heroic instant when the mind may or may not intervene with good or ill effect on bodily action. This traditional, dualist notion of willing as a mental event preceding physical action, when combined with nineteenth-century confidence in free will, resulted in what Norman Fiering has well called, "the Victorian orgy with intellectualized will" from which, at

---

30. James, "The Dilemma of Determinism," in *The Writings of William James: A Comprehensive Edition*, ed. John J. McDermott (New York: Modern Library, 1968), 610.

31. Charles S. Peirce to William James, 18 March 1897, quoted in Gerald E. Myers, *William James: His Life and Thought* (New Haven: Yale University Press, 1986), 532n.

least in our popular culture, we can scarcely even now claim to have escaped.[32] But Peirce's rejection of the model of thought as immediate self-knowledge by the mind in favor of a description of thought as an interpretive, relational process involving bodily signs left no space for the existence of an intellectualized will that made moral decisions prior to bodily action. If thinking is a bodily process, so is willing. Thinking and willing do not occur in an immaculate instant before action but are part of the body's action.

According to Peirce, willful thinking is, among other things, an interpretive action that can only influence future bodily action by thinking about that future action within a broader interpretive framework. The struggle is not between mind and body or understanding and willing but between different desires for the present and future. A drug addict, for instance, might well be enjoined by a traditional nineteenth-century moralist like James to exercise internal self-control and deny the impulse to shoot up. But a Peircean moralist would not describe the choice as one between mental self-control and sensual indulgence. Rather, the choice is between two sensations, the momentary pleasure of the drug as opposed to future well being. The difference between the persons who do and do not surrender to temptation is not that the latter have achieved greater mental self-control ("will power") over their bodies but that they think about the temptation in relation to the future as well as the present. The drug addict has not successfully considered the temptation in its relation to future well-being. Telling the drug addict to "just say no," as if his desire were an alien thing to be controlled rather than the powerful part of himself he knows it to be, is a strategy unlikely to succeed because of its false premise.

Peirce believed that there is such a thing as moral heroism. But the required strength to do the right thing does not come from a bodiless mental faculty called "the will," whose function is to deny impulses and enjoin effort. Rather, moral strength comes from a breadth of view that implicates possible courses of action in the broadest conceivable relations in order to judge their consequences: "Self-control seems to be the capacity for rising to an extended view of a practical subject instead of seeing only temporary urgency. This is the only freedom of which man has any reason to be proud."[33]

For all his greater innovativeness as a philosopher, Peirce was at least

---

32. Norman Fiering, *Moral Philosophy at Seventeenth-Century Harvard: A Discipline in Transition* (Chapel Hill: University of North Carolina Press, 1981), 303. For an example of orgiastic willing, see G. Gordon Liddy, *Will* (New York: Dell, 1981).
33. *Writings of Charles S. Peirce*, 2:261.

as traditional as James in allocating moral responsibility. Even though Peirce proved by pragmatic logic that the propositions of free will and determinism are perfectly consistent, he was "far from desiring to say that both sides are equally right. On the contrary, I am of opinion that one side denies important facts, and that the other does not." That is, advocates of free will correctly emphasize "that I ought to blame myself for having done wrong."[34]

As with many differences between them, on the question of free will Peirce seems to emerge as the traditional pietist and James as the antinomian. Peirce is ready to accept responsibility for his actions without undue concern as to the fairness of the burden. James, on the other hand, seeks encouragement: "Free-will thus has no meaning unless it be a doctrine of *relief*. . . . Our spirit, shut within this courtyard of sense-experience, is always saying to the intellect upon the tower: 'Watchman, tell us of the night, if it aught of promise bear,' and the intellect gives it then these terms of promise."[35] James's metaphor of the courtyard and the tower is, as usual, aptly chosen and telling. For him, the individual human spirit depends less on supposedly empirical relations with the world than a hopeful assertion that the will is free because the "intellect" says so.

Human beings, in James's pragmatism, were as isolated within society as they were within the universe at large. The enormous difference between the social implications of Peirce's philosophy and James's can perhaps best be seen in James's assessment of the place of his pragmatism in the history of philosophy. In order to show that his pragmatism occupied a middle ground between the traditional philosophical extremes of rationalism and empiricism, he reduced these extremes to the temperamental attitudes of tender-mindedness and tough-mindedness. Yet James's position was not as centrist as he liked to think. In the famous lists of attributes he placed under the headings of tender- and tough-minded in *Pragmatism* (12), it is easy to place him on one side or the other of most of his antinomies:

Tender-minded	Tough-minded
Rationalistic	✓ Empiricist
Intellectualistic	✓ Sensationalistic
Idealistic	Materialistic

34. Ibid., 3:267.
35. James, *Pragmatism*, 121. Page numbers to most subsequent citations of this work will be given parenthetically in the text.

✓ Optimistic	Pessimistic
✓ Religious	Irreligious
✓ Free-Willist	Fatalistic
Monistic	✓ Pluralistic
Dogmatical	✓ Sceptical

The balanced position which James believed he occupied was only a matter of occupying roughly the same number of extreme positions in both categories, some of which were traditionally rationalist and others empiricist.

How much more balanced Peirce's pragmatism was is suggested by characterizing him according to James's lists:

Tender-minded	Tough-minded
✓ Rationalistic	✓ Empiricist
✓ Intellectualistic	✓ Sensationalistic
✓ Idealistic	✓ Materialistic
✓ Optimistic	Pessimistic
✓ Religious	Irreligious
Free-Willist	Fatalistic
✓ Monistic	Pluralistic
Dogmatical	Sceptical

In the first three antinomies, which are among the most metaphysical in the two columns, Peirce fits on both sides. He was a rationalist, intellectualist, and idealist in James's sense since he believed general ideas were real and knowable. Yet if "empiricism" means "going by 'facts,'" as James put it, Peirce was also the most empiricist of philosophers since he believed logic was best learned by studying the relations of external symbols rather than our own thoughts. (In this respect his empiricism surpassed James's.) He was "sensationalistic" in that he believed all thought was based on feeling. And he was "materialistic" in that he always denied that "secondness" (physical events) and "thirdness" (mental events) were possible in the absence of "firstness" (matter).[36]

Peirce's philosophy belies almost everything in James's description of pragmatism. In *Pragmatism,* James stated that the allowance of "real novelty or chance" meant "that pragmatism must turn its back on absolute monism, and follow pluralism's more empirical path" (160–61). Peirce disagreed. He was a monist, though not a philosopher of the Absolute, who believed in "real novelty or chance" as factors in the universe. James

36. "Faith requires [us] to be materialists without flinching" (*Peirce on Signs,* 188).

believed that because our ideas of many realities "can only be symbols and not copies," the test of truth could not be correspondence between thought and reality but only whether thought guides us satisfactorily through life (212). Peirce, on the other hand, never abandoned a correspondence theory of truth. James believed that a correspondence theory of truth implied that "reality stands complete and ready-made from all eternity" and that the correspondence theory therefore further implied that philosophy should look backward to immutable principles rather than forward to the results of actions (226). Peirce, despite his correspondence theory of truth, had an evolutionary cosmology and believed that "total oneness would appear at the end of things rather than at their origin" (159).

James's opposition to a correspondence theory of truth, his belief that "you can't weed out the human contribution" (254) to reality, led to dangerous pridefulness. In the absence of triadic, interpretive relations to constitute knowledge, James confounded reality and knowledge. If knowledge is an immediate rather than interpretive relation with reality and if there is an unavoidable human element in knowledge, then one passes, as James seems to have done almost unconsciously, to the conclusion that reality unavoidably involves an element of human subjectivity. Thus he passed from unexceptionable statements that "all our theories are *instrumental, are mental modes of adaptation to reality*" to notorious statements such as "Truth *happens* to an idea. It *becomes* true, is *made* true by events. Its verity *is* in fact an event, a process" (194, 201). James's enthusiasm for the idea that truth did not exist "*ante rem*" carried him toward statements suggesting extraordinary human control over reality: "We break the flux of sensible reality into things, then, at our will. We create the subjects of our true as well as of our false *propositions*" (220, 254). James's opponents made so much of these statements that he collected his replies in a subsequent volume, *The Meaning of Truth* (1909). There he defended his extreme statements about human control over reality and insisted that they did not contradict the idea of a reality independent of human beings.[37]

The controversy forced James to address questions basic to any social theory, questions of human relations and communication. He seems to have realized that, given his nominalist faith that sentient experience, not logic, is the explicator of meaning, nothing other than an independent, objective reality satisfactorily answers key questions: What would "prevent us from flying asunder into a chaos of mutually repellent solipsisms?

---

37. James, *The Meaning of Truth,* 117.

Through what can our several minds commune?" And his answers were clear and direct: "Through nothing but the mutual resemblance of those of our perceptual feelings . . . which must also resemble their realities or not know them aright at all. . . . To find such sensational *termini* should be our aim with all our higher thought. . . . Without them we are all at sea with each other's meaning." Where Peirce gave up the whole notion that meaning was immediately experienced in favor of inferential (logical) interpretation of signs, James rejected reliance upon any "conceptual sign" in favor of "sensible things" which "are the only realities we ever directly know."[38]

Peirce, on the other hand, allowed for a sensational element in experience but believed that it achieved meaning solely through semiotic interpretation or thirdness. In a letter to a friend he distinguished his view from James's: "my point is that the meaning of a *concept* . . . lies in the manner in which it could *conceivably* modify purposive action, and *in this alone.* James, on the contrary, whose natural turn of mind is away from generals . . . in defining pragmatism, speaks of it as referring ideas to *experiences,* meaning evidently the sensational side of experience."[39]

Thus James, with no concept of thirdness or semiotic relations, could not conceive of reality as containing generals as well as particulars. He was of course perfectly entitled to elevate "experience" above logic, but it is doubtful that he would have become so great a cultural hero to early twentieth-century social and political theorists if the extent of the nominalism created by his universe of dyadic relations had been understood. "Empiricism," he proudly announced, "lays the explanatory stress upon the part, the element, the individual, and treats the whole as a collection and the universal as an abstraction."[40] In the course of writing about external relations in *A Pluralistic Universe* (1909) he reflected that though his manuscript was clearly "on" his desk, "the 'on' fails to appear to our senses as one of those unintelligible 'betweens' that have to be separately hooked on the terms they pretend to connect. All this innocent sense-appearance, however, we are told [by Hegel, Royce, Bradley, etc.] . . . is a tissue of self-contradiction which only the complete absorption of the desk and the manuscript into the higher unity of a more absolute reality can overcome."[41] Leaving aside the question of how "absolute" reality must be in order to relate the manuscript to the desk, it is noteworthy

38. Ibid. 30–31.
39. Quoted in Christine Ladd-Franklin, "Peirce at the Johns Hopkins," *Journal of Philosophy and Scientific Methods* (1916): 718.
40. James, *Radical Empiricism,* 22.
41. James, *Pluralistic Universe,* 41.

that the type of relation in question called into being the theory of grav-ity. The actual existence of the kind of thirdness that gravity represents can never be "experienced" in James's sense of the term.[42] We do not sense gravity itself but only the floor under our feet or, to continue James's ex-ample, the manuscript on the desk. Yet without the real existence of some such unsensed thirdness as gravity, we authors would seem to have been astonishingly fortunate that merely dyadic relations between nominalist particulars have so far resulted in every known manuscript's remaining "on" its desk (and authors' feet on the floor) rather than some of them drifting away to the moon or to Mars.

The social significance of this seemingly esoteric, metaphysical differ-ence between Peirce and James can be seen in the penultimate lecture of the series that became *Pragmatism.* James could not conceive of society or even his audience as real but only as a rationalist fiction. He informed his audience that any "*thing*" could be broken down into further particu-lars. Therefore, his audience's group identity "seems quite arbitrary. . . . So of an 'army,' of a 'nation.' But in your own eyes, ladies and gentlemen, to call you 'audience' is an accidental way of taking you. The perma-nently real things for you are your individual persons. To an anatomist, again, those persons are but organisms, and the real things are the organs. Not the organs, so much as their constituent cells, say the histologists; not the cells, but their molecules, say in turn the chemists."[43] This fact that there seemed no end to the degree to which seemingly unitary phe-nomena could be split into further units might have convinced a more rigorous thinker that it was the relations between the units rather than the units themselves that constituted reality. Such a conclusion would have allowed for the reality of general ideas such as "society," would have allowed that James's audience was something more than a roomful of "in-dividual persons." But to have gone down this path would have been an obvious departure from empiricism and thus have run the gnostic risk that always frightened James, the risk of a reality that could not be known immediately but only interpretively.

Within a few years of his death, James was ruled useless to sociology by one of that discipline's early greats. In a 1913–14 series of lectures en-titled "Pragmatism and Sociology," which was not published until long after his death, Emile Durkheim pointed out the inability of James's phi-losophy to account for general social categories. Durkheim, who knew more of Peirce than most contemporaries, noted the difference between

---

42. For Peirce's analysis of gravity as a type of thirdness, see *Peirce on Signs,* 241–42.
43. James, *Pragmatism,* 253–54.

James's conception of truth as subjective and Peirce's traditional view of truth as correspondence between thought and its object. It was "curious," Durkheim thought, that "James has continued to call himself his [Peirce's] disciple, has saluted him as the father of pragmatism and has never pointed out these differences." Although Durkheim would suggest that logical categories were derived from communal social practices of primitive peoples—not the social principle from logic, which was Peirce's view—he clearly saw the difference between Peirce and James on the possibility of generals or, in Durkheim's term, "reason." James's psychological, subjective notion of truth made it an individual affair which left the question "How could reason, in particular, have arisen in the course of the experiences undergone by a single individual? Sociology provides us with broader explanations [than James's pragmatism]." [44]

James, however, had settled for the individual as the most real thing he knew and argued that the individual's immediately known experience ought to occupy the center of a pragmatic philosophy: "To shift the emphasis in this way means that philosophic questions will fall to be treated by minds of a less abstractionist type than heretofore, minds more scientific and individualistic in their tone yet not irreligious either." [45] This was indeed the type of mind that came to dominate social theory in the twentieth century, which is no surprise given the influence of James upon the education of social theorists. Progressives would not look to society for solutions to what they called the "social problem" but only to charismatic individuals, thinkers who to a significant degree modeled themselves after the illogical thought and character of William James.

44. Emile Durkheim, *Pragmatism and Sociology*, ed. John B. Allcock (Cambridge: Cambridge University Press, 1983), 6, 67. Cf. Anne Warfield Rawls, "Durkheim's Epistemology: The Neglected Argument," *American Journal of Sociology* 102 (September 1996), 476.
45. James, *Pragmatism*, 123.

DEWEY'S IMPLICIT NOMINALISM

I saw in Louisiana a live-oak growing,
All alone stood it and the moss hung down from the branches,
Without any companion it grew there uttering joyous
   leaves of dark green,
And its look, rude, unbending, lusty, made me think of myself,
But I wonder'd how it could utter joyous
   leaves standing alone there without
   its friend near, for I knew I could not.
—Walt Whitman, *I Saw in Louisiana a Live-Oak Growing*

Dewey was James's Saint Paul, the chief spokesman in the first half of the twentieth century for the illogical, implicitly nominalist pragmatism that James had devised and that became the intellectual justification of pragmatic liberalism. A moderate by nature and temperament, Dewey never imitated James's announcement that he was abandoning logic, but there was also never any danger that Dewey would fall victim to Peirce's passion for exactness. Although he adopted, as Peirce had, the notion of science as the preeminent logic of the modern world, Dewey differed from Peirce by strongly opposing formal logic. Unlike Peirce, Dewey had no experience as a working scientist to make him skeptical that the philosophical implications of science are easily discerned. And although Dewey often voiced opposition to nominalism, he had no well-developed theory of communication comparable to Peirce's to support belief in the reality of community and general ideas. Consequently, Dewey's scientific instrumentalism amounted to a weak pragmatism. Dewey's social philosophy was a combination of James's empiricism and implicit nominalism with the enjoining of a willingness on the part of society as well as the individual to respond intelligently to whatever experience was delivered up by a world impossible to know with certainty.

Bequeathing to American social science (and "intellectual" history) a logic less interested in thought than the social context of thought, Dewey left his liberal disciples ill equipped to understand that social context. In the absence of any detailed analysis of the logic of the relations by which society is constituted, Dewey's emphatic assertions as to the reality of society were only assertions, not explanations usable by later liberals. Absent such logical guidance, there was nothing to prevent later liberals and sometimes Dewey himself from slipping into implicitly nominalist language tending to deny the social reality they explicitly avowed. Those liberals like Reinhold Niebuhr who were more nominalist than Dewey to begin with would not find any convincing antinominalist arguments in his philosophy but only assertions answerable by counterassertion, by the religious doctrine of the atomistic soul. Others like Walter Lippmann, who eventually abandoned Jamesian nominalism, knew so little of Peirce and enough of Dewey that they found no satisfactory realism in pragmatism. They turned back to more absolutist philosophies to find the universalism that would sanction liberal faith in the reality of society.

Dewey missed a great opportunity for an education in logic in the early 1880s when as a graduate student at Johns Hopkins, his path crossed Peirce's. But Dewey was unimpressed by Peirce's Hopkins teaching precisely because of its exactness. A native of Vermont, Dewey had received his undergraduate education at the state university in Burlington where he had been deeply influenced by H. A. P. Torrey, the professor of moral philosophy who expounded a mix of Scottish intuitionism and German idealism. When the young Dewey arrived at Hopkins he was looking for more of the same and found it in the Hegelian idealism of George Sylvester Morris. Peirce's bold and innovative logic, on the other hand, struck the idealistic Dewey as too narrow in scope. He disappointedly informed Torrey that he was "not taking the course in Logic. The course is very mathematical, and by Logic, Mr. Peirce means only an account of the methods of physical sciences, put in mathematical form as far as possible." [1]

If Dewey's choice of Morris rather than Peirce as mentor was philosophically mistaken, Morris was nevertheless better equipped to help launch Dewey on his academic career. Morris soon left Hopkins for the

1. Quoted in George Dykhuizen, *The Life and Mind of John Dewey* (Carbondale: Southern Illinois University Press, 1973), 30–31.

University of Michigan and, in 1884, arranged for Dewey's appointment there as well. A crucial factor in Dewey's Michigan appointment was no doubt his subscribing to Morris's Hegelian idealism, which allowed the Michigan president and trustees to perceive Dewey as a safe young man who would keep philosophy in her proper place as handmaiden to theology. Dewey performed this role with sincerity in his Michigan years, and his instrumentalism did not really emerge until he began to be influenced by his reading of James in the 1890s. Moving to the University of Chicago in 1894, Dewey was well enough established by then to drop his church membership, to enter energetically upon a career as a social and political activist, and to abandon Hegelian idealism in favor of instrumentalism. Within a decade he would be called to Columbia University in New York and to the media opportunities in the nation's cultural capital that would help bring him national and international fame as the leading spokesman of pragmatic liberalism, so that by mid-century Henry Steele Commager could call him "the guide, the mentor, and the conscience of the American people; it is scarcely an exaggeration to say that for a generation no issue was clarified until Dewey had spoken."[2]

Yet the innovative aspects of Dewey's social philosophy have been overestimated, partly because of a tendency to accept Dewey's own evaluation of his philosophy as antinominalist, when, in fact, Dewey's antinominalist convictions were unsupported by a detailed, realist metaphysics. Indeed, he seems never to have attempted to develop such a philosophical basis for his antinominalism. Without a well-articulated foundation, he tended often to lapse into nominalist modes of speech regarding individuals. And he had no way of conceiving of the reality of society as a "greater person" in the manner of Peirce. His notion of a social self was simply an assertion that the individual self was formed with the help of social influences. Society was not a self for Dewey but a mere aggregation of individual selves.

Dewey's lapse into implicit nominalism was tragic, for he was capable of larger views. Unlike James, he came by the end of his career to understand Peirce's realism and to see that it was a viable option in philosophy. But by then it was too late for him to revise his social philosophy in the light of such understanding. For almost all of his active career Dewey's deep interest in social philosophy was constrained, narrowed, and channeled by a metaphysics insufficiently developed to explain the reality of generals. Consequently, Dewey could never affirm the reality of society in a manner sufficiently detailed to steer subsequent political thinkers

2. Henry Steel Commager, *The American Mind* (New Haven: Yale University Press, 1950), 100.

clear of nominalist shoals or to keep those, like Follett, who did reject nominalism from also rejecting pragmatism.

As with James, the enormity of the divide between Dewey and Peirce can best be seen in Dewey's opposition to formal logic to which Peirce devoted his life. *Studies in Logical Theory* (1903), the culmination of Dewey's philosophical work at Chicago, more or less formally announced his commitment to instrumentalism, cited James as an "inspiration," and showed that Dewey was only a bit less skeptical than James of logic. Although Dewey did not explicitly spurn logic as James tended to do, he greatly narrowed the field of logic in order to make it consistent with James's version of pragmatism and radical empiricism. Adopting the idea Peirce had rejected, Dewey held that there are "intimate connections of logical theory with functional psychology." Dewey believed that both scientific method and ordinary practical thought differed profoundly from formal logic in that "they both assume that every reflective problem arises with reference to some *specific* situation." To engage in merely formal study of logic was to miss the specific situation that prompted thought and thus to separate the form of thought from its specific content. Absent this specific functional element in thought, formal logic, Dewey believed, was bound to be abstract, artificial, and useless. James was delighted with Dewey's position, so consistent was all this with James's instinctive distrust of logic. Dewey and his students at the University of Chicago, James exclaimed, had produced a "real" school with "real" thought.[3]

But it is the formal element in logic that raises thought above the merely specific and gives it general content, making it possible for words and other signs to provide communication or social coherence among human beings in general. Even this early in Dewey's instrumentalist phase, it became evident that he would not fully escape the nominalism he denounced. Dewey's implicitly nominalist conception of thought would vitiate his supposed social emphasis and indeed had already done so in his best known book, *The School and Society* (1899), which preceded *Studies in Logical Theory* by four years. Believing there was a void in urban children's experience, he aimed to recreate for them the continuity between education, work, home, and community that he believed had been the common heritage of most children only a few generations earlier. But in fact Dewey could not really envision education as a community activity

3. John Dewey, *Studies in Logical Theory,* in *Middle Works,* vol. 2, ed. Jo Ann Boydston (Carbondale: Southern Illinois University Press, 1976), 196–297, 317; quotations on 296, 301; and Ralph Barton Perry, *The Thought and Character of William James* (Boston: Little, Brown, 1935), 2:501.

in any deeper sense than that of a group of individuals who happened to be learning the same thing at the same time. For all his talk "that really the only way to unite the parts of the system [curriculum] is to unite each to life," he had no conception of *social* life, of there being a life *among* people as well as in them.[4] His educative focus was strictly on the child's individual motivation. The experience of the individual organism responding to its environment was Dewey's model of education. He emphasized the importance of the social environment and hoped that better educating individuals would change society, but he had no theory of communication comparable to Peirce's to suggest that individuals and society were constituted of relations so similar as to give society the same kind of reality as the individual.

Dewey's distrust of any formal, general element in thought pointed him toward a radically empiricist view of the relation between mind and reality: "Neither the plain man nor the scientific inquirer . . . knows . . . two fixed worlds—reality on one side and mere subjective ideas on the other; he is aware of no gulf to cross. He assumes uninterrupted, free, and fluid passage from ordinary experience to abstract thinking, from thought to fact, from things to theories and back again. . . . The fundamental assumption is *continuity*. . . . Only the epistemological spectator of traditional controversies is aware of the fact that the everyday man and the scientific man in this free and easy intercourse are rashly assuming the right to glide over a cleft in the very structure of reality."[5]

Predictably, Peirce, who had argued for many years and made it the basis of his semiotic that logical meaning could be more general than experience, wrote a negative review of Dewey's *Studies in Logical Theory*. Dewey's focus on experience, said Peirce, made him anything but a logician: "He seems to regard what he calls 'logic' as a natural history of thought." Such an approach could not fulfill the "normative" role of logic; Dewey had illogically and negatively prejudged "the question of whether or not there be a logic which is more than a mere natural history, in as much as it would pronounce one proceeding of thought to be sound and valid and another to be otherwise." The notion that truth about an object could be arrived at by describing how it was experienced made Dewey not only a natural ally of the antifoundationalists of our time but also, in Peirce's time, of "the German school of logicians, meaning such writers as . . . Wundt, . . . Erdmann, . . . Husserl, etc., . . . [who] make

4. Dewey, *The School and Society*, in *Middle Works*, 2:44.
5. Dewey, *Studies in Logical Theory*, 305–6.

truth, which is a matter of fact, to be a matter of a way of thinking or even of linguistic expression."[6]

In his review Peirce listed a long series of questions then current in the natural sciences that exact logic might help resolve but which could not find any assistance from Dewey's mere natural history of thought. Peirce evidently meant to suggest that Dewey, for all his praise of scientific method, had little familiarity with it in practice. Peirce's judgment has stood the test of time that Dewey and his students "are manifestly in radical opposition to the exact logicians, and are not making any studies which anybody in his senses can expect, directly or indirectly, in any considerable degree, to influence twentieth-century science."[7] If Dewey's "general logic of experience" was useless in the scientific realm, what reason was there to have confidence, as many twentieth-century political and social theorists did, in Dewey's claim that his logic "alone can do for social qualities and aims what the natural sciences after centuries of struggle are doing for the physical realm"?[8]

The issue of logical theory helps make clear how profoundly different Peirce's pragmatism was from Dewey's. Not opposed to a philosophy of experience, Peirce nevertheless believed that the meaning of experience could best be comprehended by studying its constituent relations in their objective forms as well as from the subjective point of view of the individual experiencer. Unlike Dewey, Peirce did not fear that a formal approach to logic would separate form from content. For logic was the science of thought. And thought or thirdness, Peirce had concluded, was a real relation in the objective world. To study the forms of these relations—in other words, to study logic—was to study an aspect of reality.[9] With no comparably detailed metaphysics, Dewey feared that a formal, general element in thought could only be an abstraction from reality and would therefore also be a conservative reification that blocked progress.

Dewey may have inadvertently helped foster the myth that there was one school of American pragmatism that included Peirce and himself, for he seems mistakenly to have thought Peirce's interest in scientific logic

6. Peirce, "Logical Lights," in *Charles Sanders Peirce: Contributions to the Nation,* compiled and annotated by Kenneth Laine Ketner and James Edward Cook (Lubbock: Texas Tech University Press, 1979), pt. 3, 186.

7. Ibid., 185.

8. Dewey, "Some Stages of Logical Thought," in *Middle Works,* 1:314.

9. For an example of Dewey's later denial of the reality of logical forms, see the 1929–30 exchange between him and Ernest Nagel. Dewey, "The Sphere of Application of the Excluded Middle," in *Later Works,* vol. 5, ed. Jo Ann Boydston (Carbondale: Southern Illinois University Press, 1984), 107–202; Nagel, "Can Logic Be Divorced from Ontology?" ibid., 453–60; and Dewey, "The Applicability of Logic to Existence," ibid., 203–9.

was similar to his own interest in science. Like much of the rest of the philosophical world at the time, Dewey did not understand that Peirce's logic of science was based at least as much on his semiotic and his communitarian metaphysics as on his practical scientific experience. With no similar basis in semiotic and metaphysics, Dewey's conception of scientific thought bore only a superficial resemblance to Peirce's, as in Dewey's 1900 essay "Some Stages of Logical Thought." This was conceptually almost a copy of Peirce's 1877 essay "The Fixation of Belief," one of the essays in the "Illustrations of the Logic of Science" toward which James had pointed as the birth place of pragmatism. Just as Peirce had done and in the identical terms of "doubt" and "inquiry," Dewey pointed out that "The natural tendency of man is not to press home a doubt, but to cut inquiry as short as possible." Like Peirce, whom he did not credit in his essay, Dewey suggested that history showed four successive logics whose chronological order was one of continuous progress due to the inadequacy of the previous logic as a method of resolving doubt. Corresponding to Peirce's four logics of "tenacity," "authority," "reason," and "science," Dewey offered "fixed ideas," "discussion" (his only real departure from Peirce's model), "reason," and "science."[10] Completely missing, however, was any understanding of the relation between Peirce's logic, his metaphysical categories, and his semiotic.

Without a firm metaphysical foundation, Dewey's writings on logic tended to slip into forms of expression that lost the essential meaning of Peirce's pragmatism. For example, *How We Think* (1910) bore a resemblance to conceptions of logic against which all of Peirce's work had been an attack. Dewey understood, of course, Peirce's notion of doubt as a lively sensation of discomfort which the organism seeks to escape through inquiry. But consider how this vital notion of doubt and inquiry is lost in Dewey's conventional paean to open-mindedness: "the most important factor in the training of good mental habits consists in acquiring the attitude of suspended conclusion. . . . To maintain the state of doubt and to carry on systematic and protracted inquiry—these are the essentials of thinking."[11] There was nothing in this that exactly contradicted Dewey's naturalism, but there was also nothing to put the novitiate reader in logic on guard against Cartesian artificiality. Indeed, Dewey's ill-chosen expression—"the attitude of suspended conclusion"—could be read as suggesting that doubt is a form of thought put on at will, the very artifice of Descartes against which Peirce had protested: "Some philosophers

10. Dewey, "Some Stages of Logical Thought," in *Middle Works*, 1:151.
11. Dewey, *How We Think*, in *Middle Works*, 6:191.

have imagined that to start an inquiry it was only necessary to utter a question . . . and have even recommended us to begin our studies with questioning everything! But the mere putting of a proposition into the interrogative form does not stimulate the mind to any struggle after belief. There must be a real and living doubt, and without this all discussion is idle." [12]

When one considers that *How We Think* was the principal logic text in teacher training programs for decades, one can only lament Dewey's lack of understanding of Peirce at this point in his career. *How We Think* could have been the means of communicating the essentials of Peirce's strong pragmatism to the world at large. An understanding of Peirce's categorical commitment to the reality of thirdness or semiosis could have provided the metaphysical underpinnings to make Dewey's naturalism and his social commitment a real force in American education and society. Without that foundation, Dewey's philosophy came to be understood as a mere celebration of the instrumentality of thought. In turn, thought was not conceptualized as a basic category of reality that formed persons but merely as a mode of skeptical inquiry by which persons dealt with a reality that was categorically different from themselves. Dewey failed to establish the natural reality of human persons with enough precision to prevent the creeping in of a conventional notion that there was a basic estrangement between persons and reality. He asserted that nominalist conceptions of the atomistic individual fall short of comprehending social reality, but did not explain how. Having never analyzed the metaphysical basis of relations, Dewey could not arrive at anything like Peirce's semiotic, which placed representation at the heart of being, whether individual or communal.

Dewey mistrusted semiotic representation. It is easy to mistake his meaning in such statements as "To say that language is necessary for thinking is to say that signs are necessary." He believed signs are necessary not for thought in and of itself, but only so that the meaning of thought may "be embodied in sensible and particular existences." [13]

12. Peirce, "The Fixation of Belief," in *Writings of Charles S. Peirce: A Chronological Edition*, ed. Edward C. Moore et al. (Bloomington: Indiana University Press, 1978–present), 3:248.
13. Dewey, *How We Think*, 314. Dewey also differed from Peirce by subscribing to the principle of the arbitrariness of signs that has recently become the fashionable doctrine of postmodernist literary critics: "In the case of signs we care nothing for what they are in themselves, but everything for what they signify and represent. *Canis, hund, chien,* dog—it makes no difference what the outward thing is, so long as the meaning is presented" (*How We Think*, 315). Dewey evidently had no inkling of, or else did not consider important, Peirce's typology of signs—symbol, icon, and index. The only arbitrary sign in Peirce's typology is a "symbol" such as any word whose meaning is a matter of convention. The meaning of an "icon" is not arbitrary but is derived from its resemblance to its object as in the case of a portrait and its subject. An "index" gets meaning from a real, causal

When Peirce said that thought is in signs he meant literally that cognition is a semiotic process, not just that the outward expression of thought requires signs. Dewey accepted the necessity of semiotic representation as a means of communicating the meaning of thought among individuals in society, but distrusting signs, he never pursued the possibility that they might also constitute the self. Distrusting signs and their ability to unite society, he was scarcely ready for a semiotic interpretation of the self. Society might involve semiosis, but not the self and its thoughts. The result was that Dewey not only implicitly separated thought from representation but also self from society.

Dewey's antirepresentationalism underlay and undermined his educational philosophy. In *Democracy and Education* (1916), he argued that the fact that "much of our experience is . . . dependent upon signs" created a special danger of unreality in traditional education. One of the purposes of his untraditional emphasis on physical activity in school was to lower the risk that in book learning and passive classroom instruction mere signs might "encroach upon the sphere of direct appreciations."[14] In the entire 370 pages of *Democracy and Education,* Dewey never mentions, as Peirce would have, that even the seemingly most abstract signs are embodied in the organ of thought, the brain.[15] Convinced that signs are abstractions from reality rather than creators of it and well aware that social communication is a representational process, Dewey was bound to have difficulty expounding a vision of education genuinely affirmative of social reality. He could articulate the importance of educating students for society but could not teach students a way of actually conceiving of the social reality he wanted to affirm. As so often in his philosophy, Dewey's writings on education omit the metaphysical heart of Peirce's pragmatism, the intimate relation between generals and particulars, so that pragmatism came to be understood less as a logic of relations than as a merely empirical style of thinking.

In an appreciatory essay on Peirce published in 1916 and probably occasioned by Peirce's death two years earlier, Dewey drove an extra nail in the coffin by offering the first reading of Peirce I have found that makes the mistake still made by many scholars today, the mistake of thinking

connection with its object, as a bullet hole does from a bullet. (See *Peirce on Signs,* 239–40.) Dewey's superficiality in regard to semiotic is revealed by his lack of understanding that only symbols have arbitrary meanings and that, contrary to him, the meaning of icons and indices does depend on "what the outward thing is."

14. Dewey, *Democracy and Education,* in *Middle Works,* 9:240–241.

15. See *Democracy and Education,* 148, where Dewey insists on the importance of the action of bodily organs in mental activity without ever mentioning the brain.

that for Peirce the social element in truth was merely a matter of agreement within the society or community of those who investigate rather than, as he actually believed, that it was "a matter of fact." Acknowledging that Peirce was "less of a nominalist" than James, Dewey saw the difference as due to Peirce's greater interest in logical conceptions which could serve as general rules of conduct. He then associated Peirce's interest in logic with "the fact that Peirce has a more explicit dependence upon the social factor than has James. The appeal in Peirce is essentially to the consensus of those who have investigated, using methods which are capable of employment by all." [16] This was all right as far as it went, but it did not go on to explain the metaphysical basis of Peirce's view, his category of thirdness or semiotic relations. Dewey may not even have known at this point that Peirce relied on a community to investigate reality because reality itself is, so to speak, communal, that is, composed of representative relations. Of course Dewey would never have followed some of our contemporary students of scientific method in arguing that logic and science are merely social conventions, but neither did he offer sufficient metaphysical guidance to steer them past that abyss. There was nothing in Dewey comparable to Peirce's attribution of the conception of reality to the individual's experience of error, an experience which suggests that the individual is implicated in a reality larger than himself: "the very origin of the conception of reality shows that this conception essentially involves the notion of a COMMUNITY." [17]

Dewey summarized Peirce's view of reality and truth in a way that, again, shows how he tended not to pass on the essentials of Peirce's pragmatism but rather to filter them out. In Peirce's view, according to Dewey, "'reality' means the object of those beliefs which have, after prolonged and cooperative inquiry, become stable, and 'truth' the quality of these beliefs." What was missing was Peirce's foundationalist view of truth as "a matter of fact," a matter of agreement between a sign and its object. For Peirce the quality that made a belief true was accurate representation of its object. A belief was stable because it was true, not true because it was stable. Dewey, having thus subtly if no doubt unwittingly relativized Peirce in the direction of James, urged "recourse to Peirce" as a way of avoiding "our epistemological difficulties [which] arise from an attempt to define the 'real' as something given prior to reflective inquiry." [18] But if Peirce did not believe the "real" is "given" prior to reflective inquiry, that was only because he believed that inquiry or representational thought

16. Dewey, "The Pragmatism of Peirce," in *Middle Works*, 10:76–77.
17. Peirce, "Some Consequences of Four Incapacities," in *Writings of Charles S. Peirce*, 2:239.
18. Dewey, "The Pragmatism of Peirce," 10:78.

is part of reality as it is represented to us. The representational element in reality may depend on us for its representation but not for its content or meaning: "The real is that which is not whatever we happen to think it, but is unaffected by what we may think of it."[19]

Dewey's poor understanding of Peirce's notion of "social" was probably due to his lack of knowledge at this point in his career of Peirce's categorical metaphysics. Dewey seems mainly to have read Peirce's series of essays on the logic of science. There is no indication that Dewey at this time knew of the "cognition series," the review of Berkeley, or "A New List of Categories." Had Dewey known of these writings and their central importance in Peirce's philosophy, they might have helped him express and support his antinominalist faith in the reality of society. Instead, he often expressed his views in language so implicitly nominalist as to undermine his social emphasis. Unaware of Peirce's idea that representative or semiotic relations constitute the individual self as well as society, Dewey could never arrive at any such insight that just as the self is social, society may be a self. Social thought, for Dewey, could never be thought *by* society; social thought was individual, island selves thinking *about* society.

Dewey's nominalist legacy can be illustrated by his failure to consider society's interest in comparing students by uniform standards. His implicitly nominalist scepticism of the reality of generals underlay his failure to consider the social good, the value that others might place on the individual's ability. Anyone who has ever taught college freshmen astonished to be told that each student's work is not equally praiseworthy will recognize the results of the following idea: "How one person's abilities compare in quantity with those of another is none of the teacher's business. It is irrelevant to his work. What is required is that every individual shall have opportunities to employ his own powers in activities that have meaning." Individual minds required attention but comparative assessment was no part of the teacher's responsibility since the "notion of mind in general is a fiction."[20]

Content always to assert that relations existed without analyzing their metaphysical foundation, Dewey merely assumed that social relations were consistent with his biologism. It never occurred to him that while a bodily organ, a brain, is an obvious necessity for human thought, to stop there left unexplained how social relations among organisms could exist. When Josiah Royce called attention to the individualist implications of

19. Peirce, "Fraser's The Works of George Berkeley," in *Writings of Charles S. Peirce*, 2:467.
20. Dewey, *Democracy and Education*, 179.

organicism, Dewey merely replied that any organic creature has "continuity with a racial organic life" in space and time.[21] Dewey made no reply at all to the central point of Royce's challenge, the fact that the new logic of relations seemed to point toward realism rather than Dewey's organicism and implicit nominalism.

Neither did Dewey reply to Royce's statement that "the fact that Mr. Charles Peirce, one of the most inventive of the creators of the new logic, is also viewed by the Pragmatists as the founder of their own method, shows how the relation of the new logic to the theory of truth is something that still needs to be made clear." [22] Although Royce had better understood Peirce than either James or Dewey, he tried to insert Peirce's logic into his own metaphysical absolutism. Dewey, an inveterate foe of absolutism was not prepared to take Royce seriously and conceived it a sufficient reply to state that "individual man" is already saturated . . . with social inheritances and references" without examining the question how such social relations are achieved.[23]

Without knowledge of Peirce's realist metaphysics, Dewey believed that his own instrumentalism was the only feasible American alternative to what he saw as Royce's ethically empty absolutism. America, Dewey wrote in *German Philosophy and Politics,* could not get needed guidance from the Teutonic method of "supreme regard for the inner meaning of things . . . in disregard of external consequences." Kant "tells men that to do their duty is their supreme law of action, but is silent as to what men's duties specifically are." Given to innerness, Kant cannot "admit that consequences can be taken into account in deciding what duty is in a particular case." [24]

Dewey did not see Peirce's realism as the alternative it was to both instrumentalism and absolutism. Unlike Royce's absolutism, Peirce's realism recognized that values are shaped in relation to external reality. Unlike Dewey's instrumentalism, Peirce's realism recognized the reality of generals. Peirce was therefore able not merely to assert the reality of society but to explain how it could be more than a mere collection of atomistic individuals, could be a general reality formed by thirdness or real semiotic relations among those individuals.

Because Dewey did not have such a well-developed metaphysical foundation, he often lapsed into nominalist verbiage that contradicted

21. Dewey, "A Reply to Professor Royce's Critique of Instrumentalism," in *Middle Works,* 7:69.
22. Royce, "The Problem of Truth in the Light of Recent Discussion," in *Middle Works,* 7: 422–23.
23. Dewey, "Reply to Professor Royce's Critique," 78.
24. Dewey, *German Philosophy and Politics,* in *Middle Works,* 8:153, 163.

his antinominalist belief in the reality of society. In *Democracy and Education* he wrote that "such words as 'society' and 'community' are likely to be misleading, for they have a tendency to make us think there is [a] single thing corresponding to the single word."[25] Despite his professed opposition to nominalism and his often-stated commitment to continuity, when the only remaining pragmatist of the original three got down to details he was unable to describe society in any other way than as a collection of atomistic individuals.

This implicitly nominalist view of society was both a cause and a result of Dewey's conception of mind as individual and adaptive. According to Dewey, pragmatic knowledge was based not on general ideas but on "particulars as they are discriminated by the active responses of sense-organs" in adaptive behavior.[26] When Dewey wrote "Social Interests and Sympathy" in his *Ethics* (1908), the social interest he spoke of was the individual's interest in society.[27] Peirce's idea that society might constitute a kind of quasi-mind or spirit remained utterly alien to Dewey. Assert as he might in the abstract the reality of society, he could not conceive of it in the same way that he conceived of the individual's reality.

How was an individual mind, however deeply socialized, to exert control over society at large? Dewey's latent individualism raised a difficult question for the possibility of democracy in a complex, modern society since mind in the sense of understanding the shared uses of things "*is the method of social control.*"[28] Believing that the beginning of control lay in comprehension, Dewey proposed an education that would enable the individual worker to impose the greatest possible meaning on his environment. Critical of scientific management of the sort espoused by F. W. Taylor, Dewey moved beyond Taylor's concern with physical efficiency but not beyond his focus on managing the individual worker. The efficiency that came with the division of labor was acceptable so long as it was more than mechanical, so long as "workers see the technical, intellectual, and social relationships involved in what they do, and engage in their work because of the motivation furnished by such perceptions."[29]

Yet even with such motivation, the individual worker would scarcely have control, so Dewey found another use for mind in "recognition of mutual interests as a factor in social control." Shared interests within a group and as many contacts as possible with other groups were Dewey's

25. Dewey, *Democracy and Education*, 25.
26. Ibid., 353.
27. John Dewey, *Ethics*, in *Middle Works*, 5:70.
28. Dewey, *Democracy and Education*, 38.
29. Ibid., 92. Cf. John Dewey, *Experience and Education*, in *Later Works*, 8:32.

two criteria for the worth of a society.[30] These criteria pointed directly to democracy as the highest form of social life and to the need for education that would make it possible for human beings to understand their shared interests and enhance their contacts with other social groups. In the end, Dewey's notion of democracy boiled down to a commonplace notion of groups of atomistic individuals associated by the broadest possible understanding of their common interests.

What if interests are not shared? How can a democracy composed of individual minds alone deal with opposing interests which, after all, are the real challenge to democratic government? Against the background of his implicit individualism and nominalism, Dewey's faith in education and intelligence seems as weakly sunny and impractical as Reinhold Niebuhr found it from the perspective of Christian orthodoxy.

The largest indictment of Dewey's implicit individualism was his apparent belief that individual leaders had to speak to society rather than with it since society, not being real in the same sense as individuals, did not have a mind of its own. Such a conception of intellectual leadership tended inevitably toward elitism, and Dewey succumbed to the temptation that lies in wait for all elites by mistaking his opinion for the country's. "In a Time of National Hesitation," written early in the feverish spring of 1917, defended President Wilson against the criticism of interventionists who feared even then that he would not lead them into war. Dewey's stirringly written essay might have become a famous document had events not proven him wrong in his assertion that slow progress toward war reflected the nation's thoughtful deliberation: "Never has the American people so little required apologizing for, because never before has it been in such possession of its senses."[31]

Yet soon after war was declared, the outbreak of hysterical fear of domestic enemies led the innately decent Dewey to warn that pacifists "deserve something better than accusations." Appalled at the outburst of intolerance, Dewey had to admit that he had misunderstood the situation: "what I wrote for these columns a few weeks ago on the conscription of mind is strangely remote and pallid." Yet even this turn of events did not lead him to stop confusing his desires with facts. Attributing the lapse of democratic values merely to a misguided "haste to get into the war effectively," he was soon arguing that the passion with which Americans threw themselves into the war effort suggested the kind of increases

30. Ibid., 89.
31. John Dewey, "In a Time of National Hesitation," in *Middle Works,* 10:257.

of productivity that would be available in an intelligently ordered society where the worker "took anything like a personal, not to say vital, interest in his work." [32]

After the Versailles Treaty had demonstrated the futility of Dewey's hope for progressive results from the war, he seemed for a time at least to lose hope in the possibility of democratic discourse. Sympathetic to the League of Nations, he was nevertheless skeptical of the arguments for American participation for reasons bordering on solipsism: "the reasons which governed a small group in this country in leading them to advocate our entering into the late war were not shared by the mass of this people . . . and were very different to those which animated the ruling statesmen of our Allies in desiring us to get in. The result was when the war aims were gained, the peace aims were lost. The present seems to me closely to *parallel* the former situation." [33] There were of course few parallels between going to war and joining a league to prevent war, especially in regard to the attendant risks to peace. The only "parallel" would have been Dewey's situation if he advocated joining the league; he would have been at odds with the people. Having erred once by assuming that he could speak *for* the people, Dewey did not seem to consider it a possibility that he might speak *with* them and participate in a democratic dialogue.

Dewey's postwar chastenment was limited to his politics and did not include his philosophy, which proceeded undisturbed along the path of his prewar work. In his book of 1916, *Democracy and Education,* he had formulated the concept of "education as reconstruction" as a counter notion to the old idea of education as merely preparatory to life and based on mastery of past knowledge. [34] In his first major book after the war, Dewey applied this concept of reconstruction to philosophy itself. Considered as an activity vitally involved with the environment, what form should philosophy now take?

His answer, in *Reconstruction in Philosophy,* was essentially to reject metaphysics. As opposed to Aristotle's idea that philosophy had begun in wonder, Dewey held that it had begun in the desire to reconcile traditional morals and customs "with the matter-of-fact positivistic knowledge which

---

32. John Dewey, "Conscience and Compulsion," in *Middle Works,* 10:261; Dewey, "In Explanation of Our Lapse," in *Middle Works,* 10:293, 295; and Dewey, "Internal Social Reorganization after the War," in *Middle Works,* 11:79.

33. John Dewey, "Reply to Lovejoy in 'Shall We Join the League of Nations?,'" in *Middle Works,* 15:83.

34. Dewey, *Democracy and Education,* 82.

gradually grows up" (85).[35] This positivistic knowledge was definite, accurate, and verifiable while traditional morals and customs were "uncertain in foundation." Hence the rise of metaphysics which aimed to place morals and values on the firmest foundational basis—"the very metaphysics of Being and the Universe." Dewey proposed to take the next step in philosophy by abandoning the supposed certainties of metaphysics. He proposed "To say frankly that philosophy can offer nothing but hypotheses and that these hypotheses are of value only as they render men's minds more sensitive to life about them," especially "the struggle of social beliefs and ideals" (89–90). Only then could humanity enjoy a moral and social progress equal to its economic and scientific progress so that "life will be bathed in the light that never was on land or sea" (201).

Yet in his actual practice of philosophy, Dewey continued to be a metaphysician. The empiricism to which he remained committed was as much an epistemological theory as any of those he attacked. He offered a relational notion of being and universe that was nothing if not foundational: "Experience carries principles of connection and organization within itself. These principles are none the worse because they are vital and practical rather than epistemological."[36] That those "principles of connection" were not "epistemological" was, at minimum, debatable.

Once, just at the end of the war, Dewey had briefly asserted a metaphysical basis for democracy, and in the process gave a succinct statement of why he believed that democracy reconciles individuality and community: "If democratic equality may be construed as individuality, there is nothing forced in understanding fraternity as continuity, that is to say, as association and interaction without limit. . . . To say that what is specific and unique can be exhibited and become forceful or actual only in relationship with other like beings is merely, I take it, to give a metaphysical version to the fact that democracy is concerned not with freaks or geniuses or heroes or divine leaders but with associated individuals in which each by intercourse with others somehow makes the life of each more distinctive."[37] This metaphysics, like any other, could be put to the same test to which Dewey had proposed to subject scientific hypotheses, the test of whether they "render men's minds more sensitive to life about them," especially "the struggle of social beliefs and ideals."[38]

35. John Dewey, *Reconstruction in Philosophy*, in *Middle Works*, vol. 12. Page numbers to most subsequent citations of *Reconstruction in Philosophy* will be given parenthetically in the text.
36. Ibid., 132.
37. John Dewey, "Philosophy and Democracy," in *Middle Works*, 11:53.
38. Dewey, *Reconstruction in Philosophy*, 89–90.

In *Reconstruction in Philosophy,* Dewey's social philosophy failed his own test of sensitivity to surrounding life, for it was based on an implicitly nominalist, individualist bias that "society is composed of individuals: this obvious and basic fact no philosophy . . . can question or alter" (187). With a truth so "obvious and basic" in plain view Dewey felt no need to explore the nature of relations or to consider the possibility, as Peirce had put it, that "one can never narrow down to the individual."[39] There is a sense in which Dewey understood that the "individual" is not one thing but rather a series of relations. But having never analyzed the nature of relations he had no concept of thirdness or semiotic representation to set against relations of secondness and facts of firstness. When Dewey said that the individual was not one thing, he did not mean, like Peirce, that one could never narrow down to it but rather that one could keep on narrowing down past the individual to still more finite, organic particulars, the "reactions, habits, dispositions and powers of human nature that are evoked and confirmed under the influences of associated life." That associated life could therefore never be in any sense one general thing. To Dewey, the implicitly nominalist conclusion seemed inescapable: "Society is one word, but infinitely many things" (194).

Unwilling to deal with generals, Dewey had no way of explaining how society was possible and never even attempted to do so, but only asserted that "society is the *process* of associating in such ways that experiences, ideas, emotions, values are transmitted and made common" (198). Dewey believed this view was in opposition to the universality of Plato and Kant and that "communication, sharing, joint participation are the only actual ways of universalizing the moral law and end" (197). But did it make no difference how people communicate? It is one thing if communication is simply an exchange of signs among atomistic individuals and another thing if the communication of signs is also the process through which "individual" selves are formed. Peirce's study of semiotic relations led him to the latter conclusion and thus to conceive of the self as the same sort of process as society—a series of semiotic relations—and thus to place community at the heart of being. The nominalist Dewey saw the self as a process, but at bottom, less of a communicative process than an organic one that placed the individual body at the heart of being.

The result of Dewey's separation of the process of creating the self from the process of creating community was that he was never able to move beyond self-interest to the community's interests as motives for social

---

39. Peirce, "Lowell Lecture VII, 1866," in *Writings of Charles S. Peirce,* 1:461.

reform. Dewey believed that the reaction against the self-interest of classical liberalism had gone too far: "Interests are specific and dynamic; they
are the natural terms of any concrete social thinking." Without interests,
we are left with abstractions such as "law, justice, sovereignty, freedom,
etc." These "vague general ideas" were useless, Dewey believed, for thinking instrumentally about social reform (191). Only particular interests
could realistically guide action.

Here is the heart of the problem of Dewey's social philosophy and his
failure to conceive of society as a communicative process, a real self that
resembled in some respects the individual self. If society was an unreal
abstraction, a vague general idea, who was to take the required educative
view of institutions, and how were they to do it? The perspective of the
ordinary citizen is surely much too narrow unless he or she can be somehow, sometimes united with others. If as Dewey implicitly suggests, such
unity is not possible, then the only solution seems to lie with just the sort
of elite social engineers who have become the broad public's stereotype of
the liberals they reject.

When actually confronted with a specific proposal for such elitism,
Dewey's democratic spirit recoiled, but only to fall back on his implicit
individualism. In an otherwise favorable review of Walter Lippmann's
Public Opinion, Dewey argued that "the enlightenment of public opinion still seems to me to have priority over the enlightenment of officials
and directors." Lippmann had proposed an intelligence staff for every
government department similar to the staff of an army's headquarters.
Dewey rightly saw that this evaded the question of how political action
could be guided by an intelligence possessed only by leaders, not voters.
Lippmann, Dewey said, had given up too easily on improvement of the
press and assumed that it must remain a mere record of events rather than
an organ of intelligence. Dewey wanted to use the press to raise public
discourse to the level necessary for democracy: "Because this fundamental general education is at once so necessary and so difficult of achievement, the enterprise of democracy is so challenging."[40] Unable to comprehend how experts and voters might together constitute a larger self by
representative relations, he could only imagine the admission of expertise
into politics by impractically suggesting that all voters become experts.

How desperately Dewey needed Peirce's category of thirdness is illustrated by his belief that "the problem of origin and development of the
various [social] groupings . . . is not solved by reference to psychic
causes." This statement in his *Human Nature and Conduct* (1922) makes

40. John Dewey, "Public Opinion," in *Middle Works,* 13:344.

it hard to fathom the book's subtitle, *An Introduction to Social Psychology*. Chemistry, physics, and physiology, not psychology, were the sciences by which Dewey would explain social groups. Psychology might help in understanding history, politics, religion, economics, and so on, "but it enters . . . not into the question of what psychic forces form a collective mind and therefore a social group. That way of stating the case puts the cart a long way before the horse, and naturally gathers obscurities and mysteries to itself."[41] This is the Dewey who appeals so greatly to the antifoundationalists of our time. But to keep out "mysteries" Dewey had to exclude any psychic or spiritual element as a foundation of social psychology, and the effect on his notion of society ought to give his contemporary adherents pause.

Although Dewey insisted that, absent society, a self could not be realized in any sense at all, his social philosophy had not progressed far from the atomistic individualism of the social contract theorists two centuries earlier: "It is easy to criticize the contract theory of the state which states that individuals surrender some at least of their natural liberties in order to make secure as civil liberties what they retain. Nevertheless there is some truth in the idea of surrender and exchange. . . . Conscious agreements among men must supplement and in some degree supplant freedom of action which is the gift of nature. In order to arrive at these agreements, individuals . . . must consent to curtailment of some natural liberties in order that any of them may be rendered secure and enduring."[42] This legalistic, even mechanistic notion of the basis of society does not represent the best of Dewey's social philosophy, but it points to its basic weakness. Dewey could write stirringly about how people ought to recognize the need for better social relations and how there could be no self-realization without society. But when it came time to explain the good of society, he made it a matter of atomistic individuals reconciling debits with credits in their own, individual accounts. Excluding any psychic or spiritual factor as the basis of society kept out foundational "mysteries" but only at the expense of also excluding love and community.

Even in his most explicitly avowed metaphysics, which he presented in *Experience and Nature* (1925), Dewey fails to explore the metaphysical basis of community. Rather than attempting in Jamesian fashion to square his new universe with traditional problems of mind and body, the one and the many, experience and knowledge, Dewey simply abandons the old issues and baldly asserts that experience is relational: "Things

41. John Dewey, *Human Nature and Conduct: An Introduction to Social Psychology*, in *Middle Works*, 14:45–46.
42. Ibid., 211.

interacting in certain ways *are* experience." [43] Yet if Dewey's directness of assertion is refreshing, there is also a dissatisfying vagueness in his claim that "the only way to avoid a sharp separation between the mind which is the center of the processes of experiencing and the natural world which is experienced is to acknowledge that all modes of experiencing are ways in which some genuine traits of nature come to manifest realization." [44] It may be this sort of statement that the antifoundationalists of our time have in mind when they say that Dewey, whom they otherwise find admirable, sometimes went too far, was too metaphysical, too foundationalist. [45] But in such statements Dewey scarcely broached the metaphysical issues. What are those "certain ways" in which things interact to create experience? Are those relations perceptual, representational, internal, external, dyadic, triadic, or of still some other sort? Dewey never said.

Unlike Peirce and James (unsuccessful though the latter was), Dewey seemed to feel no need to explain how, in the absence of a transcendental self, experiential relations are possible. He was utterly Peircean in protesting against any view of experience as a matter of introspection or privileged knowledge within a transcendental self. But where Peirce moved from the weakness of the argument for the transcendental self toward the general theory of signs, Dewey was content simply to assert that experience is constituted of genuine relations and to leave the metaphysical basis of relations unanalyzed.

Although Dewey held that "mind and matter" were merely "different characters of natural events," he nevertheless tended to separate mind from most of matter. [46] Intelligence, for Dewey, was a natural event, but also a very specific and local event, limited to organisms capable of purposeful action. This limitation is evident even more clearly in his next major work of metaphysics, *The Quest for Certainty* (1929), where he wrote: "purpose like intelligence is within nature; it is a 'category' having objective standing and validity. It has this status in a direct way through the place and operation of human art within the natural scene." [47]

It would be easy to make too much of such a passage's tendency to separate humanity from the rest of nature by humanity's apparently exclusive possession of "intelligence," but it would also be a mistake to make too little of it. This century's most widely read pragmatist offered his readers

43. John Dewey, *Experience and Nature*, in *Later Works*, 1:12.
44. Ibid., 30–31.
45. Richard Rorty, *Consequences of Pragmatism: Essays, 1972–1980* (Minneapolis: University of Minnesota Press, 1982), 82–85.
46. Dewey, *Experience and Nature*, 66.
47. John Dewey, *The Quest for Certainty*, 196.

no real guidance past Cartesian dualism or at least no safeguards from slipping unawares back into something resembling it. "Intelligence" might be a natural "category," but if it was described in strictly human terms, did it differ very radically from Descartes's supernatural mind as a trait separating humanity from nature and individual human souls from each other?

Dewey can scarcely be called a dualist in any technical sense since, unlike Descartes, he did not propose that matter and mind are different substances, but his focus on intelligence as a human capacity meant that he had to deal with some of the same questions as Descartes. If intelligence is a more or less particular characteristic of human beings, then knowledge may be a "natural" relation, but it is still hard to fathom. How and why is the universe knowable by human beings if they, being intelligent, are so different from the rest of nature? Dewey's answer was that nature is knowable because it has a machinelike regularity: "Nature *has* a mechanism sufficiently constant to permit of calculation, inference and foresight."[48] By disclaiming any literally mechanist view of the universe in favor of statistical averages among varying singular events, Dewey left room for contingency, uncertainty, and intelligence to disrupt nature's regularity. But unlike Peirce who emphasized the reality of thirdness as a category containing, but not limited to, human persons, Dewey never seriously considered the possibility that contingency and intelligibility in nature might suggest an element or category of mentality in the universe at large.[49]

In a universe with no universals, no element of reasonableness at large, and where intelligence is limited to individual human beings, social interaction among human beings is the largest possible source of meaning. Despite Dewey's many invocations that communication is the measure of the good society in *Experience and Nature*, he could not arrive at Peirce's conclusion that society was a self that was constituted in communicative, interpretive, semiotic relations among individuals, just as individual selves are constituted of similar relations within the body. Dewey believed that selves could not be constituted in such relations without recourse to the transcendental selves of idealists such as Berkeley, Hegel, and Royce, against whom his naturalist soul instinctively rebelled. Not until very late in his career did he understand Peirce well enough to see the possibility that communicative relations or thirdness could possess

48. Ibid., 198.
49. For an indication that Dewey at this point did not understand the evolutionary, developmental aspect of Peirce's metaphysics, see *Quest for Certainty*, 219, where he suggests that all "realistic philosophies" place "the standard of thought and knowledge in antecedent existence."

reality, not in the mind of a transcendental self, but simply as a metaphysical category.

Rather than opting for semiotic, communicative relations as a metaphysical category, Dewey believed that the most naturalist notion of mind was an "emergent" theory according to which mind was simply the result of "increasing complexity and intimacy of interaction among natural events."[50] When feeling organisms began to express their feelings not only by bodily movements but by more abstract signs such as words, it became possible to objectify the feelings and think about them; it became possible for there to be minds.

This may have technically resolved the traditional dualist puzzle of mind and matter, but it did not come close to resolving the actual dualism that dogged Dewey's philosophy, the dualism of self and society. Society was a matter of linguistic relations, but selves were organic individuals. The physiological relations that created selves were fundamentally different from the communicative relations that formed society. Understandably, Dewey never explained how such atomistic selves might become social in any larger sense than by conceptualizing or intellectualizing "society" in the same way that they might intelligently attempt to fathom any object distinct from themselves.

The thinness of Dewey's notion of society became clear in *The Public and Its Problems* (1927) which he intended to be a democratic counterweight to antidemocratic tendencies in Lippmann's *Phantom Public* (1925). Dewey objected to the pundit's idea that the problems of contemporary democracy were due to a mistaken theory of democracy—the notion of the all-competent voter—which Lippmann wished to replace with reliance on experts. Dewey turned away from Lippmann's bleak view. Government by experts invited "oligarchy managed in the interests of the few." Yet Dewey had no alternative to offer except the omnicompetent voter, which Lippmann had correctly diagnosed as a hopeless model of democracy in a complex modern society. Individuals could not be combined into a community, according to Dewey, until they shared each other's knowledge and perspectives. Such sharing of knowledge, he believed, was only possible in small communities. Nevertheless, he hopefully asserted that the "local" community "will not be isolated" but will draw on larger relationships with the "world-wide scene in which it is enmeshed."[51] Dewey never explained how local knowledge was to establish a "Great Community."

---

50. Dewey, *Experience and Nature*, 200, 207.
51. John Dewey, *The Public and Its Problems*, in *Later Works*, 2:365, 367, 370.

The weakness that comes through most clearly of all in *The Public and Its Problems* is Dewey's inability to come to terms with the question of political leadership. He can only win our sympathy for his refusal to sign on with Lippmann's cult of expertise: "The world has suffered more from leaders and authorities than from the masses." But he could see no alternative save an utterly impractical bottom-up democracy in which a communication revolution made every citizen omnicompetent. He offered this vision only as an ideal: "There will be no attempt to state how the required conditions might come into existence, nor to prophesy that they will occur. The object of the analysis will be to show that *unless* ascertained specifications are realized, the Community cannot be organized as a democratically effective Public."[52] Dewey's empiricism and implicit nominalism, combined with his organic individualism, left him no way to project a social vision with a place for leadership. He never came to terms with any notion of Peircean thirdness whereby the public and its leaders might sometimes become one, might share something of the spirit within a "greater person" without sharing all they knew.

Instead, Dewey was thrown back on impossibly heroic beliefs in the capacity of individuals, as he revealed in *Individualism Old and New* (1930). According to his implicitly nominalist convictions, "there is no society at large. . . . Harmony with conditions is not a single and monotonous uniformity, but a diversified affair requiring individual attack."[53] In a revealing essay on the corporation, written at about the same time as *The Public and Its Problems,* Dewey rejected the legal concept of the corporation as a person. The concept of "personality" was an ancient heritage inapplicable to social groups, he argued.[54] The success of giant business corporations showed not that there could be larger persons but only that individual human persons could think socially. The same corporatism that millions of individual citizens daily practiced in their external business lives must be made "internal" so that a new individualism of socialized intelligence could have free and creative sway.[55] If there was to be social feeling it would nevertheless be a social feeling felt only by individuals. For only individuals, not society, were real.

To Dewey's immense credit, he was greatly stimulated by Peirce's writings as they became available in his old age. Well into his seventies in 1932

52. Ibid., 333.
53. John Dewey, *Individualism Old and New*, in *Later Works*, 5:120.
54. John Dewey, "Corporate Personality," in *Later Works*, 2:42–43; cf. Dewey, review of *Corporate Personality*, by Frederick Hallis, in *Later Works*, 6:268–70.
55. Dewey, *Individualism Old and New*, 65.

when the first volume was published of Peirce's *Collected Papers,* Dewey greeted the book as representative of "the most original philosophical mind this country has produced to general philosophy; to logical theory, both in the traditional form, as a theory of scientific method and a modern symbolic logic; to metaphysics, to pragmatism, to mathematics." [56] When the sixth and what was then thought to be the final volume of Peirce's papers was published in 1937, Dewey reviewed the entire set, predicting that Peirce's influence was "only just beginning and . . . will grow greatly in the future." [57]

The next year, in revising his *Studies in Logical Theory,* the book of 1903 which had won admiration from James and a negative review from Peirce, Dewey paid tribute to the father of pragmatism by retitling the book *Logic: The Theory of Inquiry,* a definition of logic with which Peirce would have at least partially agreed. Explicitly acknowledging "my great indebtedness to him [Peirce] in the general position taken," Dewey largely abandoned the opposition to formal logic that had led Peirce to say that in *Studies in Logical Theory* Dewey had abandoned the notion of logic as a normative science. [58]

Dewey's statements of praise for Peirce were not encomia but based on an increasingly thorough understanding of the greatest and most original of the pragmatists. In 1935 and 1946 (when he was eighty-seven years old) Dewey wrote impressively detailed essays defending Peirce against what he saw as misinterpretations by Thomas Goudge and C. W. Morris. [59]

The new availability of Peirce's writings enabled Dewey finally to see that the uncertainty and indeterminateness he valued so deeply did not require the implicit nominalism that had dominated his career. Indeterminateness was consistent with the reality of generals: "Peirce believed thoroughly in the objective reality of the general. But he understands it in a way which would have been abhorrent to Aristotle and the scholastics, and to some at least of the contemporary philosophers who appeal to Peirce as if he confirmed their views. For Peirce understands by the reality of a 'general' the reality of a way, habit, disposition, of behavior; and he dwells upon the fact that the habits of things are acquired and modifiable. Indeed, he virtually reverses Aristotle in holding that the universal always has an admixture of potentiality in it." [60]

56. John Dewey, "Charles Sanders Peirce," in *Later Works,* 6:273.
57. John Dewey, "Charles Sanders Peirce," in *Later Works,* 11:479.
58. John Dewey, *Logic: The Theory of Inquiry,* in *Later Works,* 12:17n.
59. John Dewey, "Peirce's Theory of Quality," in *Later Works,* 11:86–94; Dewey, "Peirce's Theory of Linguistic Signs, Thought, and Meaning," in *Later Works,* 15:141–52.
60. Dewey, "Charles Sanders Peirce," 6:276.

Despite his new understanding of Peirce's realist commitment to generals and to communities, Dewey never revised his social philosophy, never specifically revoked his implicitly nominalist scepticism about the reality of communities. Perhaps it was too late for the aged Dewey to do more than he had already so generously done in coming to terms with Peirce.

There are no doubt as many missed opportunities in intellectual history as elsewhere, but Dewey's lack of clear understanding of Peirce for most of his career was surely one of the most significant and far reaching missed opportunities in American intellectual history. Dewey, the preeminent pragmatist of the twentieth century missed the opportunity to interpret democracy in the light of Peircean pragmatism, the only modern philosophy to suggest how indeterminateness, uncertainty, and potentiality were consistent with a more than atomistic view of society, a belief in the real possibility of community. No wonder, then, that mere pundits and theologians similarly failed when they attempted to interpret society in the light of what they supposed was pragmatism.

CHAPTER FIVE

LIPPMANN'S DISTRUST OF DEMOCRACY

The lust of government is the greatest lust.
  —James Harrington, *Oceana*

In 1908, William James, already retired from teaching, noticed a book review in *Harvard Illustrated* by an undergraduate. When James went to meet the author to offer his congratulations, he was so charmed that he invited him to morning tea, a practice which soon became a weekly ritual. That undergraduate was Walter Lippmann. So even though Lippmann never studied with him, James became a decisive influence in both the substance and style of his thought. Even as a youth, Lippmann had James's knack of assuaging the anxiety of new ideas by invoking patriarchal wisdom: "God will forgive us our skepticism sooner than our Inquisitions," wrote the twenty-four-year old Lippmann in defense of an experimental rather than dogmatic approach to politics.[1] For the next half century, he would base his writings in political theory on James's nominalism. Only near the end of his career did he abandon James and go unsuccessfully in search of an antinominalist foundation for political theory. Besides nominalism, Lippmann got from James the raw empiricism, vestigial dualism, and intellectualist notion of willing that made James's philosophy less radical and less pragmatic than Peirce's. During nearly all of his career the most influential political commentator and newspaper columnist of the first half of the twentieth century was, like James, a weak pragmatist.

1. Walter Lippmann, *Preface to Politics* (New York: Mitchell Kennerley, 1913), 236.

There is a parallel between the direction of James's and Lippmann's basic intellectual interests over the course of their careers. James began his academic career in psychology, moved on to philosophy because of epistemological concerns, and concluded with the metaphysical radicalism of *A Pluralistic Universe.* Lippmann's enormously influential career as a liberal pundit can be divided into three similar phases. First, there was a "psychological phase" in the pre–World War I period, when Lippmann in his early twenties precociously wrote *A Preface to Politics* (1913) and *Drift and Mastery* (1914). After the war came a chastened "epistemological phase," marked by his still influential books, *Public Opinion* (1922) and *The Phantom Public* (1925). Third and finally, there was a "metaphysical phase" in which he wrote *A Preface to Morals* (1929), *The Good Society* (1937), and *Essays in the Public Philosophy* (1955). In all three of these phases, James was a prominent influence. Lippmann sometimes invoked Peirce's name but his view of Peirce was usually distorted by the lens of James.

When Henry Steele Commager remarked that for a generation no issue was clarified till Dewey had pronounced on it, he might have added with no more exaggeration that most people did not know the issue needed clarification till Walter Lippmann had said so. The *wunderkind* of his generation, Lippmann left college with socialist sympathies and by the end of his twenties was socializing with Supreme Court justices. Having begun his career writing for small elite audiences, he successfully negotiated the difficult transition from consummate insider to skillful popularizer. His column, "Today and Tomorrow," begun in 1931 with the expectation that it would last no longer than the Depression, ran for more than thirty-five years and was eventually syndicated in over two hundred newspapers. More than anyone, Lippmann was the popular voice of pragmatism, albeit its weak and nominalist form, in political thought.

In youth Lippmann set out to accomplish in political theory what he considered James to have accomplished in philosophy—the reconciliation of modern discoveries in science, especially psychology, with the nineteenth-century values of willful moralism, muscular personality, and heroic effort.[2] The first American political theorist to use Freudian ideas, Lippmann probably owed his avant-gardism to James, a close follower of developments in clinical psychology who had attended Freud's famous

---

2. Lippmann, *Preface to Politics,* 47, 113–14. Page numbers to most subsequent citations of this work will be made parenthetically in the text.

lectures at Clark University in 1909, a year before Lippmann graduated from Harvard. Like James, Lippmann was less interested in the power of unconscious thought than in celebrating the power of consciousness. Desires might be unconscious and irrational in origin, but they could be resolved consciously and rationally. His goal was to "draw the hidden into the light of consciousness" in order to achieve "mastery," which he defined as "the substitution of conscious intention for unconscious striving."[3]

In *A Preface to Politics,* James's influence on Lippmann was already evident. James bequeathed to Lippmann a pragmatism whose emphasis on immediate rather than represented experience ironically frustrated pragmatism's ostensible goal of dealing with the muddy reality of things. Nothing could be more Jamesian than Lippmann's scornful dismissal of abstract ideals in favor of the tumult of "actual life" as "raw material" for the political philosopher. He tried, for example, to make the national passion for baseball—"a colossal phenomenon in American life"—grist for political philosophy, only to be defeated by his Jamesian preferences for unmediated experience. The common street scene of a crowd waiting for the telegraphed results of an out-of-town game led Lippmann priggishly to exclaim, "What a second-hand civilization it is that grows passionate over a scoreboard with little electric lights! What a civilization it is that has learned to enjoy its sport without even seeing it!" An abstractly represented game could appeal only to people dissatisfied with the immediate "monotony of their own lives" (93–94). Given his Jamesian bias against mediation, Lippmann could not see that electronic, representative media extended rather than extinguished the experience of sports fans.

Communication, according to Lippmann, was not a matter of relations creating selves but a matter of manipulating the detached signs that separated selves: "As I have had to abstract from life in order to communicate, so you are compelled to animate my abstractions in order to understand." Lippmann conceived of communication, not as an interpretive process that created selves, but as a mimetic process whereby one atomistic self attempted to ape another: "All language can achieve is to act as a guidepost to the imagination enabling the reader to recreate the author's insight" (170). As a result of his linguistic nominalism Lippmann subscribed to a model of democratic communication in which the leader and the led mimed each other's thoughts rather than creating new thoughts together. Peircean semiosis was far more consistent with par-

3. Walter Lippmann, *Drift and Mastery* (New York: Mitchell Kennerley, 1914), 269.

ticipatory democracy than the nominalism Lippmann had acquired from James. Without much knowledge of Peirce, Lippmann would not see that a "greater person" might articulate a goal whose exact form is originally held by no single citizen but which is a result of the communicative process of them all.

The incipience of Lippmann's post–World War I distrust of popular democracy can be discerned in the pre-war years, especially in his *Preface to Politics*. Against "mystical democrats" who believed that the people's choice, as represented in an election, is always wise, Lippmann replied, "That choice is not necessarily wise, but it is wise to heed that choice. For it is a rough estimate of an important part of the community's sentiment, and no statecraft can succeed that violates it. . . . Voting does not extract wisdom from multitudes; its real value is to furnish wisdom about multitudes" (115–16). Lippmann's notion that the purpose of an election is only to supply knowledge *about* the people suggests that decision making is not the business of the electorate, a view consistent with Lippmann's nominalist philosophy of mind. Decisions must in the end be made by a mind. With no concept of a greater mind, he concluded that only individual leaders, not the people at large, could make decisions.

Individual decision makers should either be experts or at least informed by experts. Lippmann contemptuously dismissed fashionable Progressive era reforms of the political system—"the little mechanical devices of suffrage and primaries" (254). His intellectual interest was less in democratic systems of government than in the elite who ran government, albeit for the benefit of all: "The preoccupation with the 'system' lays altogether too little stress on the men who operate it and the men for whom it is run" (295).

Properly informed by experts such as Lippmann, a creative statesmanship "would go out to meet a need before it had become acute" (285). The creative statesman would mold society less according to either his own vision or the people's than according to experts like Lippmann: "The statesman acts in part as an intermediary between the experts and his constituency" (302). The statesman could get a "clue" to the people's needs through "sensitively representative machinery," but "the real preparation for a creative statesmanship . . . is the work of publicists and educators, scientists, preachers and artists" (301, 306–7). The job of these experts and litterateurs was to engage in self-examination and then self-expression which would reveal the zeitgeist and instruct the political elite about the inward lives of others: "The best way of knowing the inwardness of our neighbors is to know ourselves. For after all, the only experience we really understand is our own" (108).

Not surprisingly for a thinker inspired by James's nominalism and willful moralism, Lippmann believed that the spirit of the age revealed by artists' and publicists' self-examination and self-expression was the desire of such creative persons "to be self-governing in their spiritual lives" (309). A new culture was being forged by this striving "towards autonomy," which was the "common impulse in modern thought" (311).

Lippmann could conceive of personal autonomy in only a nominalist rather than social sense. Selves and thoughts were atomistic units, incapable of any interrelatedness that would create larger selves in either time or space. Like James, Lippmann held to a philosophy of mind that made it impossible to relate thought to history. Like James, Lippmann agreed with Bergson that "consciousness cannot go through the same state twice" (313). This supposedly profound observation was one of the era's intellectual bromides. James had devoted many pages of his *Principles of Psychology* to the proposition that "no two 'ideas' are ever the same."[4] And by arguing for this proposition on the basis of immediatist premises, James and Lippmann vitiated any concept of communication, making it impossible to prevent the extension of this view to the conclusion that no two thoughts are ever related in any respect at all. If consciousness was unrepresented or known only immediately rather than mediately, the unrepeatability of any thought implied that it was unrelatable to anything else.[5]

Antirepresentationalism in psychology led to antirepresentationalism in political theory. Lippmann protested Woodrow Wilson's statement regarding the limitations of the statesman's mind, "Though he [the statesman] cannot himself keep the life of the nation as a whole in his mind, he can at least make sure that he is taking counsel with those who know." Lippmann held that the ideal statesman could not be satisfied with representative counsels but must vivify the nation directly, immediately in thought—an increasingly difficult feat: "To think of the whole nation: surely the task of statesmanship is more difficult to-day than ever before in history. . . . Plato and Aristotle thought in terms of ten thousand homogeneous villagers; we have to think in terms of a hundred million people of all races and all traditions." Only the influence of James's immediatism can explain how an intellect as acute as Lippmann's could

4. William James, *The Principles of Psychology,* ed. Frederick Burckhardt (Cambridge, Mass.: Harvard University Press, 1981), 1:229.
5. For a useful discussion of the contradictions in James's notion of consciousness, see Gerald E. Myers, *William James: His Life and Thought* (New Haven: Yale University Press, 1986), 63–64. See also my discussion in *Consciousness in New England: From Puritanism and Ideas to Psychoanalysis and Semiotic* (Baltimore: Johns Hopkins University Press, 1989), 209–12.

arrive at the ludicrous notion that an idea of "the whole nation" could be vivified in the statesman's "fibrous imagination" and did not require representative signs (105).

Well aware of the problem posed by insisting that the statesman must directly imagine "the whole nation," Lippmann believed the solution lay in the pragmatic model of thought as inseparable from action. With a typically Jamesian spurning of logic or "theory," Lippmann favorably resolved the "great question whether our intellects can grasp the subject. Are we perhaps like a child whose hand is too small to span an octave on the piano? . . . the facts are inhumanly complicated. . . . We are putting a tremendous strain upon the mind." Such doubts are "merely one of the temptations of theory. In the real world, action and thought are so closely related that one cannot wait upon the other. . . . Experience itself will reveal our mistakes" (105–6).

The above quotations from Lippmann were influenced by the vestigial dualism that separates James's pragmatism from Peirce's. When Peirce said that "thought" is "action" he did not mean for either rubric to exclude physiological events in the brain. He did not mean to suggest, as Lippmann comes close to suggesting, that there is no advantage in using the brain before engaging in other kinds of action. Peirce explicitly rejected such notions as Lippmann's that logic or "the temptations of theory" are useless for the purpose of detecting our errors. Such language in Lippmann betrays the influence upon him of James's assumption that thinking about the world is fundamentally different from acting in it.[6] With no knowledge of Peirce's foundational metaphysics, Lippmann followed James in implicitly separating thought from the rest of the world. Consequently, he conceived of society as separate from mind, conceived of social experience not as part of thought but only as corrective of thought.

Unlike Lippmann's and James's weak pragmatism, Peirce's philosophy was based not only on an assertion that the meaning of thought is in its consequences for action but also in an explanation of *how* thought may lead us to the experiences we desire. Thinking can be so potentially useful because, being an action itself, thought possesses a substantial or monistic identity with the rest of our universe of experience, a universe to which there is also a general logic as Peirce insisted in his emphasis on the reality or thirdness—semiotic representation or thought.

On the basis of his Jamesian commitment to a model of experience as immediate rather than representational, Lippmann justified his support

6. Myers, *William James*, 63.

for Theodore Roosevelt's third party candidacy in the election of 1912. President William Howard Taft had no knowledge "of the condition of the people" (97). Neither did Roosevelt's other opponent, Woodrow Wilson, for "like all essentially contemplative men, the world has to be reflected in the medium of his intellect before he can grapple with it" (102). A "real political genius," such as Roosevelt, knew "the actual life of men" and made government a "throbbing human purpose" (99).

But Wilson, not Roosevelt, won the election, and the ambitious Lippmann had to come to terms with the new president. Lippmann's facile pen, personal charm, and remarkable self-assurance soon transformed the earlier cultural radical into an establishment insider. In 1914 Herbert Croly, who had been impressed by *A Preface to Politics,* invited Lippmann to join his progressive magazine, *The New Republic,* as a founding editor. This influential position provided Lippmann with sufficient nectar to buzz among the great and powerful. By his mid-twenties Lippmann's friends and correspondents included Oliver Wendell Holmes, Jr., Learned Hand, Louis Brandeis, Newton Baker, and "Colonel" Edward House, the President's closest advisor. Notable parallels between administration policies and the *New Republic*'s editorials, as well as Lippmann's frequent meetings with Colonel House, fostered the widespread assumption that Lippmann himself had the President's ear, an assumption that Lippmann did nothing to discourage and that soon contained an element of truth.

In his 1916 reelection bid Wilson courted the *New Republic*'s support by inviting Lippmann to a two hour tête-à-tête and assuring the aggressive young journalist that the president had evolved from the small business values he had espoused in the 1912 campaign to an activist nationalism. Lippmann, impressed by Wilson's change from laissez-faire idealist to "constructive nationalist," supported Wilson in the 1916 campaign, wrote speeches for him, and helped bring the hitherto critical *New Republic* into the President's camp.[7]

The world had gone to war during Wilson's first term, and Lippmann believed that nowhere more than in foreign affairs had the president been transformed by the force of reality from starry-eyed to pragmatic idealist. Charles Evans Hughes, the 1916 Republican candidate, proposed — preposterously, Lippmann thought — impartial neutrality in protest of England's illegal blockade of Germany. Wilson, on the other hand, was, as Lippmann wrote to H. G. Wells during the election campaign, "frankly unneutral" and in his second term would be a "war President."[8] Within

7. Quoted in Ronald Steel, *Walter Lippmann and the American Century* (Boston: Little, Brown, 1980), 106.
8. Quoted in ibid.

weeks of Wilson's second inauguration the United States was at war with Germany. In the first number of the *New Republic* after the declaration of war, Lippmann wrote glowingly of Wilson's "Great Decision."[9]

Yet the *New Republic* editors reserved for themselves some of the credit for America's decision to go to war in their famous or possibly infamous editorial, "Who Willed American Participation?" They claimed that the highest proportion of war sentiment was to be found among "the more thoughtful members of the community." Although pacifists were already blaming war profiteers, nothing could be farther from the truth. Short-sighted self-interest had counseled neutrality, but penetrating minds had seen the wisdom of war and led the nation into it "under the influence of ideas." The decision for war "is an illustration and a prophecy of the part which intelligence and in general the 'intellectual' class has an opportunity of playing in shaping American policy and in molding American life."[10]

When Randolph Bourne indicted pragmatism as a failed philosophy, he had most in mind this claim of intellectuals like Lippmann that they had led the way to war: "An intellectual class, gently guiding a nation through sheer force of ideas into what the other nations entered only through predatory craft or popular hysteria or militarist madness!" Bourne's indictment soon seemed justified, for by the summer of 1917 the *New Republic* was complaining that Wilson was losing sight of the war aim—a league of peace—that most justified American participation. Already the course of events seemed to confirm Bourne's jeremiad against the *New Republic* intellectuals: "It is only on the craft, in the stream, they say, that one has any chance of controlling the current forces for liberal purposes. . . . Well, it is true that they may guide, but if their stream leads to disaster and the frustration of national life, is their guiding any more than a preference whether they shall go over the right-hand or the left-hand side of the precipice?"[11]

Since the craft could not be steered from the lower decks, Lippmann had clambered aboard the bridge. Flattering letters to Newton Baker, the Secretary of War, brought an exemption from the draft and a position in Baker's office. Soon, Lippmann moved on to Wilson's secret task force—"the Inquiry"—charged with planning conditions of peace in postwar Europe. There he wrote the first draft of Wilson's "Fourteen Points." But his colleagues on the Inquiry viewed him as a self-promoter and gradually

9. "The Great Decision," *New Republic*, 7 April 1917.
10. "Who Willed American Participation," *New Republic*, 14 April 1917.
11. *War and the Intellectuals: Essays by Randolph Bourne*, ed. Carl Resek (New York: Harper & Row, 1964), 13.

deprived him of influence. So he eagerly departed for France where he hoped but failed to direct the military's propaganda effort along the lines of the Fourteen Points. After the war's end, Lippmann stayed for a time in Europe but, unusually for him, did not nimbly land a choice assignment and disappointedly sailed for home.

After returning to the *New Republic,* he heard vague rumors that Wilson, closeted behind closed doors with Clemenceau, was selling out the American war aims. When the treaty was finally published in the spring of 1919, the *New Republic* liberals were crushingly disappointed. Europe's new map reflected not the Fourteen Points but the national interests and territorial ambitions of France, Italy, and Poland. "This Is Not Peace," declared the *New Republic.*[12]

Two brief years had confirmed for others, if not for Lippmann, the truth of Bourne's mocking reference to the title of Lippmann's second book: "how soon their 'mastery' becomes 'drift,' tangled in the fatal drive toward victory as its own end."[13] Lippmann attempted to cut his losses by opposing the Versailles Treaty and laying the blame on Wilson for the failed peace. Lippmann helped to secure for William Bullitt the opportunity to offer damning testimony about the peace negotiations to the Senate, and the *New Republic* printed excerpts from *The Economic Consequences of the Peace,* John Maynard Keynes' withering critique of Wilson's diplomacy.

To have acknowledged liberal responsibility would have been not only to admit the justice of Bourne's criticisms but to deny the possibility of a career for the "public man"—the expert and publicist. No, the problem lay not with the public man but with the democracy that had insufficiently appreciated his counsel. As many of Lippmann's fellow intellectuals sank into postwar self-flagellation and criticized the "technique of liberal failure,"[14] Lippmann took a much more aggressive stance and offered a structural remedy for democracy's failings—a remedy that would make more rather than less use of the expert and the publicist. He began to pen his most famous and influential book, in which he abandoned his erstwhile antirepresentationalism and argued that in a democracy, reality required representation by people like himself.

After the debacle of the war into which he had grandiosely believed intellectuals had "willed" the nation, Lippmann moved from his psychological to his epistemological phase. Now he sought to be an advisor not merely to statesmen (who seemed suddenly to have decided they had no

---

12. *New Republic,* 24 May 1919, 441.
13. Bourne, *War and the Intellectuals,* 47.
14. Harold Stearns quoted in Steel, *Walter Lippmann and the American Century,* 165.

need of him) but to government bureaucracy, provided that it included a secure niche for experts. Gone was the psychologically naive notion that the creative statesman must immediately possess an idea of the "whole nation." For he believed that the experience of the war had revealed a problem of knowledge or epistemology in modern democracy. There was a problematic relation between the environment and its "representation" in the minds of the masses, a problematic misrepresentation between "The World Outside and the Pictures in Our Heads"—the title of the first chapter of *Public Opinion* (1922).[15]

Lippmann's best-known book has long enjoyed a mostly undeserved reputation as a radical critique of traditional democratic theory. The basic point of the book is the simple observation that in the complex modern world the individual citizen cannot have a valid opinion on every issue pertinent to the commonweal. Despite his usual invocation of Freud and Jung, Lippmann's critique of traditional democracy had nothing to do with new notions of mind and personality. He merely criticized what he wrongly conceived of as the typical belief of eighteenth-century democrats, the simple-minded belief "that the knowledge needed for the management of human affairs comes up spontaneously from the human heart" (248–49).

Yet Lippmann's own critique of modern democracy was based on the same nominalist and dualist premises as the eighteenth-century views he was ostensibly criticizing, for the weak pragmatism of William James continued to be his guiding philosophy. Despite his abandonment of James's antirepresentationalism, Lippmann continued to advocate liberal experimentalism and to cite James's open universe as his justification for not joining other liberals in postwar pessimism. "all the *ifs* on which, as James said, our destiny hangs, are as pregnant as they ever were" (262).

To seize the future, however, human beings had to have a correct understanding of the world, had to have an accurate "picture in our heads." The central difficulty of modern self-government, according to Lippmann, was that in a complex society most of the environment is "unseen," too large or distant to be immediately experienced (165). A newspaper reader during the war was unable to conceive directly of three million armed men. Instead, the ordinary citizen symbolized multitudinous armies in the personalities of their commanders, fastening "upon Joffre and the Kaiser as if they were engaged in a personal duel" (9). Lacking contact

---

15. Lippmann, *Public Opinion* (New York: Harcourt, Brace, 1922). The reference to the relation between the environment and its representation is found on p. 10. Page numbers to most subsequent citations of this work will be given parenthetically in the text.

with reality, the ordinary citizen feebly represents it with a "pseudo-environment," a false picture based on simplistic symbols (16).

At the end of the twentieth century the possibility of overemphasizing personalities and symbols is not news to those citizens disgusted with politicians' misrepresentation of themselves and their opponents via mass media. But Lippmann proposed an alternative to symbolic politics that seventy-five years later seems even more dangerous. He wanted an official corps of experts—people like himself—to be charged with getting accurate pictures into the heads of government decision makers. Lippmann's proposal to dispense with symbolic politics in favor of expert information seems dangerous precisely because modern government relies on a sprawling bureaucracy of experts against whose potential tyranny symbolic politics seems, to many, their only defense.

Where Lippmann had earlier favored those statesmen with immediate knowledge, now in *Public Opinion,* he leaned toward representation of the world by experts. Traditional democratic theory had preceded the modern newspaper, international news services, photography, cinema, psychoanalysis, and modern science: "the key inventions have been made for bringing the unseen world into the field of judgment" (165). Human beings did not have to represent the external environment in inaccurate symbols. By substituting accurate representation of the unseen world for the grotesqueries of the pseudo-environment, democratic society could replace symbolic politics with a politics of substance.

But the modern world made available so enormous a number of accurate representations that the representations themselves needed representing by experts. Otherwise, government officials and legislators would suffer information overload. Lippmann cited the new class of corporate managers and their reliance on experts. Industry's "more enlightened directing minds have called in experts . . . to make parts of this Great Society intelligible to those who manage it." Accountants, engineers, managers, and scientists gathered and summarized data for "an executive who sits before a flat-top desk, one sheet of typewritten paper before him, and decides on matters of policy presented in a form ready for his rejection or approval" (233–34). Like the modern business executive, the modern legislator and government official needed bureaucratic experts to winnow out informational chaff.

If today government experts are numerous beyond Lippmann's dreams, they have nothing like the power he wanted for them. He proposed not that experts resolve all of our problems, but only that they short list the solutions: "The Many can elect after the Few have nominated" (149). Each department of the executive branch should have an "intelligence section" whose employees would have great security and enormous power. Government experts should be impartial and therefore should have life tenure. Since intelligence is useless without access to facts, the intelligence bureaus should have the right to examine all papers and to question "any official or outsider"—in other words, any citizen (244). So equipped, intelligence bureaus would be both "the Congressional eye on the execution of its policies" and "the departmental answer to Congressional criticism" (243–44). Experts like Lippmann would not only represent reality but would govern the government.

Earlier in the book Lippmann had attempted to anticipate the obvious charge that his proposal was elitist by asserting that democratic governments, like all others, are run by elites. He proposed only to replace an informal and invisible inner circle with a formal and visible bureaucracy. Traditional democratic theory had missed the fundamental role of elites in politics. Americans, almost from the beginning, had swallowed the Jeffersonian view of the Constitution, overestimating its commitment to mass democracy and underestimating its Hamiltonian commitment to authority. The very maneuverings by which Hamilton brought the Constitution into being showed the importance of the insider in any political system. In Lippmann's own time, reformers who deplored machine politics missed the point that machines existed because public life was impossible without an "organized hierarchy" (146–47).

In weak and nominalist pragmatism, Lippmann found support for his egotistical commitment to government by the insider and the expert. He could not conceive of a decision-making process—that is of a mind—in any other than individual terms. Rejecting any notion of an "Oversoul regulating everything" as an explanation of the democratic process, he believed the only alternative explanation lay in the actions of well-placed insiders "who perform all the duties usually assigned to the Oversoul" (146). The less-well-placed people—that is, the democratic masses—had no place at all in Lippmann's political calculus except to fall in line behind their leaders. Because of his nominalist, atomistic conception of the self, Lippmann could not conceive of a community as a corporate mind, a self or "greater person" created by social relations and making decisions different from the original intention of even its leaders.

Critical of the "ordinary doctrine of self-interest" because it "usually omits altogether the cognitive function," Lippmann himself mostly omitted the cognitive function in his discussion of the self (116). When he spoke of the self as constructed or conceived through an interpretive process, he was not referring to Peirce's radical notion of the self as literally created out of cognitive relations in the brain (114, 116). All that he meant by "cognitive function" was the conventional notion of James and Dewey that the self is created in social relations between individual human beings. Lippmann was unprepared to explore the role of cognitive relations within the brain in creating the self because he owed his pragmatism to James and Dewey rather than to Peirce.

When Peirce said that the self is created in thought, he meant literally that the self is an interpretive relation of thoughts, that the individual mind is "a community of [brain] cells" and that "consciousness is a sort of public spirit among the nerve cells."[16] The self was constituted relationally, interpretively, semiotically. Such relations of thirdness may be carried beyond the individual self by representative media such as language and instruments of mass communication. Thus even the larger community could be a self, a mind, a "greater person." Nationalism, a *zeitgeist,* or a group spirit of any kind originates neither with an Oversoul nor with an insider but in a community of thought.

Lippmann's view of the self, like James's, was not so profoundly communicational and therefore not as profoundly communitarian as Peirce's. As with Dewey as well as James, Lippmann's view of the relations constituting the self were inter- rather than intrapersonal: "The selves, which we construct with the help of all who influence us, prescribe . . . prepared attitudes." Accordingly, he could see that society is a series of interrelations among individuals, but he could not conceive that those interrelations among persons might also be intrarelations within a greater person, a society that was itself an emergent self. Society, in his view, was not a self or mind but only a nominalist collection of individuals, each of whom must be educated or "taught" by another individual mind, an expert like Lippmann: "Each generation will go unprepared into the modern world, unless it has been taught to conceive the kind of personality it will have to be among the issues it will most likely meet" (114–16).

Three years after *Public Opinion* Lippmann published *The Phantom Public* (1925), in which he persisted in his nominalist description of society as a "bewildered herd" whose confusion originated "in the attempt to ascribe organic unity and purpose to society. We have been taught to think of society as a body, with a mind, a soul and a purpose, not as a collection of men, women and children whose minds, souls and purposes are variously related. Instead of being allowed to think realistically of a complex of social *relations,* we have had foisted upon us by various great propagative movements the notion of a mythical entity, called Society, the Nation, the Community" (155–56).[17]

16. *Peirce on Signs: Writings on Semiotic by Charles Sanders Peirce,* ed. James Hoopes (Chapel Hill: University of North Carolina Press, 1991), 188.

17. Walter Lippmann, *The Phantom Public* (New York: Harcourt, Brace, 1925). Page numbers to most subsequent citations of this work will be given parenthetically in the text.

He saw that the alternative to the organic emphasis in romantic nationalism was to conceive of society as a series of relations, but just as James had been baffled by the problem of "the One and the Many," Lippmann could find no principle of unity among the relations constituting society. Rejecting the static "spirit of Descartes," he held that change is the origin of social problems and pragmatically added that "change is significant only in relation to something else" (81, 88). But in dismissing organic unity in favor of relations, Lippmann dismissed social unity in general. For in Jamesian fashion, Lippmann conceived of relations as strictly dyadic contacts between atomistic units. Because society was a series of dyadic relations between atomistic individuals, society must lack any quality of personal unity. In the absence of Peirce's notion that triadic or semiotic relations constituted persons, Lippmann could not conceive of broad social phenomena as real or as possessing any unitary qualities approaching personality or mentality. If persons were not relations, social relations could create no larger person.

By Lippmann's nominalist understanding of reality, wide-scale social movements such as nationalism and socialism were necessarily unreal because of their reliance on symbols. Nationalism and socialism were a "veil of imagery" behind which worked individuals, the "real agents" of history, such as "the nationalist leaders and their lieutenants, the social reformers and their lieutenants." These historical insiders had worked a "deception," a deception they "often practised sincerely" but a deception nonetheless. They foisted on the people the notion that there really were such things as a "nation's purpose," a "spirit of mankind," or even a public opinion (156–57).

Lippmann tried to portray himself as an honest insider, ready to state openly that the "public" was just a "collection" of atomistic individuals, not a reality itself (156): "I hold that this public is a mere phantom. It is an abstraction" (77). Because liberals had mistaken the public for a reality when it was only an illusion, they had never accepted "the reality of individual purpose." A sure sign of the influence of James's nominalism was Lippmann's wording when he said that liberalism had been frustrated by the "problem of the One and the Many." Lippmann added, however, that "the problem is not so insoluble once we cease to personify society" (171).

The solution lay in omitting the phantom public from any active role in government, that is, in recognizing that government was strictly an affair for individual leaders and bureaucrats. Then it could also be recognized that the real key to political science was not the contrast between public and private action but "between action by and through great masses of people and action that moves without them [i.e., individual action]." On the basis of this distinction between individual and mass action, Lippmann argued that voting was not an executive act: "The work of the world is carried on by men in their executive capacity, by . . . transforming A into B and moving B from X to Y. . . . But in governing the work of other men by votes . . . they [the voters] cannot create, administer and actually perform the act they have in mind" (51–52). Blinded by nominalist theory, even Lippmann with all his acuity, failed to see that when the masses' vote a person into public office they do so precisely to execute or "perform the act they have in mind." Failing to see that an election was a governmental act or function, Lippmann dismissed "the dogma of democracy," the "fiction" that "identified the function of government with the will of the people." Public work no less than private work is individual work: "government consists of a body of officials, some elected, some appointed" (53, 71–72).

Lacking executive capacity and even the same kind of reality as individuals, the phantom public has no real interest in any particular law. Rather, the public's interest is simply that there be laws to govern the relations between individuals so that they can get on with their daily lives and work. The public may sometimes question the fairness of a law, but "in what way the rule is defective the public cannot specifically determine." Indeed, "the inconvenience due to meddling in the substance of a controversy by a crude, violent and badly aimed public opinion at least may teach those directly concerned not to invoke [public] interference the next time" (124, 137).

Similarly, the nonelite atomistic individuals who compose the phantom public ought to be taught that on matters of substance it is best if they keep their opinions to themselves: "Education for citizenship, for membership in the public, ought, therefore, to be distinct from education for public office. Citizenship involves a radically different relation to affairs" (151). Citizens ought to be taught to focus strictly on watching to see that the laws are obeyed, while leaving the substance of those laws to the parties concerned and to government experts: "the proper limits of intervention by the public in affairs are determined by its capacity to make judgments" (140). On questions of substance the public had no capacity to make judgments since, in Lippmann's nominalist view, the public did not constitute a mind.

Lippmann opened his next phase, his metaphysical phase, by carrying his Jamesian nominalism into an attack on the reality not just of society but of spirit in general. He copied James's tactic of expressing so much sympathy for traditional religion that it gave no offense when he made clear that he was not a traditional believer. His best-selling book of 1929,

A Preface to Morals, helped mark the end of a decade of hedonism by a Jamesian invocation of religious sentiment: "It is evident that life soon becomes distracted and tiresome if it is not illuminated by communion with what William James called 'a wider self' through which saving experiences come" (18).[18] After such a show of Jamesian broad-mindedness Lippmann could safely reveal his doubt that "saving experiences" came from the spiritual world. Modernity contradicts the notion "that behind the visible world of physical objects and human institutions there is a supernatural kingdom" (143–44). The God of popular religion, Lippmann might have said, was a "pseudo-environment," a "phantom" on which he refused to attempt to base morality.

To the conventional list of science and the "acids of modernity" that had dissolved traditional notions of God, Lippmann added an additional solvent—democracy (8). The modern political movements of democracy and republicanism had made "incredible the idea that the universe is governed by a kingly person" (56). An analogous collapse of hierarchical authority had occurred within the individual. It was impossible for a modern person to conceive of the soul as "an immortal essence presiding like a king over his appetites" for his life was "a play of many characters within a single body." The cult of Freud in the 1920s meant that "popular psychology to-day is republican. Each impulse may invoke the Bill of Rights" with victory awarded to the strongest desire (112–14).

Mistakenly invoking the authority of Peirce, Lippmann held that science could not replace religion as arbiter of morality, for science does not "yield a certain picture of anything." He quoted the definition of "truth" offered "by the late Charles S. Peirce" as merely "the opinion which is fated to be ultimately agreed to" (129). Lippmann had got the quotation from the first published anthology of Peirce's writings, a slim volume compiled by Morris R. Cohen called *Chance, Love, and Logic* (1923). Unfortunately, that volume treated Peirce as a philosopher of science in a narrow sense, offering in the introduction only a vague, one-paragraph discussion of Peirce's semiotic. Cohen made no mention of Peirce's categories, including his category of thirdness—semiotic representation or thought—which had turned Peirce as a young man against the nominalism to which Lippmann subscribed. On the basis of his belief in the reality of thirdness Peirce defended the reality of generals such as scientific laws and held that they were a form of mind or spirit. Lippmann was therefore mistaken in his supposition that Peirce's philosophy supported

18. Walter Lippmann, *A Preface to Morals* (New York: Macmillan, 1929). Page numbers to most subsequent citations of this work will be given parenthetically in the text.

the conclusion that science "does not pretend to justify the ways of God to man" (133).

The dissolution of ancient beliefs and the uncertainty of modern science meant that modern people must look to themselves, not the community, for the "saving experiences" that would provide moral authority. Having prepared to write *A Preface to Morals* by dipping into classical philosophy, medieval theology, and Renaissance humanism, Lippmann offered an ancient etiology for the morally disordered psyche. He cited Socrates in the *Phaedo* as authority for his conviction that the "body and the lusts of the body" are the source of immorality (159). Since the problem lay within atomistic selves, Lippmann offered a Jamesian, individualist solution—self-control.

Self-control was to be achieved by consciousness and understanding. Like those ancient moralists who favored the faculty of understanding, Lippmann believed that the intellect should dominate the passions: "For when our desires come into contact with the world created by the understanding, . . . they are made rational by the ordered variety with which the understanding confronts them" (182–83). As with his earlier books, *A Preface to Morals* was littered with references to Freud, but was less interested in the unconscious origin of conflict than in its conscious resolution: "To be able to observe our own feelings as if they were objective facts . . . is somehow to rob them of their imperiousness" (219). Lippmann admired the psychological faculty most characteristic of himself, the understanding. Dispassionate, knowing, and keen, the understanding should dominate the passions just as the expert should dominate society. The passionate conflict and tumult of democracy were no more acceptable in moral than in political life.

Yet with the coming of the New Deal, its Brain Trust, and alphabet agencies, Lippmann had cause to think again about the role of the expert in public life and began a long process of withdrawal from belief in the intellectual as the prophet/savior of modern society. A best-selling author and columnist did not need a secure niche in a bureaucracy of experts. Although Lippmann supported the New Deal's early bold initiatives and also admired Roosevelt's wartime leadership in the 1940s, in the middle years of the Roosevelt presidency he became so skeptical and suspicious of the centralizing tendency of the New Deal that he was provoked to write his best book on political theory.

An Inquiry into the Principles of the Good Society (1937) marks an obscure and complex but fundamental shift in Lippmann's philosophy, a transition away from his quarter-century-long faith in pragmatism but not entirely away from the nominalist spirit of William James. At the

outset of the 1920s *Public Opinion* had announced Lippmann's abandonment of the antirepresentationalism he had learned from James. Yet
Lippmann had still believed in a pragmatic, experimental, and activist
government of experts and bureaucrats. Now he rejected that pragmatic,
experimental, and activist government in favor of judicious regulation of
a vital private sector. In philosophical justification of this shift, Lippmann recurred not to James but to an eighteenth-century dualism and
nominalism from which James could not save him because of James's
own atavistic dualism and nominalism.

In *The Good Society,* Lippmann presciently predicted "that if ever the
time comes when Russia no longer feels the need of mobilization, it will
become necessary to liquidate the planning authority and to return
somehow to a market economy" (179).[19] Written during an economic
crisis that for some political theorists validated Soviet-style planning, *The
Good Society* asserted that "a directed society must be bellicose and poor"
(xii). Adam Smith, not Karl Marx, was the great social scientist of modern times, according to Lippmann. Unlike Marx, Smith saw that the social tensions arising from the specialization and division of labor could
not be regulated by a dictatorship, whether of the proletariat or planners,
but only by the free market. Civil war and foreign intervention had sanctioned Lenin's authoritarianism and had enabled the Soviet Union to ignore the harsh truth that a planned society must fail.

Lippmann was no harder on communists than on classical liberals.
The Spencerian prophets of laissez-faire mistakenly "identified the existing laws of property with the new mode of production." Indeed, these
"latter-day liberals" were more culpable than Marxists for the widespread
assumption "that the status quo *was* a liberal society achieved" (181).
Classical liberals failed to recognize that property was a civil rather than
a natural right, failed to see that the capitalist social order was a product,
not of laissez-faire, but of positive action by the state (180). In missing all
this, they made themselves forces of reaction who stood in the way of further positive actions that the state should take in modern society.

As always with Lippmann, the question that interested him in *The
Good Society* was *who* should direct the state in its positive actions. He
was appalled at the opening for interest group politics offered by New
Deal activism. Appeasement of every interest group restricted society's
ability to produce wealth and at the same time fostered the illusion that
the seeds of plenty had been sown. The result could only be heightened

19. Walter Lippmann, *An Inquiry into the Principles of the Good Society* (Boston: Little, Brown, 1937).
Page numbers to most subsequent citations of this work will be given parenthetically in the text.

tension and lower civility among opposing interest groups, the environment most likely to stunt liberal democracy (115–18).

Lippmann's long-term skepticism of democracy had been increased by the Depression. In January 1933 he advised his column's readers of the need for a strong executive by belittling, on nominalist grounds, the legislative branch: "Any group of 500 men, whether they are called Congressmen or anything else, is an unruly mob unless it comes under the strict control of a single will." Lunching soon thereafter with Roosevelt, he startled the president-elect by saying, "The situation is critical, Franklin. You may have no alternative but to assume dictatorial powers."[20]

Yet Lippmann's rightward drift was in no fundamental danger of becoming authoritarian, thanks to his loss of faith in the ability of the creative statesman to comprehend all of society. A quarter century earlier, in his youthful *Preface to Politics,* Lippmann had said that the creative statesman's task—to "think of the whole nation"—had become increasingly difficult since the time of Plato and Aristotle.[21] Now in *The Good Society* he believed that task impossible, for even though "President Roosevelt has a greater reach than Pericles, he needs a very much greater reach" (26). The communication revolution had more than offset the increased power it gave to government by making the society to be governed almost infinitely more complex. In so densely interrelated a society it must be profoundly destructive to give government experts autocratic powers.

His newfound and healthy distrust for expert authority had a weak philosophical basis, for Lippmann's epistemology was still nominalist: "The mind . . . evolved . . . for the mastery of specific details" (21). Being specific rather than general, "no human mind has ever understood the whole scheme of a society" (31). The planner who ponders the proper organization of society while eating his breakfast, said Lippmann, is incapable of completely understanding even the mere interrelation of citrus groves, coffee plantations, dairy farms, ships, railroads, and trucks that provide him with orange juice, coffee, and cream. Beyond Lippmann's ken lay any notion that these relations might be, among other things, mental and constitutive of the community's emergent mind or self.

The answer to the question of how to maintain a civilized society without central planning lay in "higher law" which was not to be ascertained through Peirce's pragmatic logic of external relations but through the individual's supposed interior light of reason in which Descartes had placed his faith (347). No longer believing in the ability of the creative statesman to "go out to meet a need before it had become acute," Lippmann needed

20. Quoted in Steel, *Walter Lippmann,* 300.
21. Lippmann, *Preface to Politics,* 104.

a principle of social order and direction.[22] Never a believer in pure democracy and equally fearful in the late 1930s of authoritarianism, he hoped to find a principal of social order within the individual. Human beings need only look within, he stated in *The Good Society,* to find "a profound and universal intuition of the human destiny which, to all who have it, is invincible because it is self-evident" (372).

Rejecting the experimental spirit of pragmatism but still bound by the kind of nominalism he had learned from James, Lippmann had found his way back to the philosophical basis of the market economy he now espoused. The Englishmen and Americans of the seventeenth and eighteenth centuries who had defeated tyranny and created free societies had done so on the basis of "self-evident truths" (372). They had drawn courage from the Cartesian and Lockean faith in the mind's immediate, unrepresented knowledge of its own thoughts. What had above all been self-evident to eighteenth-century freedom fighters were human rights which were "simply the expression of the higher law that men shall not deal arbitrarily with one another" (281).

Government regulation was therefore justified when it prevented arbitrariness in human relations and unjustified when it created arbitrariness in human relations. If the collectivists were mistaken in their idea that everything should be administered by the state, rugged individualists were equally mistaken in their idea that nothing should be regulated by the state. In modern corporate capitalism "the potentialities of regulation are as numerous and varied as the points at which the corporation has relations" (281). But to be just, such regulation must be shorn of "willfulness and caprice" (372).

The surest way to inject caprice and arbitrariness into society was for the government to overreach itself by attempting not merely to regulate but to administer society, the temptation to which the New Deal had surrendered in Lippmann's view. In a free society the state's task is to resolve social problems "by the readjustment of private rights rather than by public administration" (282). In a free society, the state does not administer human affairs; the people administer their own affairs. The state merely administers justice under law when the people's interests conflict. Knowing the regulations and laws, the disputants will often settle the matter themselves rather than go to court.

Lippmann justified his sensible preference for government regulation over government administration by recurring to the faulty philosophical foundation of nominalism. If the human mind is an individual affair, then it is not capable of administering a complex society but only of judging among contending interests. All of modern history testifies, Lippmann believed, to the profound error of the notion of the legislature as representative of the people's sovereign will, directing the executive to administer affairs in this way or that. On the other hand, "it is proved by experience that men can render good decisions as judges in affairs which they would be entirely incapable of initiating and administering" (297). Legislators should not create administrative bureaucracies but rather should "judge among visible claimants" (283).

This superficially attractive theory of the liberal state as essentially judicial came apart at the seams when Lippmann tried to describe how the legislature might enact statutes conforming to the higher law against arbitrariness. Everything depends on the legislator's understanding that his job is to judge: "the more clearly he understands . . . that he is not there to impose his will but to judge among visible claimants and invisible interests, the more likely he is to set himself a sound and workable criterion of the public interest" (285). But the legislator who, because of public interest, judiciously opposes the interest of his constituents is more, rather than less, likely to incur their political wrath and be voted from office. In short, Lippmann's faith in the possibility of the judicious legislator was contradicted by his nominalist scepticism toward public spirit. The selfish constituency that wants its interests guarded can simply elect an injudicious legislator.

For a quarter of a century Lippmann had unsuccessfully devoted his acute intellect to the question of how democracy can be guided by mind. As a nominalist, he could not conceive of mind as anything other than individual, which meant that everything depended on the leader. In 1912 he had conceived of the task of statesmanship as "to think of the whole nation."[23] By 1937 this grandiose conception had been narrowed enormously: "the primary task of liberal statesmanship is to judge the claims of particular interests."[24] But his judicious legislator of 1937 was no more realistic or practical than his creative statesman of 1912. And in terms of a role for mind, the judicious legislator was a big comedown, a mere arbiter of claims among conflicting interests in a Hobbesian war of all against all. Still guided by James's sort of nominalism, Lippmann could only back away from the ideal of the planned community by backing away from the ideal of community altogether.

In 1955 Lippmann finally rejected the nominalism that had dominated his career when he returned to political philosophy with *The Public Phi-*

23. Lippmann, *Preface to Politics*, 104.
24. Lippmann, *An Inquiry into the Principles of the Good Society*, 284.

losophy, his final attempt at a deep analysis of politics. In its rejection of nominalism, its insistence that the unperceivable can nevertheless be real, and its consequent assertion that the public is no phantom but is a reality, *The Public Philosophy* marks his final if not quite complete departure from James. Having abandoned James's antirepresentationalism in *Public Opinion* and liberal experimentalism in *The Good Society,* Lippmann now abandoned the nominalism he had also learned, at least initially, from James. Yet Lippmann pontifically announced the mistakenness of nominalism without admitting that it had dominated his career or acknowledging his abandonment of James. Too politic to cast doubt on the substance of his previous writings, Lippmann may also not have understood how far he had travelled intellectually from his mentor. He continued as in his past books to support his own ideas with pithy quotes from James. The irony was unintentional but real; James was Lippmann's authority for abandoning James.

Yet Lippmann did not offer an alternative, foundational metaphysics to the nominalism he abandoned and therefore could not accomplish a genuine revision of his political philosophy. Holding that the reality of the community could be denied only by those "who are strongly nominalist," Lippmann nevertheless failed to offer a philosophical argument against nominalism. He cited Mortimer Adler, the neoscholastic philosopher at the University of Chicago, as an antinominalist authority, but he did not actually employ any philosophical arguments, either Adler's or others'. Lippmann merely countered Bentham's assertion that "the community is a fictitious *body*" by invoking Burke's declaration that a person is bound to his country by "ties which though light as air, are as strong as links of iron." Altering James's metaphor for the continuity of consciousness into a figurative description of the political community Lippmann in *The Public Philosophy* held that "the people is . . . the stream of individuals, the connected generations of changing persons" (34–36).[25] As with James's argument for the continuity of thought, Lippmann's argument for the continuity of social relations rested on nothing stronger than the fact that that was the way it seemed to him.

Just as James's belief in the stream of consciousness was illogically contradicted by his belief that experience is a matter of disjunctive, dyadic relations, Lippmann's newfound belief in the reality of society was illogically contradicted by his continuing belief that mentality is strictly limited to atomistic individuals. With no realist metaphysics such as Peirce could have provided, Lippmann maintained in *The Public Philosophy* the

25. Walter Lippmann, *Essays in the Public Philosophy* (Boston: Little, Brown, 1955). Page numbers to most subsequent citations of this work will be given parenthetically in the text.

same position as in *Public Opinion*—the public is not capable of executive decisions because the public is not a mind. Not being a mind, the
public is incapable of acting in the public interest. Naively defining the
public interest as "what men would choose if they saw clearly, thought
rationally, acted disinterestedly and benevolently," Lippmann added that
the public's being unable to do any of these things explained why the
century of mass democracy had shown "a general tendency to be drawn
downward, as by the force of gravity, towards insolvency, towards . . . fac-
tionalism, towards the . . . erosion of liberty, and towards hyperbolic
wars" (42, 46).

Lippmann exhorted the community to apply natural law even to those
to whom it was not self-evident. The Cold War made it difficult for
Lippmann to share classical liberalism's faith that the free exchange of
ideas would lead to the truth. Communists not committed to the value
of rational debate were not entitled to the protection of free society. Indeed, Lippmann believed that democracy itself was destroying the values
on which freedom depended, the values of civility and rational discourse.
By enjoining the temporal power not to interfere in the "realm of the
mind" democracy had made itself powerless to preserve "the character of
its citizens" (99). In his previous book he had avowed his faith in the economic marketplace, but in this book he seemed to have lost faith in the
traditional liberal notion of the marketplace of ideas.

Possibly owing to Adler's influence, Lippmann mistakenly invoked
Peirce as an ally when he defined the public philosophy as "*natural law*"
(101). Peirce would never have agreed with Lippmann's definition of natural law as "a common conception of law and order which possesses a universal validity" (104). Peirce indeed defined the truth of any question as
the opinion all would agree upon if inquiry proceeded long enough and
with sufficient information to reach the answer. But Peirce did not maintain that there were universals because, as Lippmann put it, it was "rational" (133). Peirce rejected the interior light of rationality—Descartes's
"clear and distinct" ideas—in favor of the objectivity of thought. Not the
interior light of reason but the logical method of thinking by signs was
Peirce's logic. Modern science was one example of this method of thinking by signs, and its success, not its appeal to subjective rationality,
confirmed the merit of symbolic logic.

Lippmann is probably as good an example as history offers of the damage wreaked on liberal thought when James's nominalism, dualism, and
subjective style of thought became the more or less official version of
pragmatism rather than Peirce's realism, monism, and external, formal
logic. Even after Lippmann finally abandoned nominalism in favor of

realism, he remained essentially Jamesian in his commitment to a subjective, dualist philosophy. He could not find a foundation for the political community in modern philosophy and could only assert it on the basis of a long outdated belief in self-evident principles of natural law which in turn rested on an atomistic, individualistic conception of human beings. The individual human mind had only to look inward, not outward toward the world of others, to find truth.

Lippmann's understandable lack of confidence that a logic which was so individualist would protect the community against Communist untruth made him suspicious of the civil liberties held dear by those same eighteenth-century thinkers whom he thought of as progenitors of the public philosophy. In the absence of Peircean foundations, the newly converted antinominalist of *The Public Philosophy* remained as wary of participatory democracy as the nominalist author of *Public Opinion.*

CHAPTER   SIX

NIEBUHR'S DISBELIEF IN SOCIETY

. . . to believe only possibilities, is not faith, but mere philosophy.
—Sir Thomas Browne, *Religio Medici*

Nothing better illustrates the attractiveness of William James's fence-straddling moralism in the early twentieth-century than his appeal to the rustic, young Reinhold Niebuhr, who discovered James when he was a divinity student at Yale in 1914. For more than a generation James had salved the fears of traditional believers by affirming their right to a vestigial dualism like his own. His essay "The Will to Believe," which had held belief acceptable so long as it did not contradict verifiable observations, appealed to many Christians attempting to reconcile science and religion in the late nineteenth and early twentieth centuries. James's approach seemed to leave room for faith in human "personality," a term which in the theological schools came to mean something like Descartes's atomistic, immaterial soul, operating above and apart from nature and mechanical physics. This uninspired formula inspired dozens, possibly hundreds, of religious writings including the thesis Niebuhr submitted for his Bachelor of Divinity degree: "The revolt of men like William James against the determinism of the universe . . . is the revolt of a growing moral consciousness in men, that is becoming increasingly impatient with a universe in which its struggles are without effect and its powers not its own." [1]

1. Quoted in Richard Wrightman Fox, *Reinhold Niebuhr: A Biography* (New York: Pantheon, 1985), 32.

The son of German pietists who had immigrated to the midwest accepted at face value the teachings of his Yale professors, including their notion that James was the leading philosopher of the time, an avant-gardist who, because of his courageous wrestling in the thickets of advanced thought, had found a path for faith. In maturity, Niebuhr came to see the other side of James, the overzealous empiricist who supposed that though the "will to believe" was permissible for the scientifically informed, a scientific viewpoint nevertheless excluded general, intangible things of the spirit.

Yet even after the mature Niebuhr got a clearer perspective on the limitations of James, he did not abandon the dualist doctrine that "personality" was above and opposed to nature, the doctrine that his teachers had led him to believe was sanctioned by James. Dewey's naturalism was of course not an acceptable alternative for a "neo-orthodox" theist like Niebuhr. With no thorough knowledge of Peirce's categories, Niebuhr could not find in the canon of American pragmatism anything better than James's illogical individualism as a way of preserving a place for human "personality." Niebuhr leaned on this doctrine all his life, with damaging effects on his theology.

As opposed to Lippmann, the drama in Niebuhr's intellectual life was not due to philosophical quest but only to shifts between political realism and idealism. A pacifist during the early years of the First World War, he bivouacked at the feet of Mars after America entered the war in 1917. An opponent of coercion in the struggle for industrial justice in the 1920s, he endorsed the morality of force as an instrument of class struggle in the 1930s. Sympathetic to Marxism during the Depression, he subsequently became a Cold War liberal.

Niebuhr, a charismatic preacher and gifted writer, pioneered what became an alternative intellectual style for American liberals, an alternative to the optimistic naturalism of Dewey. Niebuhr was tough mindedly conservative in regard to traditional cultural values such as those offered by Christian orthodoxy, yet he nevertheless adopted a liberal and even radical social critique. As a young pastor in Detroit in the 1920s, he gained a national reputation in his denomination, the German Evangelical Synod, through strenuous organizational work and by eloquent articles in religious periodicals. He was called to Union Theological Seminary in the 1930s, and he used New York's media resources, much as Dewey had, to find a role and audience beyond both church and academe.

Niebuhr was soon a force in liberal politics and in the struggle for social justice in New York and even nationwide. In the late 1940s and 1950s he concerned himself with fighting communism at home and abroad while never sacrificing his liberal credentials. His "neo-orthodox" skepticism of liberal theology helped legitimate his liberal politics. His centrist credentials were accepted by the moderate right as well as the left, and *Time* magazine even honored him with a cover story. As the country's most famous theologian and American Protestantism's leading anti-Communist intellectual, Niebuhr became a prized presence at think tanks and establishment conferences. He served as an official consultant to the State Department, helped found Americans for Democratic Action, and lent his prestige to countless liberal causes. By this time he was antipragmatic in his theology, but, in the general "practical" sense of the word, one of the country's leading pragmatic liberals.[2]

Beneath Niebuhr's changing politics there was one continuous and unquestioned conviction: however tainted the moral life of the individual, it was immeasurably superior to that of society. This was the theme of a prize-winning essay from his student days, "The Paradox of Patriotism," the theme of one of his first publications in a national magazine, "The Nation's Crime against the Individual,"[3] and the theme of his most famous book, *Moral Man and Immoral Society* (1932). In fact, this theme comes up again and again: "personality fails to make its appeal to the conscience when considered in the mass and when regarded at too long range";[4] unlike the individual, the community "knows nothing of a dimension of the eternal";[5] the "group is more arrogant, hypocritical, self-centered and more ruthless . . . than the individual";[6] "individual vitality rises in indeterminate degree over all social and communal concretions of life."[7] This one, lonely concept of the moral superiority of individuals over groups runs through and undergirds all of his political phases—pacifist, patriot, class warrior, and cold warrior.

Since Niebuhr did not engage in any philosophical quest in the way that Lippmann did, his thought can be treated as all of a piece. Without ignoring the chronological order of his writings, in this chapter I will discuss the sources of his confidence in the moral superiority of the individual over society. Then, in the light of that discussion I will attempt to

2. Ibid., passim.
3. Reinhold Niebuhr, "The Nation's Crime against the Individual," *The Atlantic Monthly,* November 1916.
4. Reinhold Niebuhr, *Does Civilization Need Religion?* (New York: Macmillan, 1927), 126.
5. Reinhold Niebuhr, *The Self and the Dramas of History* (New York: Scribner's, 1955), 35.
6. Reinhold Niebuhr, *The Nature and Destiny of Man: A Christian Interpretation* (New York: Scribner's, 1941), 1: 208.
7. Reinhold Niebuhr, *The Children of Light and the Children of Darkness: A Vindication of Democracy and a Critique of Its Traditional Defense* (New York: Scribner's, 1944), 49.

shed some new light also on his famous dispute with Dewey, a dispute which is often taken as a defining moment in the history of twentieth-century pragmatic liberalism.

For all the social emphasis in Niebuhr's writings there was a profound individualism at the core of his theology. Like Dewey, whose optimism he criticized from the vantage point of religious tradition, Niebuhr explicitly protested against nominalism while implicitly tilting toward it. Just as biologism implied that only the individual organism was real and prevented Dewey from ascribing reality to human society, Niebuhr's faith in transcendent human personality left him believing that only individual souls, not society, were real. As some recent scholars have suggested, Dewey and Niebuhr arrived at some similar conclusions. But there was no real possibility of a common liberal tradition involving both thinkers, for they argued for different moral capacities of individual human beings and based their arguments on very different philosophical foundations. Although both the young Niebuhr and Dewey sought the philosophical support of James, they meant to use him to shore up different foundations—naturalism in Dewey's case, and individual human transcendence over nature in Niebuhr's.

This reliance on a transcendent element in the individual human soul had an ironic effect on Niebuhr's supposedly neo-orthodox social criticism, for it left him positing higher qualities to the individual human being than to society at large. Where orthodox Christians had once supposed social organizations, be they churches or temporal governments, were needed to watch over morally flawed individuals, Niebuhr believed that individuals must guard against the moral imperfection of social institutions. Where Peirce, a sort of neopietist in this respect, believed that logic required the individual to have faith in the community of inquirers to find truth, Niebuhr believed the search for truth was a strictly individual affair.

Although Niebuhr paused often to profess belief in the failings of individual human beings, his strongest emphasis was always on the moral inferiority of groups. His argument was that individual souls are capable of imagining and sympathizing with the suffering of others but that groups, not being minds, are incapable of such sentiments and therefore incapable of ethical action. For Niebuhr religion was always an individual affair. Even when he spoke of religion's needing "an ethic which is not individualistic" he meant simply an ethic that would require individuals to act morally in relation to groups, not that groups may act ethically.[8]

---

8. Niebuhr, *Does Civilization Need Religion?*, 207. Page numbers to most subsequent citations of this work will be given parenthetically in the text.

The ethic which Niebuhr believed was needed but impossible to achieve in the modern world was the extension of the individual's social imagination to embrace as brothers not only other individuals but other groups. Religion, Niebuhr wrote in *Does Civilization Need Religion?* (1927), encourages human beings to regard each other as brothers by placing a high value on God-given "personality" (37). The difficulty in the modern world was that improvements in commerce and communication had vastly extended social relations, but the individual human conscience could not engage itself with groups or across great distances. Worse, now that social relations occurred not only within groups but between them, there was a new scope for "the expansive desire and unethical attitudes which develop naturally within the group as a corporate entity" (129). The consequent "lust and greed of the group" led Niebuhr "almost to despair" (142).

Niebuhr wanted to believe that his discouraged social view was based on his personal experience as a young pastor in Detroit. In a 1926 notebook entry he claimed to have been saved from "cynicism by knowing individuals, and knowing them intimately. If I viewed humanity only from some distant and high perspective I could not save myself from misanthropy. I think the reason is simply that people are not as decent in their larger relationship as in their more intimate contacts." [9] In the same notebook passage he compared the lovingness of middle-class family life with middle-class unconcern for the distant pain of industrial workers as further proof of the moral superiority of human beings in close social relations as opposed to distant ones. When he developed these ideas in books such as *Does Civilization Need Religion?* and *Moral Man and Immoral Society,* he felt that his views were supported by his everyday experience as a pastor in an industrial city.

Yet his discouragement with the ethics of intergroup relations had another basis than personal experience; its philosophic narrowness went straight back to his Yale indoctrination in "personality," the old atomistic soul with a new name. Niebuhr seems not to have been cognizant of any possible argument against "personality" conceived as individual soulfulness. The only possible escape from his discouragement with the moral potential of groups would have been through a metaphysics that made it possible to conceive of both individuals and groups as having minds capable of moral feeling. This, Niebuhr was never prepared to do because of the nominalism and psychological atomism implicit in his doctrine of

9. Reinhold Niebuhr, *Leaves from the Notebook of a Tamed Cynic* (New York: Harper & Row, 1980), 76.

"personality." It is obvious that there was considerable truth to Niebuhr's notion that individuals find it easier to act morally than groups do. But because it was only the obviousness of the proposition rather than any well-considered philosophy on which Niebuhr drew, he made the argument bleakly absolute and almost certainly underestimated the moral capacity of groups.

Distance between individuals was the dynamic factor in Niebuhr's social theory. His frequent declamations against the distance and complexity of modern social relations resemble Lippmann's priggish failure to see that electronic, representative media extended the experience and community of baseball fans. Religion and general human brotherhood, not baseball, were Niebuhr's concern, but he was no less skeptical than Lippmann of the possibility of real relations across great distances. Religion, being respect for "personality," could not prosper in a society of impersonal relations: "The industrial worker," he stated in *Does Civilization Need Religion?* "is indifferent to religion, partly because he is enmeshed in relations which are so impersonal and fundamentally so unethical that his religious sense atrophies in him" (15). Unlike Dewey, and probably more realistically than Dewey, Niebuhr held out no hope that hands-on education in the whys and wherefores of modern life would make the lot of a worker more satisfying by aiding and vivifying his comprehension of the impersonal relations in which he was enmeshed.

Left with no clear philosophic approach to the issues of modern society, the young Niebuhr eclectically pieced together a makeshift combination of traditional Protestant self-denial, faith in spiritual transcendence, and Jamesian inconsistency. The special dangers of aggressiveness in the modern world showed the mistakenness of religious liberalism's abandonment of pietist self denial in favor of celebration of the self: "it is no longer possible to veil the immoral implications of a self-centered religion" (32). Yet the Protestant ethic had erroneously tied Christianity to industrialism and therefore had to be supplemented by a religious "quest for the absolute" as "a necessary factor in social reconstruction" (76). Human aggression could only be restrained by new social and international organizations which were less a matter of law and political structures than new "attitudes . . . which . . . religion must create" (153). Religion would have a far easier job of creating these new attitudes if it could overcome the logical constraints of secular philosophy, which was where James came in.

The young Niebuhr believed that an illogical philosopher such as James was religiously useful not despite but because of his illogicality. Niebuhr wanted to heap scorn on secularists' denial of spiritual transcendence while simultaneously condemning liberal religionists' underestimation of the evil and necessitarianism at work in the world. Finding this difficult to achieve on the basis of a consistent philosophy, Niebuhr took hope from James's inconsistency. Confident that "the real facts of life" conformed to his picture of the universe as divided between creative personality and resistance to it, Niebuhr held that "the pluralism of William James, which has been criticized as scientifically inaccurate and metaphysically inconsistent, seems to have both scientific and metaphysical virtues." Inconsistency in metaphysics was a religious virtue because "religion is always forced to choose between an adequate metaphysics and an adequate ethics" (210, 213, 214). Just as the universe was divided between personality and resistance to it, so must religion deal with conflict between ought and is. A mistaken emphasis on metaphysical consistency would cost religion its moral fervor. Hence James's metaphysical inconsistency seemed just the thing for religion.

Like James, and for similar reasons, Niebuhr was skeptical of logic. James, believing that empiricism supported both dyadic, disjunctive relations and metaphysical continuity, decided to "give up the logic" that made them seem inconsistent. Niebuhr, believing that experience proved both personality and resistance to it to be facts, preferred to abandon "highly rationalized" religion in favor of a "religious dualism" whose inconsistency mirrored the contradictions of lived experience (214, 215; cf. 183, 200). By so recognizing the moral division of the universe, dualism threatened religious comfort and assurance, but religious discomfort, Niebuhr believed, was a positive good. Like James, Niebuhr assumed that if faith "makes the triumph of righteousness certain, it may incline men to take 'moral holidays'" (215). A dynamic religion that would fight evil was "not always compatible with a completely consistent metaphysics" (218–19).

Niebuhr never saw the danger in this adventurous dualism, never saw that to accept the separation of atomistic personalities from nature in order to insure their opposition to evil was to help isolate them from each other by denying that they possessed potential for community within the natural world in which they lived. From his point of view the greater danger was a naturalist, scientific viewpoint which would deny personality altogether (183). Unaware of Peirce's categories, which explained the difference between mental and material phenomena as a matter of different relations rather than different substances of mind and matter, Niebuhr believed it impossible "to do full justice to the two types of facts by any set of symbols or definitions." Since "life gives the lie to any attempt by which one is explained completely in terms of the other," the only recourse Niebuhr could see was a dualism that not only separated human beings from nature but also from each other (210).

This atomistic individualism underlay his celebrated book of 1932, *Moral Man and Immoral Society*. Niebuhr's assertion of the inability of groups to act morally was owing to his belief that spirituality stopped with the individual. So too with his belief that only force could dislodge the established power of one class in favor of another. His famous attack on Dewey was based largely on his belief that Dewey's optimistic instrumentalism ignored the central problem of modern politics, immoral relations between groups. There was a tension in *Moral Man and Immoral Society* between Niebuhr's admiration for Marxist fanaticism and his skepticism of its claim of moral superiority to bourgeois ideologies, a tension rooted in his individualism. Marxism had an admirable effect on the moral fervor of individuals, but its claims to a universal mission for the working class, a mere group, violated Niebuhr's nominalist faith in individuals. The clarity of Niebuhr's Christian commitment to the atomistic soul as the exclusive locale of spirit enabled him to address social and political issues with a bold radicalism that would have been death to the careers of clergymen less firmly grounded in nominalism and individualism.

Depression-era radicals, attracted by the broad-mindedness of a theologian sympathetic to Marxism, largely missed the traditional atomistic individualism in *Moral Man and Immoral Society*. It was noteworthy that a Christian theologian sympathized with Marxism but not news that he subscribed to an individualism that made him view Marxist goals as unachievable. What he criticized as "group egoism" was not the egoism of a group.[10] He never even considered the possibility that a group might have an emergent ego, or what Peirce called a "quasi-mind," different from the individual minds comprising it. Rather, Niebuhr lamented only the inability of individuals in groups to hold themselves to the same standards in intergroup relations as in interpersonal relations: "Individuals are never as immoral as the social situations in which they are involved and which they symbolize" (248).

The result of Niebuhr's nominalist skepticism toward society was the rhetorically interesting paradox with which he concluded *Moral Man and Immoral Society*. Originally, the book's final passage stated that the illusion that "the collective life of mankind can achieve perfect justice" was a vitally important illusion, for "nothing but such madness will do battle with malignant power and 'spiritual wickedness in high places.'" Some readers interpreted this as an embrace of fanaticism. Stung by such criticism, Niebuhr added three more sentences to subsequent editions: "The illusion is dangerous because it encourages terrible fanaticisms. It must

10. Reinhold Niebuhr, *Moral Man and Immoral Society* (New York: Scribner's, 1960; orig. pub. 1932), xxii. Page numbers to most subsequent citations of this work will be given parenthetically in the text.

therefore be brought under the control of reason. One can only hope that reason will not destroy it before its work is done" (277). Wanting social change but powerless to imagine it occurring through a social process because of his own individualist ethos, Niebuhr offered nothing more than the hope that everything would work out for the best, that the antireligious force of reason would bring to heel the religious passion of Marxism at just the moment Marxism shifted from being a force for good to being a force for evil.

Unlike Lippmann, Niebuhr held out no hope that a spiritual leader might provide an ethic for the group. Religion, being an affair of the individual soul, focused on the "inner needs of the human spirit," and therefore did "not concern itself with the social problem" (263). The moral leader of a group might sacrifice his own interests in a just cause. But the moral leader was still an individual and therefore could not justly sacrifice the group's interests which were necessarily "other than his own" (267). Individualism, combined with Christian humility, would prevent a statesman from leading the group toward generosity in its relations with other groups.

The limited range of the individual human mind was the source of both the individual's and the group's moral weakness, but it led to far more weakness in groups than in individuals. Human sympathy fails in our encounter with alien groups because of our intellectual shortcomings. We do not well understand groups different from ours because "human imagination cannot be extended too far beyond the actual experiences of an individual or a class" (230). Like the individual, a group has impulses, "but unlike the individual, little reason to restrain those impulses" (35). Self-criticism, "a kind of inner disunity," can be practiced by individuals, but "the feeble mind of a nation finds difficulty in distinguishing [it] from dangerous forms of inner conflict" (88).

Devoid of mind, soul, reason, and spirit, groups could only be expected to resort to force in order to settle differences between them. The necessity of realpolitik was the heart of Niebuhr's message to liberal, optimistic Christians who hopefully counseled peace and good will: "They do not recognise that when collective power . . . exploits weakness, it can never be dislodged unless power is raised against it" (xii). A wise Christian moralism would not wring its hands over the use of force but would join battle on the better side. Despite the focus of *Moral Man and Immoral Society* on class struggle and Marxism, the reason for Niebuhr's later attractiveness to Cold War liberals can be discerned in this early work. His emphasis that Christian moralists must not deplore but work within the world of realpolitik could be applied to international struggle as well as class struggle; in the forties and fifties he would counsel that the liberal democracies must meet the Communist threat of force with a similar threat.

Largely because of the verve and boldness of *Moral Man and Immoral Society*, Niebuhr became a renowned figure not merely within religious circles, which had been his previous sphere, but within American and even Western culture at large. In 1939 he became one of a handful of American thinkers—William James had been the first—invited to Edinburgh to deliver the prestigious Gifford lectures, which resulted in his largest, intellectually most ambitious project, *The Nature and Destiny of Man*. World War II began during Niebuhr's half year in Edinburgh, and his lectures were punctuated by Nazi bombings that confirmed for him the folly, as he saw it, of liberal optimism and failure to recognize the necessity of force.

Yet his commitment to realpolitik, combined with a world crisis in which immorality and injustice in American society were dwarfed by the sinister evil of fascism, moved him far from some of the themes that had dominated *Moral Man and Immoral Society*. Although he had devoted a chapter of that book to the morality and lack thereof in nations, his main focus had been on injustice between social classes, the usefulness of revolutionary fanaticism in class struggle, and of course the appropriateness of force as a means toward justice among social classes. Now the terribleness of fascist fanaticism and, after the Hitler-Stalin pact, the confirmation of what Niebuhr had always known—that Marxism no more than any other ideology could prevent cynicism and self-interested diplomacy—moderated his sympathy for extremist visionaries. Some societies, it turned out, were more immoral than others. Above all, his interest as a social moralist was shifted from domestic class struggle to the international arena. The outlines of Niebuhr's post–World War II, establishment, Cold War liberalism were taking shape in the late 1930s.

Despite the reorientation of his politics, Niebuhr's underlying philosophy remained essentially dualistic as became clear when he took up the question of the self in *The Nature and Destiny of Man*. Eager to present a description of the self as unified and yet also as divided between nature and the supernatural, he was confident that no monism could do justice to the real facts of life. Unaware of Peirce, Niebuhr was unaware of any monistic alternatives to idealism and materialism. Idealism wrongly denied creatureliness to humanity and materialism wrongly denied spirituality. Humanity's creatureliness was proven by the body and human spirituality by self-consciousness. The self was therefore a unity but a fissured unity: "There are obviously not simply two selves in conflict with each other. But in every moment of existence there is a tension between the self as it looks out upon the world from the perspective of its values . . . and the self as it . . . is disquieted by the undue claims of the self in action" (1:278).[11]

By now Niebuhr had largely given up his earlier admiration for William James's metaphysical inconsistency. He had finally discerned the Janus-faced quality of James's philosophy, the way James allowed for the possibility of supernaturalism only by the depth of his commitment to an empiricism that read out of philosophy anything that could not be directly experienced. Naturalists' tendency to lose sight of the soul could be seen in "James's assurance, that the hypothesis of a substantial principle of unity is superfluous" for integration of human personality, which was an example of the way not only psychology but every natural science affirmed "its character as a pure science by its metaphysical scepticism" (1: 73; cf. 1: 23).

Yet Niebuhr remained more deeply influenced than he understood by the same sort of empiricism that informed James's psychology. Niebuhr's notion of the self as torn between its transcendent and creaturely sides depended not only on Biblical revelation but on his belief that revelation confirmed, and was confirmed by, empirical self-knowledge. There had been no real progress in human psychology since the establishment of the "Biblical viewpoint," according to which a "dialogue of the self with itself is an *empiric* fact . . . in the internal life of the self." [12] The fact was that Niebuhr accepted not only the Biblical viewpoint, according to which self-knowledge was a difficult achievement, but also the Cartesian model of mental life as immediately known and requiring no interpretation. This was the model that Peirce, not James, had challenged by suggesting that everything, including our own thoughts, are not immediately present but can only be known mediately, through the interpretation of signs.

Niebuhr, however, continued to think of experience, especially "the internal life of the self" as known empirically and therefore certainly. In *The Nature and Destiny of Man* he appealed less to the Bible than to consciousness to assert the reality of the soul: "As a creature who is involved in flux but who is also conscious of the fact that he is so involved, he [man] cannot be totally involved. A spirit who can set time, nature, the world and being *per se* into juxtaposition to himself and inquire after the meaning of these things, proves that in some sense he stands outside and

11. Niebuhr, *Nature and Destiny of Man.* Page numbers to most subsequent citations of this work will be given parenthetically in the text.
12. Niebuhr, *The Self and the Dramas of History,* 4. Italics added.

beyond them" (1: 124). Wed to this notion that the soul's existence was empirically proven by the self-consciousness of individual human beings, Niebuhr remained committed to atomistic individualism. Christianity's distinction between the natural and the supernatural was the only possible way to maintain a "genuine individuality . . . which can do justice to the immediate involvement of human individuality in all the organic forms and social tensions of history, while yet appreciating its ultimate transcendence over every social and historical situation" (1:23).

What Niebuhr lost by his lack of knowledge of Peirce becomes clear in his deep reliance on James's style of thought—confidence in the empirical evidence of consciousness—even after he had repudiated James. For example, he cited the empirical fact of humanity's fear of death as an imaginative feat that proved the soul's "transcendence over nature" (2: 8). The argument seemed to be that since no living being has any experience of death, the fear of death had to be a feat of transcendental rather than natural imagination. It was a little like saying that if one has never experienced an airplane crash it is a feat of transcendental imagination to be afraid of being in one. Lacking any knowledge of Peirce's philosophy, Niebuhr never considered the possibility that imagining the unexperienced might not require a supernatural, transcendental capacity of the soul but might merely be a representation similar to notions of other things of which we have no sensory knowledge, such as zero or infinity. One of Peirce's earliest logical and metaphysical discoveries, which had helped move him toward the theory of signs, was that "we can syllogise upon whatever we can define. And strange as it is we can give intelligible comprehensible definitions of many things which can never be themselves comprehended" such as zero and infinity, all of which went to prove "that we can reason upon the nature of god."[13]

Niebuhr, however, was stuck with his atomistic soul—transcending nature but also trapped in it—with the result that he, no more than Dewey, could conceive of society as real. Where Peirce's notion of the self as itself a community of interpretive relations allowed for the reality of groups as "greater persons," Niebuhr could conceive of social sentiment only within individual human beings. He sometimes spoke of a "social mind" achieving "a result, different from that at which any individual, class or group in the community would have arrived." Yet even this use of the expression "social mind" was never more than a metaphor for compromise, a process of self-denial which "disproves the idea that the

13. *Peirce on Signs: Writings on Semiotic by Charles Sanders Peirce,* ed. James Hoopes (Chapel Hill: University of North Carolina Press, 1991), 14.

approach of each individual or group is consistently egoistic" (2: 249). Into the question of whether the relations between individuals might actually constitute something worthy of the name "mind," Niebuhr did not delve until his last major book.

In *The Irony of American History* (1952), Niebuhr briefly took up the question whether the debates and discussions that constitute the intellectual life of a nation or community might not constitute a single mind, and he showed surprising open-mindedness on the question. Community-wide discussion "has analogies in individual life. For the individual is also involved in a perpetual internal dialogue about the legitimacy of his hopes and purposes, and the virtue or vice of his previous acts. In this dialogue, contrition and complacency, pride of accomplishment and a sense of inadequacy, alternate in ways not too different from the alternation of moods in a community." [14]

Again, it becomes clear how Peirce's philosophy might have enlivened and usefully informed Niebuhr's thought. Niebuhr was moving in a primitive way toward a relational notion—"perpetual internal dialogue"— of what it means to be a human being. Such a relational notion of human beings puts individuals on a footing similar to those of groups and nations, which are obviously nothing if not relational. But Niebuhr had no philosophical assistance, such as Peirce might have provided, for exploring how relations might constitute the individual.

Niebuhr therefore remained certain that despite there being an analogy between individuals and communities, individuals differ fundamentally from social groups, composed of mere relations. Individuals differ from nations and groups in that the latter "obviously do not have a single organ of self-transcendence," that is, a soul. [15] He never considered the possibility that spirituality might be a matter not of a "single organ," a soul, and he therefore continued in the line of his nominalist skepticism of society. Without the sort of insights Peirce might have provided, Niebuhr remained a dogmatist.

Against this fairly deep analysis of Niebuhr's thought, it is interesting to examine his famous dispute with Dewey which was initiated by *Moral Man and Immoral Society*. According to the standard account of the Niebuhr-Dewey dispute, Niebuhr, with his neo-orthodox skepticism about human nature, threw down the gauntlet to Dewey's naive confidence that "intelligence" could lead social reform. By taking this more re-

14. Reinhold Niebuhr, *The Irony of American History* (New York: Scribner's, 1952), 83.
15. Ibid.

alistic approach to social reform, Niebuhr is supposed to have created a defining moment in the history of liberalism. His realpolitik would survive his thirties radicalism and, tempered by the Second World War, it would set the mood for pragmatic liberalism in the Cold War.

The Niebuhr-Dewey dispute is one of the more dramatic and best-known confrontations in American intellectual history, but its philosophical basis is not well understood. It is generally assumed that since it contained so little actual argument their disagreement must have originated less in philosophy than in attitudes toward human nature. The standard interpretation misses how the political differences between Niebuhr and Dewey were based on different foundational positions about the individual and society that could only have been resolved by Peirce's realism. Both Niebuhr and Dewey were nominalists and owed their nominalism at least partly to the influence of James, or rather the failure of James to pass on Peirce's realism to American political theory. Only Peirce's realism could have reconciled Dewey's naturalism with Niebuhr's theism. Only Peirce's realism could have enabled Dewey to think that society might have a reality surpassing that of the individual human organisms that comprised it, while similarly enabling Niebuhr to think of society as capable of a mentality surpassing its individual souls. With no realist metaphors to bring their ideas into relations, Dewey and Niebuhr were doomed to play out their roles as, respectively, expounders of hopeful intelligence and Calvinist pessimism.

Unfortunately, Niebuhr's attack on Dewey has seemed to some to discredit the pragmatic tradition as a basis for American liberalism. For more than half a century Niebuhrians have suggested either that neo-orthodox theology is the only possible foundation for a realistic American liberalism or else that since the difference between Niebuhr and Dewey was only attitudinal, pragmatism need not stand in the way of realpolitik. Now there is an attempt underway to revive pragmatism as a liberal political resource, but it proceeds in the tradition of weak pragmatism by suggesting that the gap between Niebuhr and Dewey was not all that wide to begin with. Our neo-pragmatic revival is in danger of failing to derive any new, interesting, or useful lessons from the history of pragmatic liberalism.

There were large philosophic differences, not merely differences in attitude between Niebuhr and Dewey. These philosophic differences helped determine their different "attitudes" toward an appropriate American liberalism and prevented them from agreeing on a common liberal program. Both of them were individualists, but they arrived at that position from very different philosophical foundations. Where Dewey's individualism derived from his naturalist organicism, Niebuhr's was based on belief in human transcendence over nature. Both of them were implicit nominalists who conceived of the individual's reality in a different way than they conceived of society's. But for Dewey the boundary between individuals was found at the body's edge and for Niebuhr at the soul's.

Niebuhr's celebrated attack on Dewey in the opening pages of *Moral Man and Immoral Society* reflected his conviction that Dewey's faith in "experimentalism" as a method of social reform was merely a secular form of the excessive optimism of liberal religionists. Both Dewey and liberal Christians overestimated human goodwill and underestimated "how much social conservatism is due to the economic interests of the owning classes." Dewey's faith that intelligence and scientific method would be as effective in understanding and controlling society as it had proven in understanding and controlling nature missed the different bases of conservatism in the social and physical sciences. Traditionalism in physical science, Niebuhr thought, had been based on ignorance and error. Conservative social viewpoints, on the other hand, were based on an accurate understanding of social reality by upper class groups who would lose their privileges in a more just regime. Intelligence and reason could not alone prevail against group selfishness: "Conflict is inevitable, and in this conflict power must be challenged by power. That fact is not recognized by most of the educators, and only very grudgingly admitted by most of the social scientists." [16]

Dewey's high stature in the thirties is indicated not only by Niebuhr's picking him out as chief errant liberal but by how much was and has been made of these scanty introductory remarks to *Moral Man and Immoral Society.* The main body of the book mentions Dewey only twice and briefly. The introduction attacked a number of other liberal notables— Kimball Young, Floyd Allport, and Howard Odum among others. None of these men, however, was nearly so deeply entrenched as Dewey in established educational, institutional, and professional networks of power and prestige, nor did any of them personally symbolize liberal hope as did Dewey. Niebuhr's brief attack on the preeminent liberal philosopher was brashly courageous, and he never recanted. Many of his later writings would contain similar, and equally brief, criticisms of Dewey. Niebuhr derived extraordinary intellectual prestige from an attack on Dewey that was little more than posturing and dogmatic assertion with virtually no sustained argument.

Lack of clear, systematic argument was one of the reasons that the philosophical differences between Niebuhr and Dewey have been largely

16. Niebuhr, *Moral Man and Immoral Society,* xiv–xv.

missed; their failure of expression was partly due to the tradition of weak pragmatism within which they worked, the tradition deriving from James rather than Peirce. From the early James, Niebuhr had gotten his idea that "personality"—the traditional unitary, individual soul—could coexist with pragmatism. Dewey rejected that view in favor of James's radical empiricist universe of relations between bits of experience. Unlike Peirce, however, Dewey did not explore in depth the nature of the relations out of which he believed the universe was constituted. Dewey had no category comparable to Peirce's thirdness to explain how thought and spirit might be distinguished from physical events yet nevertheless be part of the same monistic universe. Consequently, he could not offer an alternative account of spirituality that might have proven attractive to a theist like Niebuhr.

The result of this failure of philosophical expression on the part of both Dewey and Niebuhr was that they themselves missed how their dispute originated in their different philosophical foundations. Dewey, rejecting any essentialist account of human nature in favor of a relational theory, had some grounds to hope that intelligence might enable people to do better in the future than in the past. But because Dewey failed to articulate that relational theory with foundational depth and precision comparable to Peirce's, Niebuhr interpreted Dewey's faith in intelligence as naiveté. Niebuhr, given his essentialist and atomistic notion of the soul, had no reason to expect an originally sinful humanity to do better in the future than in the past, a view which Dewey in turn found naive because of his belief that essentialism had been philosophically discredited.

Because there are scarcely more than hints of these underlying philosophical differences in the exchanges between Dewey and Niebuhr, they themselves propagated the mistaken interpretation of their dispute that was dominant until very recently, the notion that the disagreement between them amounted to nothing more than who was the greater naïf about human nature. Niebuhr's criticism of Dewey for failing to see how "our predatory self-interest" stands in the way of social intelligence was criticized as too pessimistic by religious liberals, to whom Niebuhr replied that his position was that of traditional religion whose view "of the depravity of human nature" resulted from "taking the perspective of the divine." [17] Thus Niebuhr himself gave the impression that has become intellectual historians' conventional wisdom, the view that the difference between him and Dewey had no philosophical basis and was nothing

17. Niebuhr, *Moral Man and Immoral Society*, xiv; and Niebuhr, "After Capitalism—What?" *World Tomorrow* 16 (March 1933), 401.

more than one of religious pessimism versus secular optimism about human nature.

Dewey gave a similarly misleading impression that the difference between himself and Niebuhr was merely a matter of who was the greater realist in his view of human potential. Defending himself against Niebuhr's charge that his confidence in intelligence was naive, Dewey admitted that blind clashes of impassioned and opposing forces "have played a role in comparison with which the influence of intelligence is negligible." But the social order against which Niebuhr protested was a result of such blind clashes: "The new outcome of the domination of the methods of institutional force, custom and illusion does not encourage one to look with great hope upon dependence on new combinations among them for future progress."[18] By emphasizing force rather than intelligence as a means of social improvement, Niebuhr, according to Dewey, unrealistically hoped that the method that had produced present injustice would do better in the future.

George A. Coe, an ally of Dewey, came a bit closer to the philosophic heart of the matter when he rightly said that Niebuhr's vaunted realism about human nature hung "upon a single thread. . . . For, having granted that genuine . . . good will is possible, he maintains merely that we have not sufficient capacity for imagination to . . . realize the weal and the woe of far away men." Pointing out that Niebuhr offered no evidence, especially no psychological evidence, for his idea that people cannot sympathize with suffering fellow humans en masse and at a distance, Coe cited psychological studies suggesting the opposite. Niebuhr weakly replied that modern psychology emphasized "the force of subconscious impulse."[19] But as Coe had already stated, Niebuhr's social discouragement rested not on the force of subconscious impulse but on the supposed difficulty of sympathizing with different and distant human beings. Niebuhr's reference to subconscious impulse entirely missed the point and helped reinforce the notion that his difference with Dewey was due to nothing more than pessimism versus optimism on human nature.

Since Niebuhr and Dewey themselves left the impression that their dispute was simply a matter of who was more naive in their view of human nature, historians have assumed that was the heart of the problem. Arthur Schlesinger, Jr., helped set this direction of interpretation in an influential essay in 1956, "Reinhold Niebuhr's Role in American Political Thought." Schlesinger was one of the Cold War liberals attracted by

18. John Dewey, "Intelligence and Power," in *Later Works,* ed. Jo Ann Boydston (Carbondale: Southern Illinois University Press, 1986), 9: 107.
19. George A. Coe and Reinhold Niebuhr, "Two Communications," *The Christian Century* 50 (15 March 1933), 362, 364.

Niebuhr's realism, his divorce of what "the Social Gospel and Dewey had joined together: . . . love was the strategy of religion, pragmatism the strategy of society." As a personal friend and political ally of the theologian, the historian accepted Niebuhr's account of his struggle with Dewey: "Scientific intelligence and moral piety . . . could not abolish social conflict."[20] Schlesinger's essay was published in a festschrift celebrating the life and achievement of Niebuhr, who had suffered a stroke in the early fifties and whose active life was obviously nearly done. This may help account for the lack of any very penetrating treatment of Niebuhr, not only in Schlesinger's essay but throughout most of the volume.

Paul Tillich's essay on Niebuhr's epistemology and ontology was one of the few pieces in the festschrift that had much philosophical or theological depth. Tillich pointed out that despite Niebuhr's Jamesian distrust of any logical metaphysics, his "neo-orthodoxy" nevertheless implied an ontological viewpoint that was negative for religion. Niebuhr understood that the "way in which philosophers deal with being . . . has an open or hidden religious character." Niebuhr therefore feared "that the content of ontology clashes with the content of revelation."[21] Actually, according to Tillich, everything in revelation important to Niebuhr about humanity's condition of being both free and determined could be justified in strictly ontological terms if he would only rise above his static, materialistic conception of being. Conceived as power and dynamism, being could be ontologically described in a way that made room for the self and spirit. Failing to see this, Niebuhr refused to employ philosophical tools and was left with no basis for his insistence on the essential truth of the doctrine of sin. For he admitted that the fall was a myth and insisted only on its symbolic truth. By failing to employ philosophy, Niebuhr denied himself the ability to relate symbol to fact.

Niebuhr confirmed Tillich's criticism by refusing to engage in a real discussion and simply invoking his old opposition to using "science" in human affairs: "since ontology is the 'science of being,' it has its limitations in describing any being or being *per se* which contains mysteries. . . . If it is 'supernaturalistic' to affirm that faith discerns the key to specific meaning above the categories of philosophy, ontological or epistemological, then I must plead guilty of being a supernaturalist."[22]

An equally unsatisfactory exchange with Henry Nelson Wieman, a

20. Arthur Schlesinger, Jr., "Reinhold Niebuhr's Role in American Political Thought," in *Reinhold Niebuhr: His Religious, Social, and Political Thought*, ed. Charles W. Kegley and Robert W. Bretall (New York: Macmillan, 1956), 134.
21. Paul Tillich, "Reinhold Niebuhr's Doctrine of Knowledge," in *Reinhold Niebuhr: His Religious, Social, and Political Thought*, 40.
22. Reinhold Niebuhr, "Reply to Interpretation and Criticism," in *Reinhold Niebuhr: His Religious, Social, and Political Thought*, 432–33.

theological naturalist, showed that Niebuhr did indeed have a superficial understanding of science. Believing that science had shown that everything of this world had a mechanistic explanation, he was certain that the existence of spirit and mind was proof of the supernatural. Wieman, a Deweyan, argued that Niebuhr's faith was only a psychological ploy, since for Niebuhr, God was above life rather than "in any actual process."[23] Niebuhr predictably replied that to locate the divine process in this life was inconsistent with "the mystery of creativity and grace."[24] Niebuhr did acknowledge an element of mystery in Whitehead's process theology, but he gave no sign of understanding how it was rooted in an ontology of this world. Niebuhr was so utterly constrained by traditional metaphysical dualism that he could not conceive that there was any way to account for spirit and mind as part of the natural world.

Subsequent historians ignored the more telling analyses of Tillich and Wieman in favor of Schlesinger's view, which was derived from Niebuhr's and Dewey's own superficial description of their dispute as based only on different opinions as to the relative goodness or badness of human nature. Morton White picked up the Niebuhr-Dewey dispute in a new epilogue when his 1949 *Social Thought in America* was reissued in 1957. White, a Deweyan, concluded that the supposed differences between Dewey and Niebuhr on human nature were not very great and amounted to nothing more than the fact that "while Niebuhr puts us closer to the serpent, Dewey puts us closer to the dove."[25] But instead of looking for deeper philosophical differences White went on to suggest that the disagreement between Dewey and Niebuhr was only due to an unreasonable and illogical commitment on Niebuhr's part to the doctrine of original sin. This, to say the least, was superficial commentary, and Niebuhr responded, not in print but in person, as Daniel Rice has shown, by asserting that White had missed the whole point of his attack on Dewey, his opposition to Dewey's belief that scientific method could be shifted from the study of nature to the study of society.

Recently, two intellectual historians have gone a bit farther than the conventional account by minimizing not only the attitudinal but also the intellectual differences between Niebuhr and Dewey. Richard Fox and Robert Westbrook, like White before them, agree that the supposedly immense difference between Niebuhr and Dewey on human nature was

23. Henry Nelson Wieman, "A Religious Naturalist Looks at Reinhold Niebuhr, in *Reinhold Niebuhr: His Religious, Social, and Political Thought*, 350.
24. Niebuhr, "Reply to Interpretation and Criticism," 448.
25. Morton White, *Social Thought in America: The Revolt Against Formalism* (Boston: Beacon, 1957), 255.

not all that great. But they then add that Niebuhr and Dewey were also intellectually similar. "Like Dewey," says Fox, Niebuhr "was a pragmatist, a relativist, and a pluralist at heart. . . . Had Niebuhr unhardened his heart on the subject of liberalism, he would have discovered that he was firmly cemented in the liberal tradition of John Stuart Mill: resistance to dogmatism, tolerance for diversity, openness to correction."[26] Westbrook agrees: "what is often overlooked . . . is the degree to which Niebuhr's criticisms were advanced from within a set of assumptions and commitments he shared with Dewey."[27]

Given the vagueness with which the theologian and the philosopher conducted their dispute, these claims as to their similarity are understandable. One might object, of course, that to make them both into pragmatists misses or at least undervalues Niebuhr's basic commitment to a dualism and supernaturalism irreconcilable with Dewey's commitment to monism and naturalism.

The problem with trying to bring Niebuhr and Dewey together into one usable mainstream tradition of liberalism is less that it obscures the genuine differences between them than that it misses their common failure to articulate a viable notion of community. If one must find some similarity between Dewey and Niebuhr, surely the most important one is that neither the philosopher nor the theologian offered a useful conception of community because of their implicit nominalism. With no theory of communication comparable to Peirce's to implicate the formation of individual selves in the same sort of interpretive process that creates society, neither Niebuhr nor Dewey could articulate a political philosophy in which the boundary between self and society is fluid and permeable. Dewey insisted on the obvious reality of society, but his metaphysics was insufficiently precise to prevent his followers and often even himself from backsliding into an implicit nominalism. Niebuhr insisted on the obvious reality of the individual self and, for support, reverted from pragmatism to the supernatural notion of the atomistic soul that made community an impossible ideal rather than a sometimes achievable reality.[28]

The Niebuhr-Dewey dispute represents a real schism in the liberal tradition, a schism with deep philosophical foundations where both sides, contrary to their pious avowals, held implicitly nominalist convictions

26. Fox, *Reinhold Niebuhr*, 165.

27. Robert B. Westbrook, *John Dewey and American Democracy* (Ithaca: Cornell University Press, 1991), 524, 352.

28. Westbrook, *John Dewey and American Democracy*, 530; Daniel F. Rice, *Reinhold Niebuhr and John Dewey: An American Odyssey* (Albany: State University of New York Press, 1993), 27.

that denied society any measure of the same kind of reality ascribed to individuals. Neither side, consequently, could articulate a social theory that satisfactorily related self and society. The Niebuhr-Dewey dispute was indeed a defining moment in the history of American liberalism, but not in the way it is usually thought to have been. It reflects not the strength but the weakness of the liberal intellectual tradition built on the James-Dewey nominalist variant of pragmatism.

FOLLETT'S LOCAL DEMOCRACY

Little do men perceive what solitude is, and how far it extendeth; for a crowd
is not company . . . where there is no love.
  —Francis Bacon, *Essays*

The final major figure in this study had a nearly unique combination of
intellect, organizational skill, and enormously varied experience; she had
the most ambiguous relation to pragmatism of all. Unlike the nominalists Niebuhr and Lippmann, Mary Parker Follett (1868–1933) was convinced of the reality of society as a series of relations that amounted to
a genuine social mind, what Peirce called a "greater person." Weak, Jamesian pragmatism had failed to steer either Lippmann or Niebuhr past the
shoals of nominalism, and therefore both of them believed in atomistic
personality. The theologian supposed that groups were incapable of
morality and were bound to settle conflict by force, while the publicist
supposed groups incapable of thought and therefore in need of leadership by individual experts. Follett, through her twenty years of intense
urban social work that far surpassed the hands-on reform experiences of
Niebuhr and Lippmann, came to believe groups capable of morality and
of a level of decision making that made the expert not superfluous but
auxiliary to a democratic polity. Although intellectually more balanced,
Follett, like Lippmann and Niebuhr, knew of no better pragmatism than
James's weak and nominalist variant. Unlike those two men, she tempered that weak pragmatism with an idealism that saved her from their
wild swings of position. Unfortunately, even her modified version of
weak pragmatism proved incapable, finally, of articulating a foundational
basis for the democratic reforms she espoused. As a writer on politics,

Follett exerted less influence than Lippmann and Niebuhr, which may explain why she has been largely ignored by intellectual historians. But she deserves attention because her writings reveal as well as anyone's the problem created for political theory when James and Dewey's pragmatism eclipsed Peirce's.

At least as philosophically acute as Lippmann and Niebuhr, Follett may well have been the intellectual equal of James and Dewey. If she did not write much philosophy, she clearly saw the social weakness of pragmatic nominalism and tried to salvage pragmatism for social and political theory by mixing it with philosophic idealism. She saw that neither nominalist pragmatism nor absolute idealism offered a satisfactory political philosophy and therefore eclectically employed pragmatism when it was useful and idealism when it best served her purposes. She pragmatically qualified her idealist, holistic notion of democracy: "from a philosophical point of view there is no whole, only an infinite striving for wholeness, only the *principle* of wholeness forever leading us on."[1] Similarly, she announced that her embrace of pragmatism was in support of her commitment to German idealism's vision of the state as the highest human group: "We are pragmatists because we do not want to unite with the state imaginatively, we want to be the state."[2] Untenably, she held to both a realist emphasis on the possibility of universals and a Jamesian emphasis on their impossibility.[3]

Follett's political writings, less voluminous than Lippmann's and Niebuhr's, surpassed their work in acuteness and originality but in the end, like theirs, were vitiated by the influence of James's weak pragmatism. She would not be led by James's nominalism to rely on authoritarian expertise as was Lippmann. Neither did she allow nominalism to lead her toward realpolitik, as did Niebuhr. Still, if she was not a nominalist, she had no knowledge of Peirce's realism. She had no understanding of relations as semiotic interpretation or representation (Peircean thirdness), which made relations possible across distances of time and space. In the absence of such metaphysical foundations, she tended like James to conceive of relations as a matter of proximity, if not of what Peirce called secondness or immediacy. In the end she found it impossible on the basis of her mixture of idealism and weak pragmatism to arrive at an under-

1. Mary Parker Follett, *The New State: Group Organization the Solution of Popular Government* (New York: Longmans, Green, 1918), 249.
2. Ibid., 253.
3. For a similar view of Follett as attempting an untenable mix of pragmatism and idealism, see James A. Stever, "Mary Parker Follett and the Quest for Pragmatic Administration," *Administration & Society* (August 1986): 159–177.

standing of relations that would allow her to articulate a viable notion of community larger than the local neighborhood.

Follett's gifted mind had as wide a range of experience to interpret as any in her generation. Raised in Quincy, Massachusetts, she spent a lonely and oppressive upper-class girlhood caring for an invalid mother whom she disliked and who did not allow her to play with other children lest the distraction interfere with her nursing duties. She found a substitute mother figure and role model in her history teacher at Thayer Academy in Braintree, Anna Boynton Thompson, who was a philosophical idealist and follower of William James's idealist opponent, Josiah Royce. An inheritance provided Follett with the means to test the offerings of the greatest universities of two nations—Cambridge in England and Harvard (or, rather, the nascent Radcliffe) in America. Her undergraduate education, interrupted by her mother's illnesses, took ten years to complete, and she even published her pioneering book *The Speaker of the House of Representatives* two years before she graduated from college. Thereafter, Follett worked for Boston municipal reform in the best tradition of good-government progressivism, serving on many committees and boards. Her urban reform work led to contact with Boston businessmen, which in turn involved her in industrial relations and brought her into the field of management theory, where her writings still exert great influence. She spent the last five years of her life in Europe, studying the League of Nations and the International Labour Office as well as lecturing on business administration at the London School of Economics.[4]

Her writings on human relations in all the different fields that interested her are far less abstract and theory ridden, far more intensely focused on the problem of human interaction and connection, than Lippmann's or Niebuhr's. Perhaps partly because as a woman she was somewhat marginalized, Follett never had the opportunity of a Lippmann or Niebuhr to be drawn more and more deeply into the ranks of the high and the mighty, however liberal and sympathetic their outlooks may have remained. From nursing her mother to serving on minimum wage boards, she was brought into contact, as Lippmann in his romantic youth put it, with "actual life."[5] Although by birth she belonged to the generation that preceded Lippmann's and Niebuhr's, as a woman, she encountered distractions that made her a slow starter intellectually. By dint of long years of concern and care for others, she made her most important contributions to political theory in her middle age but at about the same time

4. "Mary Parker Follett," *Notable American Women* (Cambridge: Harvard, 1971).
5. Quoted in Ronald Steel, *Walter Lippmann and The American Century* (Boston: Little, Brown, 1980), 106.

when the young Lippmann and Niebuhr were launching their careers. Whether studying politics, society, or business she focused, with an intensity foreign to Lippmann and Niebuhr, on the practical problems of relations among human beings, but she brought to those practical concerns an intellect as acute and well informed as theirs.

At Cambridge University in 1890–91 she had written an essay involving the Speaker of the House of Representatives that led to her groundbreaking and still useful book of 1896. To appreciate the temerity of this hitherto sheltered young woman, it is important to note that she had undertaken study of a subject of enormous scope. These were the days of "Czar" Thomas Reed when authoritarian rules enabled the Speaker completely to dominate the lower house and made it a debatable question whether the President was the most powerful government official.

The Speaker of the House of Representatives[6] was deeply influenced by the realistic perspective of Professor Albert Bushnell Hart, with whom Follett studied at Radcliffe. The real source of the Speaker's power, she held, was his ability to bring order out of chaos: "It would be absurd to retard our development by a too strict adherence to an ideal of democracy impossible for a great nation" (314). Some wanted to pass a constitutional amendment to create a governing council involving both Speaker and President, but Follett opposed the idea both because it was unlikely that such an amendment could be passed and because it was unnecessary: "the advantages of an over-committee may be had by private understanding" between the Speaker and the President (330).

Although Follett's tone of tough-minded realism would soon give way to the reformer in her, she remained skeptical of those like Woodrow Wilson, fellow political scientist and student of Congress, who believed that reform could be effected by simple institutional change imposed from the top. In this first book she attacked the historical basis of Wilson's belief that the early dominance of the executive branch had been due to the importance of foreign policy in the young American republic. The dominant voices in the Washington and Jefferson administrations, Hamilton and Gallatin, had both, Follett pointed out, "concerned themselves principally with home affairs" (320). Later, after Wilson became President and failed to bring the United States into his cherished League of Nations, she remained passionately interested in the League but deeply critical of Wilson for his top-down, institutional approach to peace: "we shall never be able to make an international settlement and

---

6. Mary Parker Follett, *The Speaker of the House of Representatives* (New York: Longmans, Green, 1896). Page numbers for subsequent citations to this work will be given parenthetically in the text.

erect some power to enforce it; the settlement must be such as to provide its own momentum."[7] Even when Follett began to write on business administration, she cited Wilson as her primary example of the error of leaders who supposed leadership occurred only at the top of an organization; by contrast, she believed leadership to be everyone's job. When leaders did not understand that "followers must partake in leadership" and that there must be "followership on the part of leaders," disaster must result: "One of the tragedies of history is that Woodrow Wilson did not understand leadership."[8]

Upon graduating from college Follett developed her practical experience of leadership through energetic social work. She founded the Roxbury Debating Club for Boys and several other neighborhood associations. One of these, the Roxbury League, was a pioneer in the after-hours use of public school facilities for community activities. Later she chaired a committee of the Women's Municipal League which persuaded the Boston school board to open evening centers in other neighborhoods. Follett also worked to develop a vocational guidance program in the Boston schools. She was a founder and financial contributor to the privately funded Boston Placement Bureau, which provided placement career-counseling to the city's youth and which eventually became an official agency of Boston's city government. Placement work brought Follett into contact with businessmen such as Lincoln Filene and Henry S. Dennison, who helped involve her in industrial relations. Massachusetts passed a minimum wage law for women in 1912 which created wage boards to determine minimum rates in different industries. Serving on several of these wage boards gave Follett some of the practical experience in negotiation that helped make her writings on management theory still influential today.[9] Thus in the twenty years between her graduation from college in 1898 and the end of the First World War in 1918, Follett had, at the neighborhood and urban level, practical experience in politics and social work surpassing that of any other thinker discussed in this book.

On the basis of this intense experience of local politics she greeted the last year of the Great War with a boldly prophetic book, *The New State: Group Organization the Solution of Popular Government* (1918), that was both one of the highest intellectual achievements of progressivism and also the movement's death knell. With a verve equal to anything that Lippmann or the other brilliant young men at the *New Republic* might

7. Mary Parker Follett, *Creative Experience* (New York: Longmans, Green, 1924), 206.
8. Mary Parker Follett, *Dynamic Administration* (New York: Harper, 1941), 290.
9. See for example *Mary Parker Follett—Prophet of Management: A Celebration of Writings from the 1920s* (Cambridge: Harvard Business School Press, 1990).

have mustered, she broke entirely with their notion of leadership, with their vision of a special role for intellectuals, and above all with what they mistakenly supposed were the political implications of pragmatism. Where they wanted to graft a role for the best and the brightest on to the gnarled tree of modern democracy, she proposed to make a place for all by beginning with an axe: "We talk about the evils of democracy. We have not yet tried democracy" (3).[10] Much rot had to be chopped out of the existing democratic organism—political parties, simplistic ballot box models of democracy, government by "consent" of the people, the idea that the people's sovereignty could be exercised by a monistic state, and even "the notion of individual rights" (141).

In place of political parties she proposed to substitute neighborhood organizations, not out of any naive do-gooder opposition to urban political machines but because she believed her own experiences in social reform movements had revealed a path to greater social harmony than could ever be achieved by political parties. The problem with any political party is that "it wants merely a crowd, a preponderance of votes" (5–6). The same sin bedeviled typical progressive political movements: "Both wanted voters not men" (6). A majority of the voters, on which parties and political reform movements counted, was a mere "crowd," an assembly of atomistic individuals connected by the fact that they had all voted the same way but not necessarily for the same reason. As opposed to political parties' reliance on the crowd, democracy ought to rely on the "group," by which Follett meant a number of people who not only favor the same action—such as voting the same way—but do so for the same reason.

Groups, as opposed to crowds, are formed by what Follett eventually called "integration," a concept central to her mature work in political science and management theory. Integration is essentially resolution of conflict by joint adoption of a larger point of view than that with which either antagonist began, a point of view large enough to include or "integrate" the originally conflicting viewpoints of the former antagonists. To explain integration she quoted two acquaintances, the first of whom said:

> If you are trying to decide whether you will go to New York by boat or by train, and are weighing the advantages—fresh air, etc., on the one hand, speed, etc., on the other—and a friend comes along and offers to take you in his aeroplane, where you will have the advantages of both train and boat, that is an integration.

10. Follett, *New State.* Page numbers to subsequent citations of *The New State* will appear parenthetically in the text.

The second acquaintance, a businessman, corrected the first:

> If you or your friend had *invented* the aeroplane to take you to New York, it would have come nearer the process as I see it taking place. That is, when we cannot decide in one of our committees what to do, because part of the members wish to take one course and the rest another, I find that the best way out is always when someone invents something new.[11]

The businessman gave as an example of integration the resolution of a dispute among his corporate managers over the right price to charge for a product. Agreement came neither through compromise nor the victory of one side over the other but by agreeing on a new standard of quality—in essence, a new product—for which there would have to be a new price.

Not through debate, compromise, arbitration, referenda, and all the mechanical devices of traditional progressives would the new state achieve a more perfect democracy but through integration of ever more powerful personalities. In *The New State,* Follett scarcely proposed to dispense with ballot boxes, but she wished to see democracy aim higher than the confrontational, adversarial, us-versus-them approach of the traditional political system. That approach was based on old-fashioned notions of the atomistic, individual self which, in dealing with others, must either dominate or be dominated because of its unchangeable, inviolate personal identity. This atomistic conception of the self was a result of traditional metaphysical dualism and led to what Follett called "political dualism" which pitted the individual against the state (137). Disagreeing with the old notion of the atomistic self, Follett believed that the individual self grew in power and freedom only insofar as it was brought into an ever broader network of social relations in which the individual and society were constantly and reciprocally evolving new personal identities: "The old idea of natural rights postulated the particularist individual; we know now that no such person exists. The group and the individual come into existence simultaneously" (137).

The "new psychology" taught Follett a new concept of personal identity, for "we are now looking at things not as entities but in relation" (13). To look at things in relation is to see that there "is no 'individual,' that there is no 'society,'" if by these words are meant isolated, atomistic identities unrelated to anything else. Like the rest of her generation she could scarcely escape the influence of William James, but from his conclusions

11. Quoted in Follett, *Creative Experience,* 157.

about the individual, she generalized to conclusions about society far more effectively than either Lippmann or Niebuhr: "James brought to popular recognition the truth that since man is a complex of experiences there are many selves in each one. So society as a complex of groups includes many social minds" (20). The old psychology had taught that the individual is a psychological atom who lives in physical relations with other people but "thinks, feels, and judges independently" (19). This old, atomistic psychology according to which the individual lives physically in society but thinks alone had been the basis of the arrogant individualism of classical liberalism, which put the individual on one side and society on the other. No, said Follett, in a conclusion worthy of Peirce. The individual is inseparable from society because the same kinds of relations that create the one create the other: "individuals are created by reciprocal interplay" (19).

What distinguishes Follett from the nominalist political theorists of her generation such as Lippmann and Niebuhr is her overriding conviction that society is as real as the individual: "People often talk of the social mind as if it were an abstract conception, as if only the individual were real, concrete. The two are equally real. Or rather the only reality is the relating of one to the other which creates both" (60). Niebuhr held groups morally inferior to individuals; and Lippmann, intellectually so. Since the demos en masse could neither will the good nor think the true, Niebuhr opted for realpolitik and Lippmann for bureaucratic government by experts. Either way, the problem was that society seemed not to have the same kind of spiritual or mental unity as the individual. Follett, however, held that "the activity which produces the true individual is at the same time interweaving him and others into a real whole . . . into such genuine relations that a new personality is thereby evolved" (8).

Probably partly out of consistency with her concept of "integration," Follett was a tactful controversialist who sometimes made it difficult to know with whom she was disagreeing, but in advocating the reality of the social mind in *The New State,* she almost certainly intended Dewey for the target of such remarks as the following: "We hear a good deal of academic talk about 'the functioning of the social mind'; what does it all amount to? We have no social mind yet, so we have no functioning of the social mind" (8). Dewey, the best-known proponent of social-mindedness in his generation, used the phrase "social mind" merely to describe the individual mind thinking socially. And since the obvious reality of communication suggested to him that the individual mind drew on much socially shared information, Dewey assumed that his nominalist notion of a "social mind" was already a functioning reality. Follett disagreed and again probably had Dewey in mind, but tactfully did not say so, when she wrote that "individual ideas do not become social ideas when communicated. . . . The essential feature of a common thought is not that it is held in common but that it has been produced in common" (33–34). Tragically Follett did not win an audience sufficiently large to make her an opponent to whom Dewey had to attend. Compounding the tragedy was the fact that she did not know of Peirce and therefore supposed that her opposition to Deweyan nominalism left her no recourse but an untenable mixture of weak pragmatism and idealism.

Although Follett's antinominalism distinguished her from Lippmann, it seems likely that she nevertheless emulated his literary vitality in order to attempt to win recognition similar to his, perhaps partly out of resentment of the ease with which he had emerged as the major political theorist of his generation. Whether or not there was jealousy on her part, the disparity between their careers is striking. While she was working on vocational guidance programs for school girls in Boston, his youthful verbal pyrotechnics launched him toward starring roles at the *New Republic* and in the war councils of the second Wilson administration. The prophetic, voice-of-God style of Follett's *New State* bore some resemblance to Lippmann's youthful literary voice and may have been an attempt to win an audience and clout such as he enjoyed.

If Follett did hope to emulate Lippmann's tone of prophetic omniscience in order to win a similar role, she missed her target by a mistake in timing and by her loyalty to the language of idealism. The half dozen years by which her *New State* succeeded Lippmann's early writings had brought a war that not only destroyed the public's appetite for spiritual adventures in politics but made idealistic justification of politics distasteful. The year 1918 was scarcely a good time to use lofty language to appeal for "undivided allegiance" (318): "I live forever the undivided life. As an individual I am the undivided one, as the group-I, I am again the undivided one, as the state-I, I am the undivided one—I am always and forever the undivided one, mounting from height to height, always mounting, always the whole of me mounting" (319).

But there were other less ludicrous aspects to Follett's style, and *The New State* seems almost to have been written by three different authors—the fulsome idealist of the above passage, a tough minded pragmatist, and a pithily laconic New Englander. If Lippmann would never have erred by suggesting a "mounting" toward the ideal, neither could he have delightfully described with Thoreau-like bluntness the balance of humility and self-confidence Follett sought in her fellow reformers:

I asked a man once to join a committee I was organizing and he replied that he would be very glad to come and give his advice. I didn't want him—and didn't have him. I asked another man and he said he would like very much to come and learn but that he couldn't contribute anything. I didn't have him either—I hadn't a school (29).

And as the war wound down, the tough-minded pragmatist in Follett could presciently warn the naive idealists in the Wilson administration that rhetorical flights would not hold together an alliance born only of military necessity:

> If we go to that peace table with the idea that the new world is to be based on that community of interest and aim which now animates us, the disillusion will be great, the result an overwhelming failure (36).

There were enormous substantive differences between Follett and Lippmann even if she imitated his literary boldness. In *A Preface to Politics* he had called for a "creative statesmanship which would go out to meet a need before it had become acute." [12] Almost as if to say that Lippmann's rapid and lofty ascent had deprived him of useful knowledge that could only be gained in the kind of neighborhood social work of which she had twenty years' experience, Follett answered that "in most of the writing on American politics we find the demand for a 'creative statesmanship' as the most pressing need of America to-day. . . . but the doctrine of true democracy is that every man is and must be a creative citizen." [13]

In *The New State* Follett anticipated some of the themes Lippmann would address two years later in *Public Opinion,* but her approach was more democratic and was based on her hope that society at large could be built up from small groups. Follett and Lippmann agreed that, as she put it, "the chief need of society to-day is an enlightened, progressive and organized public opinion" (226). But where Lippmann would argue that the organization of public opinion should be the job of experts and "intelligence bureaus" in government departments, Follett held that "the first step towards an enlightened and organized public opinion is an enlightened and organized group opinion" (226). Groups and local interrelations among them, not high and mighty experts, were Follett's hope for democracy.

After Lippmann staked out his claims for experts in *Public Opinion,* Follett answered him in *Creative Experience* (1924). Using Lippmann's own phrase, she pointed out that experts were as likely as anyone else to

12. Walter Lippmann, *A Preface to Politics* (New York: Macmillan, 1913), 213.
13. Follett, *New State,* 335.

have "pictures in their heads" tainted by their own prejudices and stereo-
types. Surely she had Lippmann in mind when she warned that, "many
seem to imagine the expert as . . . one who has no emotions, no interests,
no memories and associations" (8–9).[14] In a deft footnote she turned
Lippmann against himself by saying that his "brilliant chapter on stereo-
types would completely dispel such an illusion" (9). One wonders if the
serious Lippmann even understood this sly joke at his expense. Lippmann
had argued that the people should vote only after experts in government
intelligence bureaus had swept away the chaff of misconceptions, stereo-
types, and prejudices—false pictures in our heads—to reveal the real
choices that the people had to make. Follett's opinion of that approach
may be gathered from the title of her opening chapter, "Vicarious Experience: Are Experts the Revealers of Truth?" Without mentioning
Lippmann by name she made clear that he was her target by questioning

> the assumption that we are obliged to choose between the rule of that
> modern beneficent despot, the expert, and a muddled, befogged 'people.'
> If the question were as simple as that, . . . we should have only to get
> enough Intelligence Bureaus at Washington . . . and all life would become
> fair and beautiful. For the people, it is assumed, will gladly agree to be-
> come automata . . . by abandoning their own experience in favor of a su-
> perior race of men called experts (3).

Not necessarily opposed to adding new institutions, including even intelligence bureaus to government, Follett nevertheless maintained that
"our hope for the future lies not in increasing institutions but in im-
proving process" (229)

Follett's most basic objection to the cult of expertise was the tendency
to sever the dense web of social relations in which both the expert and
the public were inextricably enmeshed by supposing that the expert
stood outside and above society. Again, she deftly skewered Lippmann by
saying that the notion that the pictures in our heads should represent
facts was

> one of his [Lippmann's] most valuable contributions to political sci-
> ence. . . . The 'objective situation' cannot be overemphasized if we un-
> derstand it as part of a total process; I am objecting here merely to those
> who speak of it as if there were an inherent nature in a 'fact' to be revealed

14. Follett, *Creative Experience*. Page numbers of most subsequent citations to this work will be
given parenthetically in the text.

to the devout. This is opposed not only to psychology but to science as well, for was it not several centuries ago that scientists began to look at objects as processes? (152–53)

To suppose that the expert could aloofly, from on high, make decisions was to cut the expert out of the social process.

Equally repugnant to her and for the same reason was Dewey's resolution of the problem of the citizen's role. Just as Lippmann erred by supposing that the expert could step outside the social fabric, so too did Dewey overreach the mark in supposing the citizen could sometimes live outside politics. The citizen, no less than the expert, was inextricably involved in the social relations of which government was a part:

> Professor Dewey says that it is the role of the public in government (I am using his words) to intervene not continuously but at certain junctures. He explains the phrase 'not continuously' by saying that the public has its own life to lead, it is preoccupied with its own work and amusements. I do not think that there is any possible way in which Professor Dewey can support this statement. We have our own work? As a Vermont farmer, I go out and shear my sheep, but at Washington they are putting a tariff on wool—I hope. My amusements? I go to the movies and at the same time the government is censoring them—I fear.[15]

It is unfortunate that Follett died in 1933 just as Niebuhr was achieving national prominence as a political theorist, for a Follett-Niebuhr debate most likely would have far surpassed in interest and substance the Dewey-Niebuhr standoff. Opposed to the nominalism of the weak pragmatists and with a notion of society as potentially capable of a unity, an identity, no less real than that of individual persons, she was far better equipped than Dewey to answer Niebuhr's pessimistic assessment of groups as morally inferior to individuals. In *The New State*'s penultimate chapter, "The Moral State and Creative Citizenship," she answered the question, How was the state to gain moral authority?: "Only through its citizens in their growing understanding of the widening promise of relation" (333). Dewey was of course capable of similar expressions, but in Follett they were never offset by the slightest deference to expertise.

The difference between Follett and Dewey—a difference that would have made her a far more effective respondent to Niebuhr—was that she did not suppose the expert's job was to save the public trouble. The in-

15. Follett, *Dynamic Administration*, 190.

dividual citizen must strive every moment to comprehend and decide the social right rather than "to do his work and then play a little . . . with the understanding that the world of industry and the government of his country are to be run by experts." [16] Calling herself a pragmatist, she invoked James's dislike of the idealists' notion of the absolute as eternally existent. Just as in religion "we are one with God not by prayer and communion alone, but by doing the God-deed every moment, so we are one with the state by actualizing the latent state at every instant of our lives." [17] Obviously, pragmatism had not carried her so far from idealism as to make her give up hope in the potential spiritual unity of people, but neither did she suppose that spiritual unity was an excuse for individual irresponsibility. The problem with the concept of the state as a collection of atomistic souls was that it encouraged people to think of their responsibility as that of one in a million or whatever number of people composed the state. Every individual must accept responsibility for the whole, just as the value of an individual piano key "is not in its being 1/56 of all the notes, but in its infinite relations to all the other notes. If that note is lacking every other note loses its value." [18]

Niebuhr would of course have replied to Follett's social holism with the same dogmatic "realism" about human nature with which he had attacked Dewey. Unlike Dewey, however, Follett would have supported her reply not with an undermining, implicitly nominalist metaphysics but with a mixture of idealism, "new psychology," and twenty years experience in social work that had taught her that groups are capable of at least some moral imagination. Niebuhr's moral criticism of groups was based on the idea that they were incapable of feeling and therefore of sympathy, an idea born of the old psychology of the atomistic soul that Niebuhr never surrendered. According to that psychological atomism, sympathy could only pass, according to Follett, "from one isolated being to another." The new psychology in which the self was not an atomistic soul but a relational process necessitated that "sympathy too is born within the group—it springs forever from interrelation. . . . [O]nly from the group comes the genuine feeling *with*—the true sympathy, the vital sympathy, the just and balanced sympathy." [19] Although Follett would have agreed with Niebuhr that social justice will never be created by altruism alone, she insisted that there was such a thing as a "collective feeling" within groups, a feeling which led people sometimes to do justice to

16. Follett, *Creative Experience*, 329.
17. Ibid., 334–35.
18. Ibid., 336.
19. Follett, *New State*, 44.

one another's interests when they were conscious of their interrelated, shared interests.

In both class relations and international relations—the two areas that dominated Niebuhr's political and social theory—she was as contemptuous as the theologian of reliance on goodwill. No less than Niebuhr, Follett cautioned that "all talk of the sacrifice of interests is ruinously sentimental." There was nothing but pathos for her in the common postwar scene of idealistic lecturers traveling about the country asking genteel audiences if they would not join the League of Nations by sacrificing a bit of sovereignty for the sake of peace.[20] Similarly, in her later career as a management consultant she deplored the "rationalization of the sentimentalist," the "fallacy . . . that the manufacturer ought to surrender a part of his power in order to gain a spirit of contentment in the factory."[21]

Unlike Niebuhr, however, she did not stop with the notion that self-interest prevented larger feelings of collective interest, for we might achieve a "revaluation of our interests."[22] No one should sacrifice anything, but everyone should examine their interests in the light of the largest perceivable series of relations. Follett's skepticism of the likelihood of self-sacrifice made her a persistent critic of the notion of compromise as the highest path of conflict resolution, for compromise involved sacrifice, even though both parties to the conflict sacrificed equally. Her concept of "integration" led her to the conclusion that "sovereignties must be joined, not sacrificed."[23] And joining of different interests was possible not out of altruism but out of people's "consciousness of themselves as a new unit [group]."[24]

She developed this line of argument fully in *The New State*. Action rather than moralistic injunctions to self-sacrifice was what would bring to consciousness new collective feelings of group interest. The old dualism of mind and matter was responsible for the notion that the idea of collectivity had to precede the reality of collectivity. To the question of how a communitarian sentiment was to be formed, Follett answered that "the process of forming this new unit [group] generates such realization which is sympathy. This true sympathy, therefore, is not a vague sentiment they [the group members] bring with them; it springs from their meeting to be in its turn a vital factor in their meeting" (46–47). Not by sentimental appeals to idealism nor by supposedly realistic acceptance of conflict and

20. Follett, *Creative Experience*, 171.
21. Follett, *Dynamic Administration*, 112.
22. Follett, *Creative Experience*, 171.
23. Follett, *Dynamic Administration*, 112.
24. Follett, *New State*, 46. All subsequent in-text citations in this chapter refer to *The New State*.

realpolitik was the world to be made better. The success of democracy depended on men and women seizing whatever chances there were to organize the world in ways that extended social interrelations, as Follett had done in her twenty years of useful social work and urban reform in Boston. Neither groundless hope nor dogmatic despair but only action could lead to more and still better action: "We must *live* democracy" (343).

How much more communitarian Follett's vision was than either Niebuhr's or Lippmann's can be seen in her definition of democracy as "the rule of an interacting, interpermeating whole" (156). Niebuhr believed the good society could only be achieved by the forceful triumph of an oppressed group over its oppressor, and Lippmann, by a mandarin-like intelligentsia. These solutions omitted some people from at least some parts of the process, either because of these people's oppressiveness or ignorance. Follett, however, believed that even the ignorant and the oppressive have a potentially useful relation to the whole. It does not matter whether "imperfection meets imperfection, or imperfection meets perfection; it is the *process* which purifies, not the 'influence' of the perfect on the imperfect. . . . There is no passive material within it to be guided by a few. There is no dead material in a true democracy" (158). Only by recognizing the inevitable participation of everyone in the social process, imperfect as he or she might be, could a creative citizen be an impetus toward the "Perfect Society" (158). To be democratic is to help create a holistic community in which the political process is not only influenced by everyone, but in which everyone recognizes that he or she is part of a relational process and not just an atomistic individual.

To be truly democratic is to understand that one's own life is so densely interrelated to others that one can never think of oneself as opposed to others but only as part of a larger whole. Democracy's fullest potential therefore goes further than mere inclusion of everyone in the suffrage and other mechanical devices of government by which the wish of a larger group triumphs over a smaller. Follett was an advocate of women's suffrage but for more complicated reasons than many of her fellow reformers. Women should vote not merely because it was equitable that they do so but because "we want what they may have to add to the whole" (157). But women were certain to be disappointed if they accepted the vote as part of a simplistic, ballot-box model of democracy in which the role of citizenship is exercised by atomistic individuals at discrete moments in time: "The ballot-box! How completely that has failed men, how completely it will fail women" (5).

Democracy is not merely about voting but is a work of mind, an act of thought by a group mind rather than an isolated, atomistic psyche. In

Follett's view in *The New State,* to be democratic is to recognize the possibility of such a mind and help it to come into being. The essential democratic art is not government by consent or even by majority vote but "by people learning how to evolve collective ideas" (159). Mechanical devices such as the referendum, initiative, and recall are not the recipe for rising above democracy's present imperfections, for those imperfections are themselves the result of a mechanical notion of democracy. In actuality, "Democracy has one task only—to free the creative spirit of man. This is done through group organization" (159). For a description of group organization Follett fell back on her personal experience of social work and urban political reform. In committee meetings, for example, the finest achievements came when no one was there to score points in behalf of an insecure ego or to compromise in behalf of a false humility. Rather, the exchange of ideas leads to new ideas which lead to an integration, a "composite idea" on which all agree even though none began the meeting with that result in mind. This is where the individual and the group come into a truly democratic relation:

> by the time we have reached this point we have become tremendously civilized people, for we have learned . . . to say "I" representing a whole instead of "I" representing one of our separate selves. The course of action decided upon is what we all together want, and I see that it is better than what I had wanted alone. It is what *I* now want. We have all experienced this at committee meetings or conferences.[25]

Yes, we have all experienced such wonderful coherence in small groups, but Follett failed completely to explain how such experience is relevant to the governance of a large polity. Given her belief in "integration" as the true method of democracy, she shared little of her fellow progressives' belief in direct government. Progressives gave support to the referendum "because of their belief in majority rule," but Follett saw majority rule as mere "tyranny of numbers" (179). In such a democracy of the crowd the individual would be betrayed by even his own vote, let alone the vote of others, for the individual is an integral part of a larger society and is constantly changing with it. The individual's vote will fail if it attempts to express individual will, for just as there is no atomistic individual but only relations, so also there can be no individual will to

25. Follett, *New State,* 25. For a critical assessment of Follett's vision of the liberal state as one without conflict see H. Kariel, "The New Order of Mary Parker Follett," *Western Political Quarterly,* 8 (September 1955): 425–40.

express. Therefore, *"my test as a citizen is how fully the whole can be expressed in or through me"* (179). Direct democracy would be an improvement only if it were integrated with the truly democratic method of integration. But how was integration to be made a method of governance beyond the small group or neighborhood?

Follett's deeply unsatisfactory answer in *The New State* was that neighborhood must be joined to neighborhood to form the nation, and that since this cannot be done "directly," there must be "representatives from the smallest units to the larger and larger, up to the federal state" (250). In short, she favored representative over direct democracy because there were obviously too many neighborhoods to be related directly to each other. Her notion of representation, however, was so radical and impractical that the word "representation" was almost a misnomer. In *Creative Experience* she would explain that the kind of representation she had in mind was actually a two-fold kind of integration: "first, the integration of the point of view he [the representative] brings from his constituents with that brought by the other representatives from their constituents; secondly, the representative should go back and persuade his constituents . . . that they must try to unite their old point of view . . . with that formed in the representative group."[26] The job not only of the representative but also the represented would be extraordinarily laborious under this system of perpetual integration. She herself recognized the laboriousness of her notion of representation when she advocated an integrated world state: "War is not the most strenuous life. It is a kind of rest-cure compared to the task of reconciling our differences."[27] Even seventy five years later, in our era of electronic information, Follett's notion of democracy seems hopelessly utopian.[28]

Follett's philosophical mixture of weak pragmatism and absolute idealism had let her down. Jamesian-Deweyan pragmatism was the only pragmatism she knew, and it was too weak and nominalist to describe a group mind. Idealism offered a lofty language and admirable goals but no explanation of the relations by which she knew that a social mind had to come into being. In the absence of any understanding of Peirce's notion of mental relations as semiotic representation, Follett was left with no choice but to describe her idealistic vision of a holistic democracy in

26. Follett, *Creative Experience*, 241.

27. Follett, *New State*, 357–58.

28. See "Full Democracy," *The Economist*, 341 (21 December 1996), following p. 74, for a fourteen-page survey of possibilities for combining direct and representative democracy in the twenty-first century.

terms of immediate relations, which in turn implied nominalism rather than the unified society she sought. Attempting to base democracy on a form of political "representation" that was not representative but immediate (which she did in order that democracy be integrative), she offered a vision of the path to a unified polity that, if followed, would most likely end in a buzzing, incoherent cacophony rather than the integration she held dear.

What Follett needed but never found was a way to conceive of the state as a "greater person" composed of, but different from, *any* of the "I's" that composed it, just as Peirce had described the individual mind as a matter of relations among brain cells, no one of which could know what the whole mind was thinking. The neighborhood and small-group experiences which Follett cherished suggested to her that in a true democracy "I" have to think the same thing as the social mind and that the only way this could be done is through immediate, or at least proximate, relations. Unlike Peirce she had never studied the schoolmen, and so she had only contempt for the "medieval idea of mediate articulation, of individuals forming groups and groups forming the nation." [29] Not mediating semiosis, not representational thirdness, but only immediate relations of secondness, she mistakenly believed, could realistically explain human behavior. It is painfully obvious that this brilliant woman who saw as keenly as anyone in her time the philosophical weakness of pragmatic liberalism had no viable foundational alternative.

In one way, time has treated Follett better than Lippmann or Niebuhr. Their larger reputations and greater influence in their own lifetimes were built on less substantial thought, with the result that today they are mainly symbolic fodder for the grazing of intellectual historians, beyond whose small pasture they count for little. Follett's later writings on business administration, mostly undiscussed in this chapter, drew on many of the same ideas that informed her work in political science and lived on to exert some influence in the world of corporate management. It is scarcely surprising that her notion of "integration" found an audience there. The modern corporate office, where people work together in small teams and with fairly clear normative boundaries, resembles much more closely than electoral politics the kind of Boston "neighborhood" where Follett for twenty years found "integration" the key to successful social work and urban reform. The corporate office more than electoral politics lends itself to the illusion to which Follett, alas, subscribed—that intellectual rela-

29. Follett, *New State,* 256.

tions are a matter of immediacy, what Peirce called secondness. Follett's failure to extend her influence beyond business to the still larger and more complex relations of politics should give us caution as to the viability of her philosophy. Her ideas' substantial usefulness in the modern corporation might make us wish that she had known enough of Peirce's pragmatism to articulate, in terms of thirdness or semiotic representation, a practical vision of democracy.

CHAPTER EIGHT

WEAK AND VULGAR PRAGMATISM
VERSUS THE REAL THING

Truth is the object of philosophy, but not always of philosophers.
—John Churton Collins, "Aphorisms," *English Review*, April 1914

This could have been a much larger book, filled with many more examples aimed at challenging the conventional view that liberalism, in resting on James and Dewey, rested on the best as well as the most avant-garde philosophy available at the outset of the twentieth century. Because the story I have tried to tell is not a simple one, I have kept it short. My aim has been to highlight the differences between Peirce's pragmatism and that of James and Dewey. My central point is that twentieth-century American liberalism was built on the weaker pillar. But in support of my argument that since the time of the emergence of Dewey's instrumentalism, American political thought has been a century-long wrong turn I could have offered many more analyses of major liberal thinkers.

My account of Dewey, for example, might have been complemented by an analysis of the writings of George Herbert Mead (1859–1931), a name often invoked as evidence of an indigenous American tradition of social psychology. Mead crossed paths with Dewey at the University of Michigan, and they were lifelong friends thereafter, a situation which has led to the conventional view that Mead's social psychology was essentially Deweyan. Charles W. Morris, in his 1934 introduction to Mead's posthumously published *Mind, Self and Society,* suggested that Mead belonged in a more Peircean, less nominalist camp.[1] Similarly, in 1980

---

1. Charles W. Morris, "Introduction," in George Herbert Mead, *Mind, Self and Society from the Standpoint of a Social Behaviorist,* ed. Morris (Chicago: University of Chicago Press, 1934), xxvii.

J. David Lewis and Richard L. Smith argued that Mead's social psychology was more akin to Peircean realism than Deweyan nominalism. Their argument depended, however, on not very convincing interpretations of passages where Mead vaguely seems to suggest some universality to social life.[2]

Neither Morris nor Lewis and Smith cited any forthright declaration by Mead of his supposed realism, and I do not think it likely they could have found one. Everywhere in Mead's writings there are statements showing that his views of society differed little if at all from Dewey's nominalism. Like Dewey, Mead was always ready to say that the self is social but never that society is a self. Society is more the result of biology than of mind: "Human society as we know it could not exist without minds and selves . . . ; but its individual members would not possess minds and selves if these had not arisen within or emerged out of the human social process in its lower stages of development [when] . . . it was merely a resultant of . . . the physiological differentiations and demands of the physiological organisms implicated in it."[3]

Recently, two excellent studies by Andrew Feffer and Hans Joas have, respectively, located Mead in the social context of Chicago urban reform and elucidated his scattered writings with unprecedented clarity. Feffer, whose vantage point is more or less Niebuhrian, finds Dewey and Mead guilty of overestimating the degree to which intelligence and civic cooperation might overcome power and class differences.[4] Joas, despite suggesting that Mead surpassed Dewey in attributing to society some holism greater than that of a mere association of individuals, does not reveal any metaphysical basis for this assertion.[5] Mead thus ends up looking like Dewey, an avowed antinominalist who nevertheless actually failed to move beyond nominalism toward a strongly pragmatic, realist notion that the social relations constituting the self might extend beyond individual selves to allow some holism in society, to make society a self.

What we can say of Mead in regard to Peirce's influence on him is no different than what we can say of Dewey; it is unfortunate that both of

2. David Lewis and Richard L. Smith, *American Sociology and Pragmatism: Mead, Chicago Sociology, and Symbolic Interaction* (Chicago: University of Chicago Press, 1980), 117–48.
3. Mead, *Mind, Self and Society,* 227. Cf. Mead, "Natural Rights and the Theory of the Political Institution," *Journal of Philosophy, Psychology and Scientific Methods* (18 March 1915), 149; and Mead, *Selected Writings,* ed. and intro. Andrew J. Reck (Indianapolis: Bobbs-Merrill, 1964), 140–43.
4. Andrew Feffer, *The Chicago Pragmatists and American Progressivism* (Ithaca: Cornell University Press, 1993), 268.
5. Hans Joas, *G. H. Mead: A Contemporary Re-examination of His Thought,* tr. Raymond Meyer (Cambridge: MIT Press, 1985), 111.

them seem to have understood so little of Peirce during the most productive years of their careers. Given their interest in matters social, they might well have taken Peirce's few hints as to the possibility of "greater persons" and elaborated them into a vital body of political and social theory. Peirce could have helped the other two philosophers include far more realism in their sociology than they managed without him.

My analysis of Lippmann, meant to show the failings of the weak James-Dewey variant of pragmatism for a progressive liberal, might have been supplemented by a lengthy analysis of the career and writings of Herbert Croly (1869–1930), founding editor of *The New Republic*. As his biographer has shown, Croly was deeply influenced by the pragmatists in the years between his two influential books, *The Promise of American Life* (1909) and *Progressive Democracy* (1914).[6] Not only Dewey and James, the latter with whom Croly studied as a Harvard undergraduate, but also Dewey's former colleague at the University of Chicago Albion W. Small moved Croly toward a somewhat less Hamiltonian notion of democracy. Where *The Promise of American Life* had concluded that the "common citizen" needed "some democratic evangelist—some imitator of Jesus" to lead the way to a better society, *Progressive Democracy* concluded that "the progressive democratic faith, like the faith of St. Paul, finds its consummation in a love . . . which is at bottom a spiritual expression of the mystical unity of human nature."[7]

As with so many of the progressives, Croly's writings betray not merely a frustrated religiosity but a longing for a way of conceiving of social unity, a longing that James and Dewey could not fulfill. Like Lippmann, Croly was unable to conceive of leadership as anything other than directive and individualistic. When he took up his editorship of the *New Republic,* the magazine suffered from the same arrogance, the same self-appointed elitism that had marred *The Promise of American Life.* The advocates of direct democracy erred, Croly wrote in *Progressive Democracy,* in failing to see that public opinion requires leadership: "Public opinion requires to be aroused, elicited, informed, developed, concentrated and brought to an understanding of its own dominant purposes."[8] This was the attitude that led to such smug, fatuous *New Republic* editorials as "Who Willed American Participation?" one of the pieces that aroused the ire of Randolph Bourne by its claim that intellectuals had

6. David Levy, *Herbert Croly of* The New Republic: *The Life and Thought of an American Progressive* (Princeton: Princeton University Press, 1985), 176–82.
7. Herbert Croly, *Progressive Democracy* (New York: Macmillan, 1914), 427, 453, 454.
8. Ibid., 304.

been the driving force in moving public opinion to support the 1917 declaration of war.

My discussion of Reinhold Niebuhr might have been enriched by a similar analysis of the writings of Lewis Mumford, (1896–1990) an Emersonian sort of writer and lecturer. Politically independent, Mumford was unswayed by the seeming logic of communism in the Great Depression. An early foe of nazism, he blamed the democracies' weak response to Hitler on "pragmatic liberalism," against which he wrote a ferocious attack, *Faith for Living* (1940). Mumford was a generalist in cultural criticism best known for his writings on architecture and urban planning, in behalf of which he was a relentless activist.

Yet Mumford had no way to conceive of planning as anything other than an elitist process, a failing that became a shortfall in his democratic vision. Though a few of his plans were enacted by various urban and civic associations, Mumford could never really partake in the give and take of politics, not for want of toughness but because of a deliberate aloofness. For all his admiration of Whitman, Mumford could not imagine that the masses might speak to him, but only that he might speak to them. His stance of Olympian disdain for much that was harmless in mass culture left him detached and ultimately isolated. What he needed but never had was a philosophy that would have enabled him to think of himself as merely a part of his culture, a member of society as well as its critic.

Mumford seems never to have gone through the youthful infatuation with William James that Niebuhr did before finally recognizing that some of the sins he charged to Dewey's account might also be levied against James. The "Young Intellectuals," such as Waldo Frank and Van Wyck Brooks, with whom Mumford associated usually followed Bourne in treating Dewey more severely than James. In "Twilight of Idols," for example, Bourne had asked if James might not have been less complacent than Dewey in regard to the World War. So Mumford's negative treatment of James in *The Golden Day* (1926) was boldness itself by the standards of his time: "He [James] used philosophy to seek peace, rather than understanding, forgetful of the fact that if peace is all one needs, ale can do more 'than Milton can, to justify God's ways to man.'"[9]

In that same discussion of pragmatism, Mumford also voiced his belief in Peirce's philosophic superiority to James: "his [Peirce's] philosophy

9. Lewis Mumford, *The Golden Day: A Study in American Experience and Culture* (New York: Boni and Liveright, 1926), 185. For a recent attempt to minimize the differences between Mumford and the James-Dewey strain of pragmatism, see Robert Westbrook, "Lewis Mumford, John Dewey, and the 'Pragmatic Acquiescence'" in *Lewis Mumford: Public Intellectual*, ed. Thomas P. Hughes and Anna C. Hughes (New York: Oxford University Press, 1990), 301–22.

was what his own age deeply needed."[10] But Mumford drew this opinion from the pioneering collection of Peirce's writings—*Chance, Love and Logic* (1923)—edited by Morris Cohen, a collection from which one can get no inkling that semiotic was at the heart of Peirce's philosophy and that on the basis of the general theory of signs he rejected nominalism in favor of realism. Without access to most of Peirce's writings, Mumford had no idea of the realist, foundational alternative Peirce offered to James.

With no modern foundation Mumford became, like Niebuhr, a modernist with a traditionalist foundation. Where Niebuhr called attention to the usefulness of the doctrine of original sin in the modern world, Mumford became a proponent of nineteenth-century romanticism and organicism as a basis for modern living. His *Conduct of Life*—both the pinnacle and philosophical foundation of his magisterial series on *The Renewal of Life,* the series that included *Technics and Civilization, The Culture of Cities,* and *The Condition of Man*—describes life in biological terms, limited to the individual organism in a manner not much different from Dewey.[11] As with Dewey, then, and indeed Niebuhr as well, Mumford never conceived of society as real in any sense resembling the reality of the individual mind. Society was a mere aggregation of individuals. With no realist metaphysics on which to stand, Mumford, who lived close to the ideal of "The American Scholar," saw his bid for Emersonian status slip away, and he became just one more nay-sayer.

This book's account of Mary Parker Follett might have been complemented by a similar account of the career of Elton Mayo (1880–1949), one of the pioneering figures of the human relations movement in American business.[12] An Australian philosopher and psychotherapist, Mayo came to the United States in 1922 on what was supposed to have been a brief visit. Through a combination of luck and deft careerism he parlayed his breezy speaking style and enormous personal charm into a position at the Harvard Business School at just the time when some of the faculty were becoming involved in the soon-to-be-famous experiments at Western Electric's Hawthorne Plant in Cicero, Illinois. Working conditions were varied to test their impact on productivity. To the consternation of the experimenters, reversion to inferior working conditions did not diminish productivity. Mayo contributed the decisive interpretation—"the Hawthorne effect"—of the empirical findings; people will respond

10. Ibid., 194.
11. Lewis Mumford, *The Conduct of Life* (New York: Harcourt, Brace, 1951), 28–33.
12. Biographical information in the following paragraphs is from Richard C. S. Trahair, *The Humanist Temper: The Life and Work of Elton Mayo* (New Brunswick, N.J.: Transaction Books, 1984).

positively to a worsening situation if they have strong attachment and affection for the authority figures involved.

Like Follett, Mayo was an opponent of old-fashioned individualism, an advocate of small group psychology as the answer to civilization's problems, and a proponent of the idea that a group may have a "personality."[13] The notion that groups could not have personalities was, said Mayo, a corollary of an outdated individualism which the most cursory examination of labor unions, clubs, professions, and above all, business organizations would disprove. The outmoded social code of rugged individualism had long been abandoned in business practice, but its persistence in popular social theory caused much harm. The discrepancy between individual desire for social relations within groups and the modern ideology of individualism meant that the ordinary human being and the social code were at odds. The goal of the human relations movement as Mayo conceived it, was to recreate in industrial work-groups the satisfying social experiences that human beings had enjoyed in the villages and towns of the preindustrial world.

Mayo was a critic of pragmatism and an admirer of Peirce, but like so many other social theorists in the first half of the twentieth century, he knew nothing of Peirce's metaphysics. His first known philosophical address, to the Students' Christian Union at the University of Queensland, had been on "The Inadequacy of Pragmatism," but he criticized pragmatism only for its lack of core values, not its nominalism. Although Peirce's name pops up occasionally in Mayo's writings he seems to have found Peirce more useful in psychotherapy than in social theory. He advocated, for example, exploration of the "mental hinterland" by a technique he called "musating" that he claimed to have got from Peirce, probably from Peirce's essay on "A Neglected Argument for the Reality of God."[14] Mayo knew nothing of Peirce's concept of semiotic communication as the means by which the personal identity of both groups and single human beings is established.

As a result of his lack of understanding of any representative or semiotic theory of communication, Mayo was forever distrustful of politics, which he saw simply as conflict and never as communication. Like follett, he believed that democratic institutions such as the vote were not enough to fulfill the human promise. Only social skills, as exemplified within human groups, could give meaning to democratic institutions,

13. Mayo, *The Social Problems of an Industrial Civilization* (Cambridge, Mass.: Harvard University Press, 1945), 48.
14. Trahair, *Humanist Temper*, 67; cf. *Peirce on Signs: Writings on Semiotic by Charles Sanders Peirce*, ed. James Hoopes (Chapel Hill: University of North Carolina Press, 1991), 263.

could "make these dry bones live."[15] Disdaining any model that portrayed the leader as a dominating hero, he lumped political movements together with the programs of desk-thumping executives and militant labor movements as means of conflict rather than communication and, therefore, saw them as more likely to do harm than good. Useful political control was impossible in modern industrial societies where human beings had lost the inward values necessary for social control.[16] The solution lay with administrators who would re-establish harmonious social relations in industrial settings. The antidemocratic implications of all this suspicion of politics were lost on Mayo. He had an instinctive affinity for the human group but, absent Peirce, no way of understanding how semiotic relations might establish a community in any arena larger than the workplace where, so to speak, he could touch it. As a result, his vision was one of disempowered workers aided by benign managers but left with no relief if the managers were not benign. It is not surprising that the human relations movement Mayo did so much to create soon lost sight of his emphasis on holistic relations and became a technique for human manipulation.

To have offered lengthy, detailed analyses of such thinkers as Mumford, Mead, Croly, and Mayo (as well as others such as Irwin Edman, Will Durant, H. M. Kallen, John Herman Randall, Jr., Harry A. Overstreet, and Thomas Vernor Smith,[17] all of whose thought was vitiated by the influence of James and lack of knowledge of Peirce) would have made this a bigger but more obscure book. Instead, I have discussed only a small group of important liberal political theorists against the background of a more complex description of pragmatism than is usually offered by intellectual historians writing about American political theory. Lippmann, Niebuhr, and Follett would have liked to envision a more unified society. But Lippmann and Niebuhr in their youth, due at least partly to the influence of James and his nominalism, became atomistic individualists. Lippmann was unable to envision anything better than government by elite individuals. Niebuhr could imagine no better future than morally superior individuals reluctantly reconciled to power politics. Follett believed in the possibility of community, but could see no way to establish it except by local proximity. With no metaphysical conception of representation as a matter of thirdness or semiosis, she could not conceive of

15. Mayo, *Social Problems*, 56.
16. Mayo, *The Human Problems of an Industrial Civilization* (New York: Macmillan, 1933), 167.
17. These now largely forgotten but once influential popularizers are discussed in George Cotkin, "Middle-Ground Pragmatists: The Popularization of Philosophy in American Culture," *Journal of the History of Ideas* (April 1994), 283–302.

political representation in any other way than as an impractical pyramid of neighborhoods. Lippmann, Niebuhr, and Follett represent three major strands of twentieth-century liberalism—elite managerialism, resigned acceptance of realpolitik, and impractical communitarianism.

The poverty of the pragmatic tradition in twentieth-century political theory is suggested by how little sustained it was among even its major proponents. In late career, Lippmann abandoned nominalism and Niebuhr came to understand the narrowness of James. Neither of them, however, seems ever to have understood how badly they had been let down by James's philosophy or that Peirce's realist commitment to generals was an alternative to Jamesian nominalism. Lippmann began espousing self-evident principles of natural law as the basis for a public philosophy, a philosophy so weak that he thought protecting it required curtailment of basic civil liberties. Niebuhr, never questioning his commitment to realpolitik, fell back on religious dogma which he believed was confirmed by the internal experience of self-consciousness and the external experience of social relations that were more often evil than good. Follett had never been as captivated by James's nominalism as Lippmann and Niebuhr in their youth. She, far more than Niebuhr, could have offered an alternative to Deweyan liberalism. But she had no foundational basis for that alternative and in any case died just as the controversies of the 1930s were commencing.

Ironically, it was Dewey himself who, late in life, came to understand how radically different Peirce's philosophy was from both Jamesian nominalism and from the eternal and unchanging general ideas that had made Dewey fearful that realism could only be an instrument of conservatism in political thought. But by the time he understood all this, Dewey's career was nearly over, and it was too late for him to revise his philosophy in the light of Peirce. This was tragic, for by his combination of the two roles of philosopher and prolific social commentator, Dewey was more or less the official mediator between pragmatism and political theory. Dewey is the central figure in the story of the philosophic failure of twentieth-century American liberalism.

It is therefore regrettable, if unsurprising, that Dewey's lack of a systematic metaphysics has made him a hero to the antiessentialists of our time, who urge consideration of the particular problems and injustices of our own time as an alternative to metaphysics. The problems of our own time, of any time, provide human beings with more than enough to think about, provided they give up "the assumption that our ideas need any more justification than our social practices and our needs." Metaphysics and epistemology—the attempt to explain the fundamental relations

among things in general and the knowledge relationship in particular—
are needless, even wasteful efforts according to this school: "the history of
philosophy shows them to have been fruitless and undesirable." [18]

The wrongheadedness of such a view can perhaps best be illustrated by
citing a contemporary issue—the abortion controversy—where metaphysics is not "fruitless and undesirable." The abortion issue comes down
to a metaphysical question, what is a human being? Most "pro-life" ac-
tivists have adopted, more or less unwittingly, the Cartesian doctrine of
the unitary soul. The fetus moves and is therefore a living, ensouled human being. Most "pro-choice" advocates share the Cartesian doctrine
with their opponents, focusing on the right of the pregnant woman to
control her own body as if she were a unitary, atomistic individual or soul
of the Cartesian sort: "our bodies, our selves." Since both the pro-choice
advocates and the antiabortionists embrace the Cartesian doctrine, the
antiabortionists would seem to have the strongest case. Can the pregnant
woman legitimately insist that her right to the control of her body is so
absolute as to entitle her to annihilate the body of the fetus who, having
an animate body, seems equally ensouled? Or more to the antifoundationalists' point, can one imagine the antiabortionists ever being brought
into a "conversation" with those who share their metaphysical premises
but argue illogically from them?

Against the background of the abortion controversy, Peirce's metaphysical discovery that a human being is not a unitary soul but a series of
interpretive relations is not "fruitless." Peirce's metaphysics places the
abortion issue in a different light by making it a question of relations:
relations within the fetus suggesting, for example, the likelihood of a
healthy body and the possibility of a fulfilled, satisfying life; relations between the parents and the fetus, showing that the former want not merely
to create a new "life" (which a single-celled organism can also accomplish) but over many years nurture a child into a responsible adult. A
Peircean approach gives pro-choice advocates a foundational alternative
to Cartesianism where pro-lifers have the logical upper hand.

Nonfoundational, "pragmatic" arguments have been made for moving
the abortion debate in this direction, but without the benefit of a metaphysical foundation like Peirce's, such arguments are almost certain to
fail. For example, in *The Good Society* Robert Bellah and others cite the
work of Mary Ann Glendon to suggest how individualist "rights" talk
has made the abortion issue "intractable." [19] They would therefore like to

18. Rorty, *Objectivity, Relativism, and Truth* (Cambridge: Cambridge University Press, 1991), 7.
19. Robert Bellah, *The Good Society* (New York: Norton, 1992), 129, 315n.

abandon such a way of framing the issue. This puts the cart before the horse. Pro-life and pro-choice advocates will not be easily persuaded that they should simply abandon for the sake of tractability the philosophical convictions on which their positions are based. The suggestion that the issue can be made less "intractable" by framing the discussion in a way that omits rather than addresses the discussants' concerns can only be insulting to them. The suggestion has the flavor of the elitist, managerial liberalism so distasteful to American democratic sentiment today. Indeed, it is an example of why such liberalism is on the defensive and in disrepute.

Peirce's philosophy was not only a metaphysics but a logic, an invitation to careful thought, whether about abortion or any other issue. In his 1866 "Logic Notebook," in order to show that a premise "must be an *accidental* not an *essential* proposition," Peirce offered the following example of a fallaciously constructed syllogism:

> All murder is wicked
> All abortion is murder
> ∴ All abortion is wicked

This begs the question because *wicked* is part of the essence of murder and therefore no one need admit abortion to be murder until it is otherwise shown to be wicked.[20]

One can read from end to end those who argue for abandoning foundational "Philosophy" in favor of "conversation" without finding a comment so pertinent to a contemporary major social issue as that which Peirce drops in passing in his study of logic from last century.

"Philosophy" is no less relevant to the issue of "issues in American society today," the issue of the proper balance between American national community and the many smaller communities of ethnic, religious, and voluntary association to which many citizens give overlapping and sometimes contradictory loyalty. Recently the liberal historian Martin Marty has characterized this issue as the problem of "the one and the many"— a phrase reminiscent not only of *e pluribus unum* but also, ironically of the conundrum of metaphysical relations among particulars and generals that ultimately defeated William James's philosophy.[21] This concern that the "identity politics" of the past quarter century has gotten out of hand

20. *Writings of Charles S. Peirce: A Chronological Edition*, ed. Max H. Fisch et al. (Bloomington: Indiana University Press, 1982–present), 348.
21. Martin E. Marty, *The One and the Many: Americans' Struggle for the Common Good* (Cambridge: Harvard University Press, 1997).

and threatens the national well-being has long troubled the public at large and is now being taken up by liberal historians.[22] Identity politics confirms that a national commitment to inclusive democratic discourse is a resource to be used, respected, and expanded rather than scorned and squandered merely because privileged and powerful majorities have exploited it and abused it.[23]

Peirce's realism, his foundational account of communication as a process through which "greater persons" and community identities are created, is the kind of basis on which the contestants in the struggle over the proper balance between national identity and smaller group loyalties might be brought into engagement with each other. As with the abortion controversy, it is surely futile to expect the partisans on either side, but especially the more dogmatic and intransigent partisans, to abandon their powerful convictions for no more reason than that their doing so would make the problem more "tractable" from the point of view of the other side. So, too, appeals for conversation, for recognition of the right to give voluntary loyalty to ethnic identity, for acceptance of alternative historical narratives, for visions of the nation as an association of associations, and so forth are futile in the absence of arguments that can actually suggest how such conduct contributes to inclusion and community among and between identity groups. Again, it is Peirce's strong pragmatism rather than the weak and nominalist pragmatism of James and Dewey that could do this. His semiotic would make it possible to understand how communication contributes to greater being for all through participation in the national community, a "greater person" possessing some of the same cohesion as individual personalities and lesser groups. Only Peirce's realism gives liberals a pragmatic argument they could reasonably offer to their opponents as a reason to participate in discussion that might lead to a more liberal polity.

Those who argue in Jamesian and Deweyan fashion that "conversation" should not be based on foundational "Philosophy," but should replace it, mean to focus our attention on the concrete problems of our time, but they miss the fact that "Philosophy" is intimately involved in those problems. The metaphysical nature of being and identity, whether individual or communal, does not obscure the real issues but is what the

22. The most aggressive critique of multiculturalism by a liberal historian is Arthur M. Schlesinger, Jr., *The Disuniting of America* (New York: Norton, 1992). For more temperate approaches to the question of community and ethnicity, see David Hollinger, *Postethnic America* (New York: Basic Books, 1995) and Michael Walzer, *On Toleration* (New Haven, Conn.: Yale University Press, 1997).

23. For an example of such an approach see Sacvan Bercovitch, *The Rites of Assent: Transformations in the Symbolic Construction of America* (New York: Routledge, 1993).

real issues are all about. The attempt of the antifoundationalists to lead us away from metaphysics is no doubt well-meaning. Certainly, they are right that much effort has been wasted and much damage done by metaphysical speculation. But waste and damage are scarcely limited to metaphysics. Just because there has been waste and damage in metaphysics it does not follow, any more than it did from, say, the existence of waste and damage in medieval science, that no improvement is possible or that scientific discoveries must be "fruitless."

Some sociologists have recognized the significance of Peirce's metaphysical realism for social theory, and indeed, some sociologists who have written the history of social theory have done as well as intellectual historians in distinguishing among the pragmatists and in recognizing the potential of Peirce's philosophy for social theory. C. Wright Mills, in his doctoral dissertation, distinguished well between Peirce's concern with logic and truth, on the one hand, and Dewey's concern with power and action, on the other. Mills also understood something of the significance of Peirce's "realist definition of society." [24] Mills did not go on to compare Peirce's realism to Dewey's nominalism. That task was left to David Lewis and Richard L. Smith in their book on *American Sociology and Pragmatism*.[25]

Yet until recently there has been little indication that historical understanding of pragmatism by at least some sociologists has had any impact on their discipline's understanding of society. There is now a newly awakening interest in Peirce by sociologists such as Eugene Halton, Norbert Wiley, and others.[26] They deserve what help we intellectual historians can give them, but if we are to be any help at all, our understanding of the history of American philosophy needs to be as good as theirs.

The great and still insufficiently recognized fact of American intellectual history is how much more deeply than Europeans we have been affected by the modern West's foundational "way of ideas," according to which knowledge of the external world is mediated by representational ideas and is therefore uncertain while knowledge of our ideas themselves is supposedly immediate and therefore certain. The success of the way of

24. C. Wright Mills, *Sociology and Pragmatism: The Higher Learning in America*, ed. Irving Louis Horowitz (New York: Oxford, 1969), 191, 416–17.
25. Lewis and Smith, *American Sociology and Pragmatism*, chap 2; cf. Eugene Rochberg-Halton, *Meaning and Modernity: Social Theory in the Pragmatic Attitude* (Chicago: University of Chicago Press, 1986), 7.
26. Eugene Halton, *Bereft of Reason* (Chicago: University of Chicago Press, 1994), Robert Perinbanayagam, *Discursive Acts* (New York: Aldine de Gruyter, 1991); Donald Levine, *Visions of the Sociological Tradition* (Chicago: University of Chicago Press, 1995); Norbert Wiley, *The Semiotic Self* (Chicago: University of Chicago Press, 1994).

ideas in the United States probably accounts in significant part for our tendency to frame issues in foundational terms of individual rights that makes many of us moral absolutists on abortion, affirmative action, and other controversial issues. Although the way of ideas was a European creation and Descartes its principal prophet, it was nowhere more successful than in the United States, with whose colonial and pre–Civil War history, the way of ideas is roughly coterminous. In the United States the way of ideas was, for a time, remarkably successful in suppressing ancient religious and philosophical convictions according to which self-knowledge was uncertain and required constant examination and interpretation. One reason for the American success of the way of ideas was that on this side of the water ancient and more complex doctrines had fewer supporting institutions such as an established church. The way of ideas also seemed to offer more support for the individual human autonomy to which the American republic was early committed. Nevertheless, the repressed notion that self-knowledge is uncertain and interpretational rather than self-evident returned, so to speak, in the form of Freudian theory. I have argued elsewhere that Freudian theory was a fundamentally conservative strategy for preserving the Cartesian notion of individual, atomistic selves. Freudianism preserved the atomistic self while enabling people to see the absurdity of their confident belief, which the way of ideas inspired, in the ease of human self-knowledge and self-control.[27]

Dissenting American philosophers, back to Jonathan Edwards, have opposed the established way of ideas by opposing its representationalism. The dissenters have attempted in one antirepresentational way or another to overcome lack of confidence in our ability to deal with the external world, a lack of confidence that is supposedly the legacy of representationalism. Antirepresentationalism was the strategy of Edwards's new spiritual sense for unmediated knowledge of divine ideas, of Emerson's Oversoul which provided an unmediated context for human spirituality, of William James's radically empirical universe of dyadic or unmediated relations, and even of Richard Rorty's view of knowledge not "as a matter of getting reality right, but rather as a matter of acquiring habits of action for coping with reality."[28] A recent critic has characterized Rorty's pragmatism in a way that must seem stunningly wrong to Rorty, yet with a certain

27. This paragraph and the following one summarizes part of the argument of my book *Consciousness in New England: From Puritanism and Ideas to Psychoanalysis and Semiotic* (Baltimore: John Hopkins University Press, 1989).
28. Rorty, *Objectivity, Relativism, and Truth*, 1. Rorty himself characterizes this position as "antirepresentationalism" (192).

logic owing to Rorty's antirepresentationalism. Rorty's is "not a new philosophy but a variation on positivism, a form of extreme empiricism." [29]

There is, however, an alternative to antirepresentationalism—Peirce's approach of conceiving of everything as representational and denying all immediacy. Rather than rebelling against representationalism for supposedly cutting us off from the real, Peirce conceived of reality as representational. In the second chapter of this book I took up the question of what it means to conceive of reality as representational and showed how Peirce arrived at that conclusion out of his "logic of relatives." American pragmatism originated in Peirce's attempt to make logic a matter of external and objective relations (not to be confused with certain or unrepresentational ones) rather than subjective ideas immediately known within an unworldly sphere of mind.

In the third and fourth chapters I attempted to show that weaker pragmatists such as James and Dewey, however deeply committed like Peirce to an instrumental notion of thought, weakly retained a more subjective logic with vestiges of Descartes' method of reason. Hence James's and Dewey's antirepresentational emphasis on the immediacy of experience was not as radical as many intellectual historians have supposed but resembled in some respects the antirepresentational logic of Descartes and Locke. Seventeenth-century thinkers such as Descartes and Locke may have held that the external world requires representation but they also believed that our own immediately known thoughts are the subject matter of logic. Peirce's philosophy, with its assertion that all knowledge and logic is representational, was a far more radical departure from the tradition of modern Western philosophy than was James's or Dewey's.

In chapters five, six, seven, and to some degree in chapter four as well, I attempted to show that the commitment to antirepresentational foundations by James had results that, while unfortunate, were certainly not "fruitless." Even Follett, who of all the political thinkers in this book was least tainted by James, suffered from his eclipse of Peirce in that she had no way of extending her notion of the reality of local, neighborhood groups to society at large. In the hands of Lippmann and Niebuhr, James's nominalist and antirepresentational foundations resulted in an atomistic individualism that prevented them from conceiving of social groups as anything more real than aggregations of individuals. As a result they could not conceive of social groups but only of individuals as capable of

29. H. O. Mounce, *The Two Pragmatisms: From Peirce to Rorty* (London: Routledge, 1997), 231; cf. 184.

thought and morality. Similarly, Dewey's foundational commitment to naturalism was not only antirepresentational and nominalist but had limiting consequences on his own political commentary similar to the influence of James on Lippmann and Niebuhr. Although James and Dewey are frequently cited as supposed precursors by contemporary antifoundationalists like Rorty, the historical record suggests the opposite.

Rorty, one of the most widely read and influential philosophers of our time, has been one of the principal stimulators of the resurgent interest in pragmatism and especially in Dewey and James, whom he sees as precursors of his own antifoundationalism. As is surely obvious by now, I think Rorty is mostly mistaken in his claim to stand in the tradition of James and Dewey. Although he has intemperately lambasted Peirce as an "infuriating philosopher . . . just one more whacked-out triadomaniac," Rorty has never, to my knowledge at least, criticized him as an "essentialist" attempting "to penetrate through appearance to reality."[30] But I wish to bring the two thinkers into relation on the question of essentials and foundations in order to suggest that it is erroneous to conflate antifoundationalism with antiessentialism. I believe Peirce would disagree with antifoundationalism but would consider antiessentialism sound and correct.

Peirce's philosophy provides a "foundation" without falling into a search for an occult entity or essentialist "$\alpha\rho\chi\eta$ beyond discourse" of the sort against which Rorty cautions.[31] Peirce was an antiessentialist philosopher of common sense who early abandoned the Kantian attempt "to prove that the normal representations of truth within us are really correct," because he believed them correct as a matter of faith and held that all philosophies contained an element of faith.[32] But while Peirce believed it unnecessary to prove that the normal representations of truth within us are really correct, he also believed that those representations correctly provide knowledge of the two fundamental or foundational relations underlying the phenomena ordinarily described in terms of mind and matter.

To understand why Peirce was a foundationalist but not an essentialist it is necessary to remember something of his metaphysical categories and the method by which he arrived at them. In maturity he named his

30. Rorty, "The Pragmatist's Progress" in Umberto Eco, *Interpretation and Overinterpretation*, ed. Stefan Collini (New York: Cambridge University Press, 1992), 89; Rorty, *Essays on Heidegger and Others*, 136.
31. Richard Rorty, *Philosophy and the Mirror of Nature* (Princeton: Princeton University Press, 1979), 390.
32. *Peirce on Signs*, 17.

categories firstness, secondness, and thirdness. "Firstness" is Peirce's category for the sheer, undoubted, even brutal qualities of the world. "Secondness" is the relationship that occurs when one object is related immediately to a second, including the sort of material relation which the science of his time had learned to measure and manipulate so well. "Thirdness" is a representative relation whereby one object is represented to a second by a third, a sign. This last relation includes all of the phenomena usually labeled "mental," but Peirce saw it as a natural relation, characteristic not only of human thought but of many other phenomena as well, such as gravitational force.[33] Without stopping here to explain Peirce's cosmology, the utter naturalism of this view may be noted. It posits no occult substance of mind after the fashion of Descartes, and it leaves human thought and spirit at one with the rest of the natural world. Obviously, this system of categories is "foundational" in that it claims to describe the basic relations apparent in the universe and to categorize all phenomena within them.

Although Peirce's categories are foundational, they are not "essentialist" in the sense to which Rorty objects, the sense of attempting to go behind phenomena to a "$\alpha\rho\chi\eta$ beyond discourse," an *ens entium,* or underlying substance, such as matter or mind in Descartes's system.[34] In Peirce's very first paper on the categories, published when he was twenty-seven years old, he stressed that, in the logical process by which he arrived at the categories, "nothing is assumed respecting the subjective elements of consciousness which cannot be securely inferred from the objective elements."[35] In Peirce's categories there is no going behind the world of appearances to some essential basis for them. He described his categories of firstness, secondness, and thirdness with no pretense of explaining why the world was so organized. As Carl Hausman has suggested, Peirce "cuts between" essentialism and antifoundationalism. He rejected both the essentialists' longing for a "complete God's-eye viewing" of the world and the antifoundationalists' "view that admits nothing that has a status independent of human interpretation." Peirce found space between them for foundational "realism that . . . recognizes what is vital to those who have taken the linguistic turn . . . without abandoning . . . our communal and individual habits, constraints that 'we' do not make."[36]

Peirce was the true radical of American philosophy. He abandoned the

33. Ibid., 241–44.
34. Rorty, *Philosophy and the Mirror of Nature,* 390.
35. *Peirce on Signs,* 26.
36. Carl R. Hausman, *Charles S. Peirce's Evolutionary Philosophy* (New York: Cambridge University Press, 1993), 223, 224.

strategy of the dissenters from Edwards through Emerson and James through Rorty, abandoned their antirepresentationalism in favor of a representationalism so complete as to destroy all notions of immediatism except in the sense that bodily feelings are immediate, a meaningless immediacy until feelings are interpreted as representations or signs. According to Peirce all knowledge, including knowledge of one's own thoughts, is semiotic or representational and therefore involves an element of interpretation. It had been the very possibility of interpretation that led the dissenters from Edwards to Rorty to object to the representationalism in the way of ideas. To the dissenters the more representationalism, the more interpretation, and the less chance of truly communing with the rest of the universe, including other human beings. But for Peirce, interpretation did not of necessity imply arbitrariness. There was such a thing as objective truth, and it could be found through the interpretation of signs. Representation and interpretation, rather than threatening the concept of truth, permitted the generality of truth.

For Peirce community is possible because reality and true representations of it are general rather than particular or individual. Representationalism makes it possible to understand how truth may be sharable among people, makes it possible to understand how there can be a community of spirit, including even the possibility of a community of spirit that reaches beyond ethnocentrism toward objective truth. This understanding of how community is possible more than offsets the risk of error, the risk of mistaken interpretation. Antirepresentationalism might have removed the risk of interpretation from knowledge, but it did so at the price of limiting truth to particulars, to special instances of unmediated and isolated experience. An understanding of the possibility of community is impossible in the dissenting tradition of antirepresentationalism that dominates the liberal conversation of our own time. Peirce's semiotic radicalism is the only basis the American philosophical tradition offers us for an understanding of community. Given the lack of attention Peirce's metaphysics has received from intellectual historians and social theorists, it is scarcely surprising that liberals have failed to articulate a convincing theory of community.

Even if antiessentialists such as Rorty were convinced that it is possible to be a foundationalist without being an essentialist, they might ask what is the use of such a foundation and whether it does not run the risk of creating intolerance and antidemocratic sentiments, just as did previous foundationalists. Loyola and Nietzsche are two examples Rorty has cited. But surely the greatest risk of promoting intolerance comes not from discussing but from refusing to discuss foundational issues. Refusal to discuss issues, after all, smacks of the very absolutism liberals supposedly oppose. Not to engage in conversation with foundationalists, as Rorty himself acknowledges in *Objectivity, Relativism, and Truth,* "seems to show a contempt for the spirit of accommodation and tolerance, which is essential to democracy" (190).[37]

Yet there is an additional and perhaps even more serious problem with Rorty's foundationless notion of liberal democracy—it is impractical and irrelevant to the vital questions faced by any society, whether democratic or undemocratic. Rorty wants to live in a culture of "insouciant pluralism" and philosophical "light-mindedness" where no big, essentialist ideas stand in the way of inhabitants becoming "more pragmatic, more tolerant, more liberal, more receptive to the appeal of instrumental rationality." Even essentialists, be they theological, Nietzschean, Cartesian, or moral absolutists might, Rorty says in *Objectivity, Relativism, and Truth,* "for pragmatic reasons be loyal citizens of a liberal democratic society" and "be ruefully grateful that their private sense of moral identity . . . is not the concern of such a state" (192, 193). Such a society would be the modern university writ large or, at least, the ideal of the university writ large. All that would be required of citizens of such a society would be that they, like the professoriat, value conversation to the point that even if it produced "despicable character types," citizens nevertheless would recognize that living among despicable people is "a lesser evil than the loss of political freedom" (192).

By confusing liberal democracy with academic life in its best sense, Rorty has produced a notion of democracy that is academic in the worst sense—merely academic. No such society exists or could exist. The obstacle is not merely that many, possibly a majority, of our fellow citizens are essentialists and moralists who very well may not value freedom more highly than rooting out despicable character types. Rather, the obstacle to a foundationless liberal society is that our fellow citizens are engaged in political discourse where issues of life and death are at stake. Rorty's insouciance may be fine for dealing with disagreement in a seminar, but our fellow citizens (and we academics, too, in our real political lives) have to deal with crime, violence, redistributive social policies, abortionists, antiabortionists, the military insecurity of nuclear proliferation, the political insecurity of inter- and intranational chauvinism, the economic insecurity of global competition, a medical establishment whose heroic excellence prolongs the life of the old by endangering the prosperity of the

---

37. Page numbers of subsequent citations to *Objectivity, Relativism, and Truth* will be given parenthetically in the text.

young, and so on. These difficult issues from our own time are not evidence that ours is a particularly difficult time. Our particular historical moment is mostly fortunate. Yet even our fortunate society must deal with issues of life and death.

Faced with life and death issues that are also often divisive, people use whatever values they have in common to resolve those issues while maintaining civil society. They are not likely to find professorial insouciance a value that will resolve issues of life and death. History shows that there are many values for which people will sacrifice all that is dear to them. But I have never heard of anyone, not even a professor, surrendering his own life—though there have been many instances where people have laid down the lives of others—in a spirit of insouciance.

Rorty believes, rightly I think, that "it is not clear how to argue for the claim that human beings ought to be liberals rather than fanatics without being driven back on a theory of human nature, on philosophy," on foundations. But having given up on the possibility that philosophy can provide such a foundational theory, he proposes "to simply *drop* questions and the vocabulary in which those questions are posed" (190). That approach, possible in a seminar filled with liberal graduate students, will not help liberals much in a society filled with people who *do* have a theory of human nature, most likely a traditional Judeo-Christian theory that is far from insouciant. One source of the political irrelevance of Rorty's philosophy stems from his misconception of the historical context in which we live. Refusing to debate constitutional democracy on Loyola's terms or Nietzsche's will probably suffice since they have few enough adherents. But on the issues that are actually broached within contemporary constitutional democracies, it is not clear that liberal democrats are the majority and certainly not clear that they are so prevalent a majority that they can resolve issues by simply refusing to discuss them.

Faced in real political life with foundationalist opponents, liberals cannot afford to spurn whatever reasonable foundationalist arguments they have at hand. It would of course be despicable to try to create a philosophical argument out of nothing more than political necessity. That would be the sort of whistling to keep our spirits up that seems to me too characteristic of our contemporary Deweyan moment in intellectual history. Rorty's antiessentialist position makes sense in view of what he rightly sees as the unreasonableness of the essentialist alternatives. But as I argued above there is a foundational alternative that is not essentialist. Peirce's metaphysics, a foundational alternative that does not attempt to go behind the universe of commonsense appearances, offers much to democratic theory.

Rorty says, for example, that "a notion of the human self as a center-less web of historically conditioned beliefs and desires," which is some-what like Peirce's notion, works well with liberal democracy. But "for pur-poses of liberal social theory," says Rorty, "one can do without such a model. One can get along with common sense and social science, areas of discourse in which the term 'self' rarely occurs" (192). But if the *term* "self" rarely occurs, *concepts* of the self are frequently invoked in com-monsense discourse for all the reasons I suggested above. Real political life involves issues of life and death where concepts of self, even if only im-plicitly employed, determine the frame of discussion. The concept of self most frequently invoked in commonsense political discourse— as in the abortion controversy, for example—is atomistic, individualistic, and es-sentialist rather than one guided by the metaphor of the "centerless web" that even Rorty admits works well for purposes of liberal democracy.

In real political life where there is often invoked an essentialist self that frequently conflicts with liberal values, democrats ought to be grateful for a philosophy such as Peirce's which offers a foundation, if not quite for the notion of the self as a centerless web, at least for a notion of the self as a relational process rather than a unitary soul. Such a foundation scarcely ensures the victory of liberal values, but it might make it possible for there to be a public discourse that involves both liberals and essen-tialists, a discourse in which both liberal and essentialist values could re-ceive explicit examination in regard to their implications for democracy, philosophy, and even religion.

That Peirce's philosophy permits democratic discussion with other foundationalists, even those of antidemocratic tendencies, is one of its larger attractions. I here repeat the disclaimer of my introduction. Al-though I have argued in this book that Peirce's philosophy is the most po-litically useful form of pragmatism, my original attraction to Peirce is to his logic, his semiotic, and his metaphysics. My argument for Peirce's su-perior political usefulness is the result rather than the cause of my con-viction that his philosophy is far greater than the weaker pragmatism of James and Dewey or the vulgar pragmatism of Rorty. Yet once the ques-tion of Peirce's philosophical superiority is settled, the political advan-tages seem immense. Unlike Rorty, who proposes simply not to speak about such things as minds, souls, and selves, Peirce offers a relational self that is a viable alternative to the atomistic self or soul on which is based much conservatism, not to mention political reaction. By presenting such an alternative, liberals could enter the same terrain as conservatives to dis-cuss the virtues and defects of both models of the self. With time, some thoughtful conservatives might even be convinced of the superiority of

Peirce's model. They might find that a relational model of the self has a liberalizing effect on their political and social views.

Such a discourse in which all could participate with the possibility of genuine communication would be a large step forward in the direction of realizing the possibility of society as a "greater person." It would mean more communication (what some these days call a "public culture") achieved not by moral arrogance and culture wars but by civilized discourse. Strange as the idea of society as a "greater person" may seem, there is nothing mystical or utopian about it. It is simply a result of the fact—as Peirce, alone among the pragmatists, explained—that communicative, interpretive, semiotic relations are at the heart of being. Personality is a very high form of being, a very well-organized series of relations within an organic body or within society at large. Peirce therefore opens up not only the possibility of a public discourse, but also provides the encouragement that such a discourse can create some of the same cohesion in society that we enjoy in our own personal identities, imperfect though our identities are, imperfect though social cohesion must and should be. Some will think such a public discourse an impractical dream. But it is enormously less impractical a strategy than Rorty's proposal to refuse to discuss foundational issues. That will not do for a society where many, possibly a majority, hold foundational positions that potentially clash with liberal democracy.

In fact, one should ask, Is Rorty's position itself truly without foundations or at least implicit foundations? What is the basis of his confidence in "conversation" if not a faith in the possibility of communication? Might it not be dangerous to have such a faith without examining its basis and analyzing it against the whole range of conditions that make communication both possible and uncertain? Might not Rorty's situation be the one described by Peirce: "Some think to avoid the influence of metaphysical errors, by paying no attention to metaphysics; but experience shows that these men beyond all others are held in an iron vise of metaphysical theory, because by theories that they have never called in question. . . . Since, then, everyone must have conceptions of things in general, it is most important that they should be carefully constructed." [38]

I have tried to show in this book that the intellectual foundations of twentieth-century American liberalism were not carefully constructed and that the result was unfortunate. There were two pragmatisms, not one, and modern liberal political theory was unfortunately built on the weak pragmatism of James and Dewey instead of the strong pragmatism

38. *Writings of Charles S. Peirce*, 1:490.

of Peirce. Such understanding is a key not only to better intellectual history but to better thought in the future. Persist as we might in our Deweyan moment, we will get nowhere by saying again and again that every past liberal thinker was the same as every other. The late-twentieth-century shattering of the liberal tradition has been a matter of reality as well as perception. Humpty Dumpty cannot be put back together again by saying that he was never broken. Ideas are not that simple and their power is not so easily invoked. A common liberal platform for the present and future cannot be assembled on the basis of a mythic history, unaware of the intellectual differences and errors of the past.

INDEX